THE LITTLE RED HOUSE
THAT JACK BUILT

Also by Russell Jack Smith

The Secret War
The Singapore Chance
Lodestone
Whirligig
Always Afternoon
Time's Prism
Downriver

Non-Fiction

The Unknown CIA: My Three
Decades with the Agency

THE LITTLE RED HOUSE THAT JACK BUILT

RUSSELL JACK SMITH

Bartleby Press
Baltimore - Washington

ISBN 978-0910155-46-5

Library of Congress Control Number: 2002104299

Published by:

Bartleby Press

PO Box 858
Savage, Maryland 20763
800-953-9929
www.BartlebythePublisher.com

Printed in the United States of America

To Rosemary
—her imagination
—her courage
—her fortitude

Author's Aside to the Reader

Even fifty-odd years ago, when the events of this book, took place, I would not have believed that a man would find it necessary to build his house with his own hands. And yet, circumstances somehow arranged themselves in such a way I felt I had not other choice than to do just that. Since I had always been an unhandy man and had never, so to speak, hammered a nail in anger, this was a decision born of desperation.

Sometime later, I sat down at the typewriter with the intention of recording the detailed steps of this episode. As I wrote, though, I found myself dwelling much more upon the adventure and emotion of this enterprise than the details of "How-I-Did-It-Myself." A man setting out to build his own house soon finds himself venturing into situations and meeting people previously unknown to him. It is this human adventure I have written about, not how to lay a subfloor.

Yet, anyone who has a yen to build but lacks courage to begin will probably find in these pages all the moral support he needs to start pounding nails tomorrow. It will not take him long to decide, "If *he* could do it, so can I!"

One

This story began one Sunday afternoon in August in the summer of 1950 when Rosemary and I set out for a walk in the woods. There was nothing particularly unusual in this because we often took gentle Sunday walks. We cut across the yard of our friends, Mort and Barbara Freligh, and walked up across the field beyond. Young grasshoppers took off from the yellowing broomsedge around us and flew in short arcs through the warm August air. Blackberry brambles caught at the legs of our blue jeans and tugged at our shoestrings. Ahead of us, at the top of the field, the woods lay green and cool.

The evening before we had eaten dinner with Mort and Barbara, and during the course of this quiet, neighborly evening the talk eventually came around to houses. "Why don't you buy some of my land and build a house?" asked Mort. "I doubt very much that you can find a house you would want to buy out here. You can't go on renting forever there, and we hope you'll stay around in this neighborhood."

"Sounds good," I said. "But what would I use for money?"

"Borrow money. You can always borrow money to build a house."

"I don't know a thing about it, but I suppose you're right."

"Well, anyway, why don't you and Rose go and have a look at the hillside of mine along the other road? It has a beautiful site for a house on it."

This invitation gave us as much purpose as we needed for setting out across Mort's field the next day. We entered the woods at the top of the field. We climbed over some fallen logs in a stand of old and neglected Virginia pines with the bark coming off some of the trees in great patches like alligator hide, and made our way down the hill to a stream at the bottom. There we came into a grove of very tall trees with trunks as much as four feet thick. The straight lines on the trunks rose sheer for almost fifty feet to the first leaved branches high above the woodland floor and seemed to create a sense of order and calm in the quiet woods. We lingered a while, walking slowly around and craning our necks up at the giant trees.

Then we walked on, coming soon upon a little stream running clear and quick in the wooded shade. We jumped across and shortly beyond the opposite bank we found beneath our feet the unmistakable signs of an old and abandoned wagon trail. This we followed for several hundred yards and then cut up through a part of the woods that seemed to be in its early maturity, the trees standing strong and healthy with their August-dark green leaves flecked with sunlight. As we neared the top of the hill, we came upon outcroppings of gray rock around the foot of the trees, and the ground was carpeted with moss and gray-green lichen. We stopped and looked down the hillside, through the thick leaves at the edge of the woods, down across a neglected field spotted with young evergreen trees and choked with broomsedge, across the little stream at the bottom and up across the hill on the other side. Here and there, through the thickly-leaved branches, we caught glimpses of blue-green haze that indicated a vista of considerable distance, and at last, by maneuvering for an opening, we found a place where we could see it. "What a view!" we exclaimed as we looked out across a mile or two of rolling countryside, the fields green and smooth in the afternoon light, the woods in the distance blue in the August haze.

We had never before looked at any land that had made us want to buy. In fact, we had never before thought of buying land, but even though we lacked any good basis of comparison it seemed obvious this was beautiful and desirable property. Too, Mort had probably added somewhat to its desirability by saying to us as we set out, "I wouldn't offer it to everyone." And so we found ourselves agreeing as we walked slowly back to Mort's house that this was land we would like to own and someday build a house on.

"We think we'll take it," we told Mort, having less than $150 in the bank and no notion whatever where more money might be coming from. "We'll take it."

It was anything but clear at the outset just what it was we were going to take. Mort was willing to sell a strip off the western edge of his 125 acres, a portion which almost certainly amounted to thirty acres or more. The thought of owning thirty acres of farmland with broad sweeping fields, running brooks, and handsome woodland made me dizzy with covetousness, but I knew this was completely beyond my financial grasp. No, I told myself, the thing to do was to buy enough land to build a house and still have plenty of room for minor agricultural operations—a small woods for fireplace wood, space to grow a garden, and maybe a small field in which to pasture a pony or a steer. "This would require—what would you say, five acres? About that. Then add to that as much land as you could afford to buy as a long-range investment."

As I said this over to myself, this sounded so business-like and so intensely practical that I was almost persuaded that the question of what land we were going to buy was settled. It was only when I began to apply this logic to the land itself that I began to understand its shortcomings. "What, draw the line here and not have that lovely open field that slopes to the north? Draw it there and not have that magnificent oak tree growing by the edge of the brook? On the other hand, at several hundred dollars an acre, how much investment could I afford to make?"

My difficulty in answering these hard questions was heightened by the awkward fact that I did not, at that moment, have enough money to buy, outright, a good-sized sandbox. Still, I had a reasonably good job, and I regarded myself as a good financial risk. Surely, when one took into account the undeniable beauty and desirability of the land, I ought to have little difficulty in borrowing money with which to buy it. Banks like to support investments. Well, this was an investment. An investment in me and my future and in the earth itself, you might say. I could greatly increase the value of that land with the house I planned to build, the clearing I would undertake in the fields and woods, and innumerable other projects which might be vague in my mind at the moment but would surely take precise form when the land was mine.

These reflections bolstered my confidence that the bank would regard my request for a loan as an investment opportunity. I decided to defer the question of how much land to buy until I found out how much money the bank would wish to lend me. Perhaps the bank would urge me to buy the whole thirty-odd acres.

With this buoyant hope, I sallied forth next morning and went directly to my bank in Washington. It is a large bank, a very large bank, and one of the oldest in the city. I was directed to a Mr. Harris whose desk was in a large room on the third floor. There I sat down in the company of a number of hopeful borrowers. Apparently, the bank was not wanting for investment opportunities.

As I sat waiting my turn, I scrutinized the man who was then talking to Mr. Harris. He wore an electric-blue suit, broad wing-tipped shoes, and a red and blue tie. His long black hair shone with oil. Like most other people, I have made judging human character a lifetime hobby. Like most of us, I probably have never let a day pass without passing judgment on someone. On the basis of this rather considerable experience, I would have firmly advised Mr. Harris to say no. This fellow had too much smack of the bar and grill. Offhand, I would guess he bet on horse races, possibly even did worse things. And yet, as I watched, it became clear he was getting an affirmative reply, and I caught the words "Twenty-five hundred dollars" as the two men stood up and shook hands.

It was my turn next. As I sat down beside Mr. Harris's desk I was conscious of my conservatively-cut grey flannel suit and my quiet, blue tie. I came straight to the point and said I wanted to borrow some money to buy some land.

"Improved or unimproved land?" asked Mr. Harris.

Thinking of the sweep of that hillside and the bluegreen woods shimmering in the distance, I smiled and said that it would probably be regarded as unimproved but that actually little improvement was needed or, for that matter, possible.

"Does it have sewerage, water, or electricity?"

"Oh, no!" I said, shocked that anyone might suppose I was talking about some suburban lot. "No, it's well out in the country."

"It's rural property then. Just where is it?"

I described where it was, naming with quiet pride some of the most highly regarded place names in northern Virginia countryside. Apparently they meant nothing to Mr. Harris.

"Is it past Arlington?"

Was it past Arlington! I almost blurted out, "In every respect!" But I restrained myself and merely said, "Yes."

"I'm afraid we're not interested in unimproved rural properties," he said gently.

I thought this over for a moment. "Well," I said, "but this is a good investment, and I've been a customer of this bank for four or five years."

"How much have you got invested in the property now?"

How much invested? Well, great expectations and the beginnings of deep love. But money? I answered that I had no money invested in it as yet but that was precisely what I wished to do. Invest in it.

"But you have nothing of your own in it. The bank can't lend the whole amount. You might change your mind suddenly after buying the property and leave us with the whole thing. And you would not have lost a cent."

This analysis of my potential behavior displayed such fundamental miscomprehension as to leave me with nothing to say. It was clear that Mr. Harris did not understand what I was trying to do. I was not the kind of person who took lightly the business of buying some farmland and building a house. I was serious about it. I had never before even considered buying any land. It was a unique decision for me. But apparently not to Mr. Harris and the bank.

"On the other hand," he said, "we would be glad to make you a personal loan or an automobile loan. What kind of car do you have?"

I replied that I had a green Plymouth two-door sedan which, although it was nearly twelve years old, it had an excellent engine and ran beautifully. As I said it, I put out of mind certain idiosyncrasies of our old car, such as the tendency of the horn to blow uninhibitedly when you turned left and the considerable reluctance of the engine to start after a wet night

"I'm afraid we can't lend you any money on that," said Mr. Harris with a kind smile, "but we will be glad to make you a personal loan—say, three hundred dollars—if that will be any help to you."

Three hundred! Three thousand would be a lot closer to what I needed. Still, it was something, and I thanked him and withdrew, baffled and somewhat daunted by the impersonal approach of the bank to my intensely personal problem.

Two

During the succeeding days of that week, I carried my financial problem around to several other places: another large bank in Washington, a building and loan association in a nearby Virginia town, and a local bank in another neighboring town. The replies I got were varied but they were all negative. The large bank, like my own, quickly categorized the land I wanted to buy as *unimproved rural property* and quickly disclaimed any interest in helping me acquire it. The building and loan association said very simply that all their loan funds were committed and suggested I return in six months and renew my application. This was an honest answer with a simplicity that satisfied me at least.

The little bank in the nearby Virginia town of Vienna gave me fullest measure, in good advice, that is, but not money. The bank president, George Cobb, a sharply direct man whose glance would cause anyone who was not immaculately honest to quail, heard my story through. Then he asked, "Do you have an account with this bank?"

I explained that for five years I had had an account with my large downtown bank.

"Why don't you go to them for the money?"

I told him I had but the downtown bank felt the property was too far out for them to invest in. His sharp glance became positively piercing. "That's no reason," he said. "No reason at all." He leaned forward as though he was about to jab me. "When you took your money in there to deposit it, they didn't tell you it came from too far out, did they? Well, how can they turn around now and tell you your business isn't near enough for them?"

I felt there ought to be a reply around somewhere for questions like this but before I could lay my hand on one he had gone on.

"I'll tell you what I would do," he said in a twang as rural as a kerosene lantern,"I would go right back to them now and say, 'You did not mind where my money came from when I was depositing it but now that I need a little help you say I live too far away. Tell 'em that and see what they say."

Unhelpful as this was in solving my immediate problem, I could not help admiring it as a piece of logic as well as a smashing thrust by the small country bank at the big city bank. While I was still groping for some way to move the conversation off this point, Mr. Cobb spoke again. "We would like very much to help you," he twanged,"but we are a small bank and we must reserve all our funds for helping our regular customers. Some of them have been with us for years."

He paused. Then he said,"Here's something that may help you though. Over at the county seat there are certain lawyers that have funds to invest that belong to various estates and rich old widows and so on. They get a little higher rate of interest than we do, but they might be willing to help you. Here's the name of one. Go see him and tell him I sent you."

I rose and thanked him, not quite certain whether I was being fobbed off or genuinely helped. At any rate, I had been given one more place to try, something I would otherwise have been completely without. Meanwhile, several days elapsed before I made the trip over to the county seat and during this interval I saw Mort and recounted for him my experience. As I finished, I mentioned the name of the lawyer I had been given, James Keith.

"Oh, sure," he said. "Jim's the lawyer who drew up the deed for this property and did the paper work for the transaction. He knows this property very well. Go see him and tell him I sent you."

Thus armed with introductions, I set out on the next Monday morning for the county seat. I found James Keith without difficulty, a pleasant man about my own age whose speech and a framed diploma on the wall declared him to be Virginia bred and Virginia educated. He heard my story through. "That's a nice piece of property Morton has there," he said. "How much were you figuring on buying?"

I answered that no precise amount had been set, that figure being dependent upon the amount of money I could borrow, but that in general we were thinking of ten acres, more or less.

"How much cash can you raise?"

"Cash? Oh, you mean so that I will have something of my own in it and not be able to walk off and leave it without losing a cent. "

"That's right," he said while I sat hoping he had been impressed by my understanding of business practice. "We could not loan you the whole amount, but we ought to be able to loan you approximately two-thirds of any reasonable amount."

"Well," I said, my heart thumping at the golden prospect of near success and my head whirling with the rapid addition of such varying items as the three hundred dollar personal loan Mr. Harris had offered, Rosemary's dime bank, my small insurance holdings, our miniscule bank balance, and my son Stephen's twenty-five dollar war bond,"Well, I think I could raise a thousand dollars or so."

"Good, that gives you a figure to work with. Now before you can go any further, you'll have to have a survey made of the plot you intend to buy. You can't do anything without a survey. The deed and trust we draw up for you and everything else depends on that survey. So why don't you do this. Go get yourself a surveyor and have him survey the part you and Mort are talking about. When you know how many acres there are there and when you know how much cash you can raise, you'll be able to work out how much you can buy. We will loan you about two-thirds the total purchase."

Before I could express my delight and satisfaction over these words, my lawyer-benefactor went on in his dry way. "I can give you the name of a surveyor if you want one. Of course, they're all the same—to busy and too expensive. They probably won't be able to do your survey for two or three months, and they'll charge you fifty to seventy-five dollars an acre. Incidentally," he said laconically, "you have to pay that yourself before the purchase is closed. "

Thus deflated, my delight no longer seemed greatly in need of expression, and I carried it somewhat soberly down the street with me as I walked to the nearby office of the surveyor. I found him in a small basement, room surrounded by drawing-boards, surveying instruments, and young men like himself, leather-booted, check-shirted, and somehow indefinably woodsy. "Sure," he said,"I know the property. Runs down there to a pretty little draw, don't it? Yeah, we surveyed that whole place a year or so ago. If we can locate our corner stakes again, it ought to be an easy job."

I expressed the hope that the corner stakes would be easily re-discovered and then asked him how much he would charge me for the survey.

"Oh, we charge by the hour," he said. "Averages about fifty bucks an acre in open country and about seventy five in dense woods. Like I say, though, if we can locate them corner stakes it will take a lot less time and you might get by for twenty-five or thirty an acre."

This was cheering news indeed. "Fine," I said. "And when do you think you can get at it?"

"Oh," he said largely, "we ought to be able to do it in a month."

"Wonderful," I said. Taking into account my elation of the moment and my vast inexperience, I may be forgiven for having believed him.

The news I took home that night of my triumphal negotiation with the great financial world was the cause of shrill rejoicing and the occasion for a round of martinis before dinner. "Here's to our land!" we cried and sipped the sharp, piquant liquid. "Here's to our land!"

"Won't it be wonderful to own some land? After all this moving and renting we will have a place that is really ours. For the first time in our lives we will be able to put down some roots."

"It will be wonderful. But what will we name our place?"

"Oh, we'll call it 'Sassafrass Hill' or 'Pine Tree Run' or something like that. Something pretty and unusual."

"No, it's got to be simple. But we'll think of something. What I want to know is what kind of house will we build?"

This was a harder question, requiring thought and several more sips of the martinis. The simple truth of the matter was we had not the slightest notion of the kind of house we wanted to build. We had lived in many different houses but only one had really pleased us: a 14-room, L-shaped farmhouse in New York state, the central portion of which had been built in 1795. The simple dignity and charm of that house had captured our hearts but it seemed doubtful we could duplicate it in the mid-twentieth century.

"A New England farmhouse would be nice."

"No, I want a more formal house. One that is comfortable but also sort of—well, elegant. "

"We could build a Williamsburg colonial."

"No, they're too conventional. Also, too common."

"How about a modern house?"

"Too extreme. "

And so, in our innocence, we babbled. This was only the first of a protracted series of such conversations. In months to come, our conversations on this subject took on more maturity as we gleaned information and understanding from talks with friends, hours spent perusing the Sunday real estate sections, and excursions to new housing developments. But on this neolithic night, our talk was as insubstantial as moonbeams.

After dinner, our conversation swung to a topic with more substance: how were we going to raise a thousand dollars? Moreover, how were we going to pay the remaining two-thirds of the cost of our land? This caused us to get out the family budget and investigate what adjustments could be made in it. At first glance, not many. But still, look here. That monthly gasoline bill was certainly higher than it should be. Probably included gasoline chits from our vacation trip. And that electric bill was surely higher than normal. Must have been doing a lot of baking. And the telephone bill included several extraordinary long-distance calls.

In short, it soon became clear, as it had always become clear during previous investigations of this sort, that there was a reasonably substantial amount of money coming in each month. The whole trouble was that it was going out faster than it should or at any rate, faster than it needed to. For some reason or other, our bills just at that moment were unusually high. In more *normal* times, they would be lower and we would have a margin with which to make regular payments on our land. It could be done.

But maybe we could accelerate the process if we took more drastic measures. Take our rent, for instance. It was undeniably high. Too high. We ought to be able to find a house with a rental $25 lower. That would certainly help. Of course, it might mean moving some distance away from our land, at present just over the hill, but sacrifices would have to be made if we were to reach our goal. In fact, speaking of sacrifices, we might even—and here we grew solemn at the thought—give up martinis.

Fortified by such high-minded thoughts and the decision Rosemary would begin househunting next morning, we put the subject away for the time being. We felt we were on our way. The day would surely come when we would be the owners of a small estate in the Virginia countryside.

Three

While Rose was looking for another house to rent—and finding one—and while we were engaged in that dreadfully familiar process, packing and moving, September came and went in the Virginia countryside and left us with October. By this time, the leaves in the woods we now called *our woods* were pink and red with the slow fire of the Southern autumn and the broomsedge in the fields was a mature yellow. To my eye it was tawny and handsome as it surged in the breeze but Mort had acquired enough agricultural lore to know it bespoke slovenly, wasted land.

"Got to cut it," he said. "Fire hazard. Besides, if you cut it for several years, it'll all come back into blue grass. Tell you what I'll do. You help cut mine and I'll help cut yours. With my jeep and that big mower." He paused while I considered this and then added, "Of course, you can burn it if you prefer." He grinned.

Burning broomsedge was something we both knew a little about. The previous autumn, when we were newcomers to the neighborhood, Mort held a *burning* on a Sunday morning and had invited us and a half dozen others to assist. Armed with brooms, shovels, and cedar saplings, we were to keep the fire from spreading too rapidly. On the whole, the burning went very well but toward the end the wind came up unexpectedly and at once a whole hillside was ablaze and the fire was running rapidly toward one of Mort's boundaries and a neighbor's house. It took Herculean efforts to stop it and then we were exhausted and slightly giddy. We straggled into Mort's house, a smoky, be-smudged group, and wolfed down sandwiches and whisky highballs. When Mort's whisky gave out under this onslaught, someone else suggested we move on to his house and his whisky. Move we did, and then again, and the party drew to a glorious, hilarious close in a round of square dancing about midnight. It was an epic occasion, and incidentally one which convinced us that this was a neighborhood in which we wished to live. But the *burning* itself did not commend itself to me as an ideal way of removing broomsedge.

"No," I said, "I'd rather cut it. Let's do it together, as you suggest."

"Okay, but first you've got to clear your field of those 'volunteer' pines and cedars. Got to cut them off close to the ground so they don't catch the cutter bar."

"Fine, I'll start on it tomorrow. "

Next morning, as I stood at the edge of the field with axe and bow saw in hand, I realized that I had taken on a large task. The sun was still in its first hour's ascent of the eastern sky and it marked the innumerable pine and cedar saplings with strong contrasts of light and shadow. In that light, they seemed to number in the thousands, crowds of little trees marching up the slope and mingling companionably with the blackberry briar and the broomsedge. Moreover, the task required decisions. Should I take down every tree right up to the fence or should I leave an incipient hedgerow? Somewhere I had read that small wildlife, particularly birds and small game, would leave an area if all their cover, particularly the hedgerows, were removed. Well, that argued in favor of hedgerows. But what about the rest of the field? Should I take out all the trees, including some that were clearly three or four years old and stood twelve or fifteen feet high? Or should I leave some to lend variety and interest to the field, but strive to group them in such a way as to cause as little difficulty as possible in the mowing? Well, clearly the latter.

But these were questions, I decided, that would have to be worked out as I went along. I removed the three bottles of beer I had stowed in the game pocket of my hunting jacket and placed them carefully in the swiftly running stream. Then I jumped across the little brook and climbed the hillside in the clean October sunlight.

It was intoxicating work, I discovered, work well calculated to give a man a sense of power. As a starter, I picked a pine tree about six feet tall and sat down beside it with my bow saw. There was a moment's difficulty getting the saw started but then it caught hold and in less than fifteen seconds the little tree toppled over with a soft swish and the air was pungent with the smell of raw resin. This was sport! I threw the small pine up against the fence its needles still glossy green in the keen sunshine, and attacked another tree. And so I worked for the next hour or so while the sun climbed steadily up the bright blue October sky. As I moved from tree to tree, brambles and briars caught at my dungarees, and I found myself thinking maliciously that their sudden death under the flailing knives of Mort's mower was certain and imminent. Once a large rabbit took fright at the unusual activity in the field and scurried away in elaborately erratic bounces, his tail a big round puff of white in the sunlight. For a moment I entertained myself by thinking of him as *my* rabbit, dwelling in *my* field, but I quickly cast it out as an unworthy thought.

After a good hour of felling trees, my arms were tired from the unaccustomed work and my throat was dry and dusty. So I hung my bow saw on the lower limb of a nearby pine, leaned the axe against the trunk, and walked back to the brook. My bottles of beer lay in the cold, swift water, moving gently to the thrust and sway of the current. I plucked one out and opened it and let the cold, amber liquid gurgle down my throat. My God, how good! I sat down with my back against a large oak tree and drank the rest of the bottle slowly, savoring the tingling coldness in my mouth. But I quickly became restless. It would be fun to finish that slope where I had been working and then start on the one beside it. I could let stand that line of pines that ran down the edge of that little ridge and clear out a broad sweep beside it that would run from the brook at the bottom of the field to the woods at the top. Somehow that would seem harmonious and handsome. And, slightly stimulated by the beer but thoroughly intoxicated by my new-found power to mold the landscape of an entire hillside, I jumped back across the brook and hurried up the hill.

I had been back at work for a half hour or so when I heard someone call and looked down the hill to see a man on a black horse. It was Bud. "Hi," he called, "whatcha doin'?"

"Cuttin' trees."

I strolled down the hill and stood beside the big horse. "I was just giving Blackberry a little exercise and I thought I'd come by and see how you're doin'. Mort tells me you're going to buy this piece of land. "

"Guess so. Hope someday to build a house on it."

"It's a mighty pretty piece of land. Just about the prettiest Mort has. Where you going to put the house?"

"Oh, I don't know. Maybe up there on the top of the hill where you get such a wonderful view. Or maybe lower down on that side over there where it's protected."

Bud nodded. "That's a good site. Then you can run your driveway right in along the stream here. "

I was shocked. "Oh, no! The place for the drive is right along the top of the hill there. You come right in at the level of the house and then you don't have a hill to climb in the drive. "

"Yeah, but you have all those trees to take out and besides there's rock in that hillside. You could put a drive in with a lot less trouble down here. And the ground is firm and drains well. This is the place for the drive." This was sound advice Bud was giving me, the first in a long series, but I was too uninformed to recognize it and could only wonder at his wrongheadedness. Then he laughed, a dry, farmerish laugh that was nearly a cackle. "You know, I don't really care where you put your drive but I think it's nice you've decided to stay in the neighborhood. You'll have a nice place here." He looked over at my large mound of cut trees. He paused and then said, ''You ought to think twice before you cut one down. You can cut 'em down a lot faster than you can grow 'em and once they're down they're hard to put back. "

Sobered by the contrast between this thought and the zest with which I had been slaughtering trees, I looked at the small mountain of cut pines and said, "Guess you're right."

"Well, let's go, Blackberry," said Bud. "Stop by and have a drink with us sometime. We're always home." And he rode off across the field and into the woods.

I stood watching him go, a casual lean figure on the big horse. And I grinned as I went back to cutting trees, pleased with the man and his manner and pleased with the idea of a neighbor coming to call on horseback.

I worked steadily away on the hillside until noon. By then, my pile of trees had become really formidable. The steady climbing of the sun in the brilliant sky had forced me first to take off my hunting jacket and then my heavy shirt

So by this time I was working in a tee shirt. My leather gloves were black with resin and pungent with the smell of pine. I had just felled another tree when I heard a whoop in the distance and saw Rose down by the brook with a picnic basket. Lunch!

As we sat munching our egg-and-olive sandwiches under the canopy of oak leaves far overhead, I described to Rosemary the plan I had for clearing a broad sweep of field from the brook to the woods. "That's fine," she said, "but don't forget to leave some pines for Christmas trees." Christmas trees! There was still another consideration.

"Oh, sure," I said, as though I had a fully detailed blueprint in my mind, "I plan to leave that whole grove of pines there to the right as Christmas tree stock."

In my ravenous state, lunch was soon concluded, and we lazed in the noonday sun for another ten or fifteen minutes, talking idly of our plans and dreams, noting the swift arrival and departure of a bird on a nearby limb, and testing with our fingertips the nubbly feel of the moss at the root of the oaks. But some new fever was working in my blood and I was itching to get back to the hillside and further my sculpture of the land.

I had worked for another hour, laying low another platoon of pines, when Mort came by in his jeep. "Thought I'd stop by to see how you're doing," he said. "How's it coming?"

"Fine. I doubt though that I can finish today. Probably be able to wind it up next weekend, probably Saturday morning. Maybe we can start mowing Saturday afternoon or Sunday morning."

"Okay." Mort cast a critical eye over my work. "Seems a shame to take out those little cedars," he said. "I transplanted a lot of mine and made a row down along my drive. You might make a line of them there along the fence."

I looked over to the fence, seeing in my mind's eye a line of mature cedar trees marching up the hillside, their branches etched with pen-and-ink sharpness against the blazing blue sky. Rosemary and I had always admired the line of cedars in the Virginia countryside, running along fence rows and standing stark and distinct against the autumn skies. This was surely a good idea, to transplant the cedars. "I think you're right. I'll bring a shovel and wheelbarrow next week and do that."

"Yeah." Mort looked again at my handiwork. "You're cutting them off good and close aren't you?"

"Sure. They won't give the cutter bar any trouble. Some of them I've been cutting off practically underground." I paused and my conversation with Bud came to mind. "Say Mort, Bud was by a while ago and said he thought I ought to put the drive in down along the stream. I'd kinda thought it ought to be put in up there in the woods at the top of the hill What do you think?"

"Well, " he said, pausing for an instant "you remember about The Acre up there, don't you?"

"I remember your telling me about The Acre but I don't think I ever knew exactly where it was. Where is it."

"Let's go up there now and look. Maybe we can find the corner stakes and figure out exactly where it is"

I put my tools down near the last tree I had cut, and the three of us set out up the slope in quest of The Acre. Mort had explained to me at the first how the problem of The Acre had arisen, how the old man who was selling off the family homestead had asked, as a favor, that one acre be deeded to his nephew, a young man who had grown up on the farm and who loved the land deeply. Flushed with the acquisition of almost one hundred fifty acres, Mort had quickly agreed and had given the old man the freedom of his choice. With a worn finger, the old man had pointed at the southwest corner of the plot. "There," he said.

There turned out to be the uppermost corner of *my* woods, and its boundaries comprised over two hundred feet of road frontage, a long dominating line right on the ridge of the hill and a long sweep through some of the handsomest woods back to the fenceline. Moreover, the old logging road that Rosemary and I had discovered on the occasion of our first walk through the woods had its beginning right at the corner of The Acre. There were remains of a gate still to be seen there, and the old road ran indistinctly under the leaves and the fallen trees, forming a natural entrance to my proposed building site.

"My God," I said, "this is awful! This Acre cut out of here messes up everything."

"I know," said Mort, "it is bad, but what could I do?" He was so obviously unhappy about it that I felt obliged to console him."Besides," said Mort. "He's just a young fellow. Maybe he will want to sell it sometime soon."

"Maybe," I said, "but it sure is a mess." And I walked back down the hill, disconsolate and unhappy that my future domain was to contain one acre less than I had hoped. It seemed for the moment to be a major catastrophe. After another hour of felling trees, however, its importance reduced considerably.

By the time the next weekend had rolled around and I found myself once again on that handsome hillside—the air redolent with autumn and the sky a silver-edged blue—it no longer seemed a matter to worry much about. Maybe the old man's nephew would sell me that acre someday. If he did not, there was plenty of space left in which to place a house in privacy and beauty, and if necessary I could adopt Bud's suggestion and run the road in along the stream.

The golden October morning passed swiftly as I went back to sculpturing the landscape of the hill. After five desk-bound days, my back and arm muscles took up sawing and chopping with joy and vigor, and I found as noon approached that I had nearly finished the clearing neces-sary before mowing. The new part of the job was trans-planting the cedars. I was quite uncertain as to how large the *ball* of earth surrounding the roots needed to be, but I reasoned that these particular trees were otherwise doomed and I was therefore justified in taking the smallest possible amount of earth. I drove my spade into the earth on four sides about a foot out from the red-skinned cedar trunk and pried the trees and the wedge of dirt out of the ground. Then I trundled the cedar in the wheelbarrow out across the field to the fence, dug a small wedge of dirt out of the ground about three feet away from the nearest tree, and jammed the cedar into place. This was fairly brutal treat-ment, and I had no expectation that everyone of the half dozen trees I transplanted would survive—as turned out to be the case—but such apparently is the toughness of the native Virginia cedar and such is the growing power of that red clay soil.

I was still tamping in a newly-moved cedar when Mort came by and asked, "How you coming?"

"Fine. Almost finished."

"You want to start mowing after lunch?"

"Sure. Rarin' to get started."

"Okay, come over when you're ready."

After lunch, eaten again under the oak trees beside the stream—where Rosemary had spent the morning building a small fireplace with rocks pulled out of the stream-bed— I walked through the woods to Mort's house. We got in his jeep and drove out across a field to the mower. We hitched it up and Mort explained how to work it. "I'll drive the jeep to start with—we'll trade later—and you ride the mower. All you do is watch for rocks and stumps and lift up the blade of the mower, with that foot pedal and that handle, whenever you see anything coming."

"Okay. Let'er rip."

Mort got in the jeep and eased out the clutch. With an enormous clatter the mower began to move and the scores of triangular knives on the long mowing blade shuttled back and forth in a slashing fury. Experimentally, I lifted the blade with the foot pedal and the handle and found it came up as much as two feet on the tip. Mort looked back over his shoulder and yelled, "We'll mow along this lane that runs over to the old homestead first and then we'll try that steep hillside over there."

I nodded and watched with fascination as the mower blade moved smoothly over the ground and impartially felled broomsedge, blackberry briar, pine fingerlings, and inch-thick weed stalks. Pitiless and furiously energetic, it advanced upon a stand of broomsedge and felled rank upon rank of the yellow, grain-like columns. Sometimes the broomsedge and briar were so heavy and thick that I lost sight of the blade and the slashing knives, and I amused myself with the notion that the plants and grass were seeking to resist the advance of the blade through sheer weight of numbers. But always underneath there was the sound of the furious energy and a fierce commotion in the grass. The heads of the broomsedge would vibrate briefly, then sag and fall gently to the ground. Sometimes a tall weed, its inch-thick stalk snipped off at the base, would be supported by masses of surrounding broomsedge, and it would continue to stand as though defiant and impervious to the steel. But eventually, sometimes as long as twenty or thirty seconds after the blade had passed, the stalk would succumb to the inevitable and slowly topple.

My reveries were suddenly interrupted by Mort's yell,

"Look out for that stump!" I looked ahead and saw an old pine stump standing six or eight inches above the ground.

"See it." And I pushed down the pedal and pulled back on the handle and lifted the blade, the knives still slashing, over the stump and lowered again to the ground. But I soon saw another stump coming and then another. We had moved into a part of the field where a small grove of pine trees had formerly stood and Mort's tenant, who had done the job of felling them as partial payment of his rent, had not been careful to cut them off even with the ground. I found that I had to keep the mower blade raised six or eight inches for several minutes at a time, and though this did not require any great exertion for a brief period the sustained effort soon had my thigh and arm muscles quivering with fatigue. After a while, Mort yelled back, "Want to change?"

"Yeah, I do."

He stopped the jeep and walked back. "We've got quite a bit done so far," he said, looking back over the long rows we had cut. I jumped down from the mower, my legs limp with the unaccustomed exertion, and got in the jeep. "There's nothing to it, " said Mort. "Just keep it in low-low and don't go much over five miles an hour. Keep an eye on the temperature gauge and don't let it get too hot."

I dropped into low-low and slowly let the clutch out. At once, the furious clatter set up behind me and the long blade began to slide forward against the grass and the weeds. Jeeps, like Model T Fords, are always fun to drive, and I thoroughly enjoyed myself, sitting nearly motionless amidst the uproar of the sturdy four-cylinder engine ahead of me and the clatter of the mower behind. Despite the din, it was somehow pleasant and gratifying. There was nothing to it, just as Mort had said. I kept a wary eye ahead for rocks and stumps and steered as closely as possible to the inside edge of the previous cut so as to get the maximum amount of new cut. The most interesting phase of the job came at the corners when I drove the jeep straight ahead into the part already mown and then swung into the 270-degree turn to the left that brought the mower blade smartly around at right angles to the previous direction. After several times, Mort began to kick the cutter bar out of gear with the clutch pedal on the mower, and then, with the knives still and silent, I would zip the jeep around in a quick, hard turn, slowing down just as the blade reached the unmown grass and Mort kicked it back into gear. We began to take great delight in seeing how quickly and with what precision this maneuver could be performed: Mort attempting to kick the mower out of gear the exact instant the blade reached the mown edge and to drop it back in just as the teeth touched unmown grass; I attempting to swing the jeep and mower around in the fastest, hardest turn and to bring the cutter bar up to the unmown edge fore-square and precisely in place.

After a while, Mort and I traded places again, and I resumed my fanciful reveries as the yellow broomsedge ranks fell in long and even rows and the briars twisted and writhed as though in agony under the slashing knives. We also played our little game at the corners and I experienced the fun of clutching in and out at the exact instant and of hanging on for dear life as the mower bounced around in a tight turn behind the jeep. In fact, so much did I enjoy this new-found sport—playing at farmering— that the afternoon passed with incredible swiftness and I suddenly noticed with great surprise that dusk was gathering in the corners and under the trees. Mort looked back just as I was looking at my watch, and he nodded in comprehension. "We'd better quit," he yelled.

At the end of the row, he swung the jeep out and around and, with the mower out of gear and running silently except for a clicking in the gearbox, we cut across the field to the lane and drove back to his house. I dismounted from the steel seat with stiff and aching legs.

"How about tomorrow?"

"Sure, what time?"

"Well, there's no sense in starting too early because the grass is wet and the mower doesn't cut well. What about eight o'clock?"

"I'll be there," I said, as though I had been accustomed for years to start mowing fields at eight o'clock on Sunday morning.

"Tell you what we'll do. We'll finish mowing that field we're in tomorrow morning and then we'll do yours after lunch. We can mow yours in two or three hours."

Next morning at eight o'clock, the skies were gray and hard, and the October wind was direct and sharp. I stood beside the mower as Mort packed grease into the gearbox with a stick. "Think it will rain?"

"Sure looks like it." He looked up at the gray clouds, the overcast so solid that no part of the sky was lighter than any other. "We can get started though and mow till it rains."

In a few minutes, we had the mower hitched behind the jeep, and I climbed up into the steel tractor-type seat as Mort got in behind the wheel. My flesh winced as it settled against the steel that had jounced it so hard the day before, and my leg muscles recorded stiffness and soreness as I lifted the cutter bar with the pedal. With an inquiring glance back, Mort let out the clutch, and we moved slowly and then more rapidly out across the field to the new mowing site.

Soon we were mowing, not with quite as much zest as the day before but pleasantly enough, and I fell very quickly once again under the spell of the furiously clattering mower and the steadily toppling broomsedge. My hands, however, soon felt the numbing cold of the steel handle through my thin leather glove, and after twenty minutes or so I called to Mort. "How about trading?"

"Sure." He stopped the jeep and came back. "What's the trouble?"

"Cold. My hands are about to drop off."

"Really? I didn't think it was that cold."

Once inside the jeep, running along evenly at five miles an hour in low-low, I soon discovered why. The jeep with its side curtains and its steadily turning engine was warm and snug. My hands thawed very quickly, and I had to open the collar of my hunting jacket. Soon, though, I looked back and saw Mort, his face red from the cold wind, warming one of his hands by sticking it under an armpit. When we came to the next turn, I paused and asked, "Want to change?"

We fell into a rhythm of changing at regular, short intervals and so the morning passed, time moving as it had the day before with extraordinary swiftness. Just before lunch we had a misadventure that broke with dramatic sharpness the grey evenness of the morning's work. We had noticed the day before that the cut broomsedge somehow got itself caught up and collected by the underparts of the jeep. It particularly seemed to jam itself between the frame and the muffler. Mindful of the inflammability of the broomsedge, as demonstrated at Mort's *burning*, we had stopped several times during the course of the afternoon to pull it out. Some of the stalks were charred and black.

But perhaps because of the cold, we had neglected to do this at any time on Sunday morning, and I was driving the jeep when suddenly smoke began to come wisping out from the hood and up through the cracks in the floorboards. "Hey, we're on fire!"

I jammed the jeep to a stop and turned off the switch,

thinking somehow that the danger of gasoline explosion would be lessened. Mort leaped off the mower and ran to the front of the jeep and pulled up the hood. A billow of blue smoke came up and underneath it was a lick of flame. We both grabbed up swatches of broomsedge and began beating at the fire which seemed to come from down along the side of the engine block. Our efforts appeared only to fan the flames, though, and meanwhile a spark from underneath ignited the broomsedge on the ground beneath the jeep.

"My God!" cried Mort, "the whole thing will go up! You get in and drive it down to the creek. I'll disconnect the mower."

Not liking the idea one bit, I got in the jeep and turned on the switch as Mort ran to the back and furiously began turning the set-screw on the hitch. In the heat of the moment I must have tried too hard because the jeep engine refused to start and the starter whirred over and over futilely. By this time, the smoke was coming up through the floorboards in volume. Again and again I pushed on the starter and it turned the stubborn engine over and over. Mort appeared beside me. "Here, let me try." He got in as I jumped out and began pushing hard on the starter button but with no success. I ran to the front of the jeep and again began beating frantically at the flames.

Mort jumped out of the jeep again. "Let's push it. We'll push it down into the creek." I ran to the back and pushed and soon we had the jeep moving down the gentle slope. "It's okay," said Mort, jumping in, "we've got her now." The jeep continued to roll unaided and I stopped and watched it go on down to the creek. Mort steered toward a spot where the bank was gradual and drove right into the water. Then he jumped out and sloshed water onto the burning broomsedge until the fire was out. I ran back to the spot where the fire had started and began beating and stomping on the burning grass. Within several minutes I had it under control and I walked down the hill to join Mort.

He had just got in the jeep and just as I walked up he pushed the starter button. The engine started at once, and he backed out of the creek and turned around. "Pretty exciting," he said as I got in.

"Yeah, I thought for a minute there we were going to lose her."

"It was a pretty close thing. We'll have to watch that broomsedge under there more carefully." He looked back up the hill to the unhitched mower. "How about it. Shall we finish this field now and start on yours after lunch?"

"Sure."

After lunch, we drove over to my field. There was no direct route that was passable for the jeep and mower, so we drove out along the lane to the old farmstead, fording a small stream on the way, and then on up the driveway to the little country road that ran beside my fenceline. The iron wheels of the mower grated and creaked on the gravel. As we came down the hill around an unpainted gray house, two little black children ran out, their mouths gleaming in their dark faces. "Hello!" they said in high little voices as thin as tin whistles,

"Hello!"

After we had maneuvered the jeep and the mower into the field through a break in the fence, Mort asked, "Where shall we start?"

"Let's mow this piece along the road first."

With almost professional ease, we flipped jeep and mower around into place and began mowing the field, *my* field. It went off in routine fashion and very quickly.

"There you are," said Mort as we slashed through the last stand of briar. "All mowed."

What a difference it made! Before, the uneven height of the weeds, broomsedge, and briar and the differences in color and texture had broken the broad sweep of the field into small patches, thereby reducing its visual size. Now the eye ran without a break across the mown surface, and the field seemed to have grown two or three times in size. The difference was amazing. I got down off the mower and walked slowly over the ground, enjoying the long line of the brook and the graceful upward sweep of the field to the woods at the top. The newly visible details of the meadow—the new-mown edge of the stream revealing the clear water foaming and gurgling over a rocky bed, the little rolls and ripples of the old field under the grass, the moss-green rocks that lay exposed in the falling light of the late October afternoon—made it seem more handsome than it had before.

I was still staring at it with possessive affection as Mort and I squeezed the mower through the fence and started up the road, the wheels grating on the gravel. Mort turned around and called back as we rolled slowly up the road. "Didn't rain after all, did it?"

Four

As I drove to work on Monday morning, I got to reflecting on the new meaning the weekends had acquired over the past month. Weekends in the country had nearly always been pleasant and a cause for gentle anticipation throughout the week. But they were mostly aimless and idle. Sometimes, when the weather was raw and rainy, they were boring. But ever since that August afternoon when Rosemary and I decided we would buy the land and build a house on it, the weekends had become important and valuable. They had taken on a continuity of their own, and the thread that bound them together over a succession of five-day work weeks was the progress I was making toward that distant goal: a house on my own land.

From that long perspective I had made only a meager beginning. But I had begun. In the long series of weekends lying ahead, I could look forward to slow, gradual progress. At the moment, though, all forward progress was waiting for the land survey. It was the key to everything. Until it had been done I could not even buy the land, let alone build a house on it. I decided to call the surveyor that day and prod him hard.

Our telephone conversation, the first in a long series, was not exactly reassuring. I waited while my call went into the telephone exchange at the county seat, and I could hear the Washington operator and the town operator negotiating for the number. The telephone rang in the coarse, reedy way of country telephones and a voice answered, "Hello!"

"Hello!" I said and went on to identify myself, a task that somehow seemed more difficult than I expected it to be. Finally, comprehension descended.

"Oh, yeah. You're talking about the job of surveying that place over there that runs down to that pretty little draw alongside the road."

"That's right. How are you coming with it?"

"Well, we've been pretty busy lately and the weather hasn't been too good. You know, we can't get as much done when the weather's bad."

"I suppose that's so." A pause while I wondered to myself why it should be, if it was. "Well, when do you think you can get at my job?"

"Well, I'd say pretty soon now."

"That's fine." Silence. "Well, just when?"

"Well, let's see now." A series of muffled noises came through the telephone as he talked with someone in the room while holding his hand loosely over the mouthpiece. "Well, it looks as though we ought to be able to get at it the end of this week or the beginning of next."

"That's fine. Swell. You're sure you can get started then, are you?"

"Well, we'll certainly do our best."

And with this, I was obliged to be content. That night, over our after-dinner coffee, I reported this conversation to Rosemary. ''Well, they'd better start this week or sometime soon," she said. "You can't do anything until the survey is done, can you?"

Challenged by this question whose fundamental truth was unchallengeable, I said, "Oh, there are lots of things I can get done before then. I'll keep on working on the weekends."

"What is there to do?"

"Well, I want to cut a path through the woods from the Freligh's house so we can go back and forth more easily. And I want to fix up a campsite there beside the stream. And there's quite a bit of underbrush in the woods I would like to clear out. And, oh yes," I said, grateful for another sizeable project that came to mind, "I need to cut a fair amount of fire wood for the fireplace here."

On Saturday morning of the next weekend, I jumped across the little stream that divided the Freligh's front lawn from the woods and looked for a place to begin clearing a path. In my hands I carried the bow saw, the axe, and a weed whip I had bought at a hardware store on my way home from work the night before. It was a rugged tool with a red-stained handle and a three-inch blade with a serrated edge. You swung it much like a golf club. And with no more than a brief survey of the problem before me, I set to work. The weed whip I used when the way ahead was blocked largely by weeds and pine fingerlings. When scrub oak and other more sturdy shrubs stood before me, I used the axe. And when small trees, between two inches and six inches in diameter blocked my progress, I used the bow saw.

As before, I found the task of felling bushes and toppling small trees highly pleasurable, and I fell to with considerable zest. In fact, I had to restrain myself when I came to a small pine grove because my tendency was to clear out the entire grove.

Throughout the morning I was working in a little flatland, and the stream ran some ten or twelve feet away, chuckling and amiable in the morning light. In the afternoon, having whipped through a formidable poison ivy bed, I found myself working at a fairly steep hillside and the stream was directly below me, at the foot of a little bluff some fifteen feet high. And so the day passed in progress and pleasure: the sharp green odor of the weeds, the pungency of the pine resin oozing out of the raw stumps in crystalline drops, the sounds of the running stream, and the needle-thin squeaks of the tiny birds I glimpsed now and then amongst the pine trees. At the end of the day, as the western sun was lighting the tops of the oak trees overhead in gold, I stood at the edge of the woods on the bank of the tributary stream that divided the woods from my meadow. And I realized that I had discovered a new project: to build a bridge.

Not a very complicated bridge, I decided as I drove home through the deepening dusk, but one strong enough to support a loaded wheelbarrow. Such a bridge could be made of two tree trunks—roughly six inches in diameter and about fourteen feet long—and some planking nailed across them.

Next morning, I stopped by Jack Durham's house. He came out of it to greet me, still swallowing some of his breakfast. "You mentioned some old oak planks I could have. Do you still want to give them to me?"

"Sure, by all means. Want to get rid of them; they're just rotting away. They're over here by the tool shed. Come have a look."

We found them lying alongside the shed, partly obscured by the rank grass, the remnants of a barn some predecessor of Jack's had built with purpose and pride some fifty or more years before. But they were still sound and monstrously heavy as a result of the moisture they had absorbed while lying on the ground. "How many shall I take?"

"Take them all. They're no good to me."

Laden with this treasure, I set off again and found myself with a new problem. I could either go into Mort's drive and then lug the heavy planks some eight or nine hundred feet through the woods on the path I had just cleared or I could go down the little gravel road that ran alongside *the woods* and carry the planks approximately six hundred feet through the newly mown meadow. I decided in favor of the little gravel road, and as I approached *the woods* I decided on an even bolder course: I would drive right down the old logging road that ran through the woods and come out into the meadow within twenty feet to the proposed bridge site.

I turned cautiously in at the break in the fence which marked the beginning of the old road, running obscurely beneath the heavy overlay of old leaves, and eased the car slowly along between old stumps and fallen limbs. Several times I had to get out and haul limbs out of the way, but except for one place—where an enormous chestnut trunk lay athwart the road (felled perhaps during the chestnut blight some forty years before) and I was obliged to snake the car through an exceedingly narrow opening between a large oak tree and the butt of the chestnut stump—the way was direct and easy and I brought my load directly up to the place it was needed.

Building a bridge, at least the extremely simple bridge I undertook to build, was quite straightforward. The most difficult part was the beginning: finding two six-inch trunks which were moderately straight for a length of fourteen feet. It was surprising. My general impression had been that the trees of the woods, particularly the young ones, grew as straight as pencils. But most trees, when examined with an eye to their becoming the supporting span of a footbridge, wavered in their ascent skyward to a marked degree. I spent much of an hour walking from one tree to the next and standing at their base squinting upwards. At last, I settled on a tulip poplar which grew right at the bridge site and on a young oak which grew some fifty feet away.

Felling them and trimming them and dragging them to

place was the work of another hour. Then I began the straightforward but slow and very laborious task of sawing the oak planks into four-foot lengths and nailing them onto the log spans. The nailing was extraordinarily difficult. Fifty-year-old oak takes on a degree of hardness somewhere between cement and granite, and shiny eight-penny nails curl over under hammer blows like cut dandelion stems in the sunshine. I was irreparably bending five nails to every one I drove home before my mind brought up out of the mists of the past an image of my father (a notable handy-man, as I was emphatically not) rubbing nails with a dirty bar of Ivory soap before driving them in. After I had borrowed a bar of soap from Barbara Freligh, I lowered my average of bent nails to two for every one driven home.

By the end of the afternoon the bridge was finished, and Rosemary and Steve and I walked back and forth over it again and again. Somehow, I had never before realized how intensely pleasurable it was to go from one side of a stream to another, especially on a bridge one had built himself. It really was quite extraordinary, I reflected, that one could grow to maturity without experiencing the intense satisfactions of building a bridge. Why, to build a bridge was really much akin to settling the wilderness. It was, when you come to think of it, in essence the extension of man's communications, the—. These very solemn reflections were suddenly broken as my eight-year-old son began to derive maximum value from the limberness of the supporting tree trunks by rhythmically jumping up and down on the bridge, *my* bridge.

"No," I said, remembering the wheelbarrow loads I had envisioned as crossing it, "no, it isn't that. It's just that it somehow doesn't seem—well, it's just that it's—well, it isn't what I built it for," I finished weakly. Rose smiled and Steve stood waiting. "Oh, well," I said, "go ahead and jump. I guess it's all right."

And as I gathered up my tools while Steve jumped and jumped like a trapeze performer on a trampoline, I tried to convince myself that it was something of a triumph to have constructed something which was at once so useful and the source of so much youthful joy.

Sometime during the course of the next week I put through another call to the land surveyor. Our conversation differed in details from the previous one, but the substance was entirely the same. It looked like another week, and he would surely do his best.

The next weekend I devoted to cutting wood for our fireplace at home, it then being well into November. A large tree had fallen into the stream near my new bridge, no man could say how many years before, and its stiff dead branches stuck out awkwardly into the meadow. They had, in fact, prevented Mort and me from mowing quite as close to the stream as I would have liked. It looked as though I could accomplish two purposes at once: clear the field of an obstruction and obtain firewood. And so I set to work, sawing and chopping in the brisk autumn air, reminding myself of Henry Thoreau's observation that in cutting his own firewood a man is warmed twice: Once by the spiritual satisfaction of honest toil and again by the combustion of the wood he has cut. I cut a fair quantity of firewood from the dead tree (expert opinion judged it to be a black walnut), and I managed with only a slight spinning of the wheels on the wet leaves to snake the car in through the woods and out again laden with wood. On Sunday night, I stood before a crackling fire of black walnut logs— a bourbon old fashioned in my hand, my arms and back pleasantly tired from chopping and sawing—and I told myself that this was hard to beat.

"What do you plan to do next weekend?" asked Rosemary.

"What? Oh, well, I guess I will cut some more firewood and do some clearing."

And so our weekends fell into a pattern. On Saturday mornings I would load the tools into the car and drive over to the woods. Sometimes, Rose would go along and drop me—my tools, my sandwiches, and my thermos of coffee—while she went shopping or ran errands. Occasionally, if the weather was fair, she would spend either the morning or afternoon with me, doing a little sawing but mostly exploring through the woods, looking for interesting mosses, ground pine, and partridge berries. On Sundays, almost without fail, we ate lunch at our simple little campsite in the woods. In some way it became established that baked beans was the menu for our Sunday luncheon, and each week we exchanged solemn judgments—sitting there beneath the tall oak trees with the campfire alternately warming us and smothering us with pungent smoke—on the quality of that week's beans: too much molasses? just right on garlic? cooked a bit too long? And late Sunday afternoon we drove home, the car loaded to the gunwales with firewood, thinking about the good hot baths and the old fashioneds that were to come.

One weekend in early December it rained so steadily and so determinedly that it drove out all thoughts of spending the day in the woods. I paced up and down and sulked and tried in vain to remember what it was I used to do on the weekends before the *woods* came into my life.

Another weekend in December, I was happily working away on a Sunday morning when Bud Bradley came by on Blackberry. I had spent the day before cutting fireplace wood and had taken in my quota for the weekend. On this day, I was clearing a path between the logging road and what I thought might be a new campsite. Bud rode along under the trees on the big black horse, a slender, casual figure, more than a little quizzical, and he reined the horse in to a stop not far from where I was swinging the weed whip.

"Watcha doin'?" he asked.

"I'm clearing out a path here from that old road to a place where I want to put up a camp site."

There was a long silence, broken only by the blowing and occasional stamping of the horse and the needle-like twittering of some unseen birds. "It will just grow back," said Bud.

"Well, I suppose that's so," I said, somewhat defensively, "but I intend to keep it cleared."

There was another long pause, and Blackberry snorted in a very decisive fashion. The twittering birds suddenly flew out of a nearby pine tree with a feathery flutter.

"You know," said Bud in his mild, dry way, "what you really ought to do is to build something."

"Like what, for instance?" I asked.

"I don't know. What do you need? How about a tool shed to store your tools in during the week?"

"You mean *me*, build a tool shed?"

"Sure, why not?"

"I never built anything in my life except a lop-sided set of book ends in manual training in school. And I got a *D* in that." I *looked* speculatively at Bud and Blackberry. "I'll admit a tool shed would be a fine thing and would save me hauling my tools back and forth every weekend but I would never try to build one. Maybe I can get a pre-fab somewhere and have it set up. Sure would be a help."

Bud grinned at me disarmingly. "You could build it yourself an awful lot cheaper. Anyway, the thing is to start building something permanent. Just remember, everything you cut down now will grow back next summer."

It was a sobering thought. And as Bud and Blackberry ambled slowly down the woodland road toward the new-mown field, I tried to imagine where I would put a tool shed if I had one. But it really was an alien thought, too advanced—six or eight months too advanced, as it turned out—and I left it with no reluctance and returned with pleasure to clearing a path through the underbrush.

It was a simple task, a soul-satisfying task, and it required no planning, only a willingness to expend a certain amount of energy.

The early weeks of December passed—still no land survey--and all at once Christmas came upon us. We were living in a guest house on a large farm, some ten miles away from the *woods*, and pine trees grew in abundance no more than fifty feet from our door. But nothing would do for our Christmas tree except a tree cut from our own woods, more particularly from that little grove of Christmas tree stock I had preserved on the hillside. It had snowed lightly during the night, and as I eased the car down around the old chestnut stump on the afternoon of Christmas Eve there was more slipping than ever before. But I was committed then, and I drove on down the old logging road out to the edge of the field.

Then we set out to select a Christmas tree. From the car it appeared there were a number of pretty and suitable trees, but from close range slight defects appeared and made our choice more complicated. How about this one? Well, it's too thin in the upper part. This one? Well, it's not even; one side is much fuller than the other. And so it went, and we shopped among the young pine trees, standing in the melting snow, like two old ladies in a bargain basement. For a while it appeared there was not a tree on the hillside that could meet our exacting specifications, and we looked speculatively across the meadow to Mort's hillside where dozens of perfectly symmetrical trees appeared to grow. But at last we found one which looked as though it would do, and once we had made our choice we found it grew in loveliness and symmetry right before our eyes. By the time I had cut it and carried it down the hill to the car, we were quite convinced it was the prettiest Christmas tree we had ever had.

I tied it on the back of the car and we started back up

the woodland trail. There was a somewhat ominous spinning of the wheels at first but all went relatively well until I made the sharp turn to the left and started to climb up the hill toward the old chestnut trunk. The car faltered and then stopped, the rear wheels spinning uselessly. "I didn't get a good start," I said."We'll try again." And so, after backing some way down the little road, we made another run and got perhaps three feet higher up the hill than before. "Everybody out," I said, captain of the ship, "I'll try it alone." And so I did, and there was a great slewing and skidding and spewing up of wet leaves by the back wheels, but the car got only a little way farther than before.

"We're stuck," I said, shocked by the enormity of the thing. Stuck in the woods, ten miles from home, on Christmas Eve!

"Oh, honey, what will we do?" cried Rosemary and Steve looked as though tears were not far away.

"Well, I don't know. We'll have to—oh, yes, I do! I'll go get Mort's jeep." And so I went over to Mort's house, across the bridge I had finished only weeks before and down the path, and within minutes Mort and I had come back in the jeep and were towing my defeated car around the corpse of the enormous chestnut tree and out onto the county road."

"Looks like you'll have to make yourself another road," said Mort as he unhooked the chain from the axle of my car. "Why don't you put a gate in down there where we took the mower in, and you can make a road right alongside the stream there."

"Guess I will," I said a little gloomily. "That was Bud's idea to begin with."

Five

The Christmas season passed and the early days of January 1951 were icy and bitter, and it was the middle of the month before I got back over to the *woods* again. It was a Sunday morning, clear and cold and the sky an icy blue, and I was merely walking over the land— "overseeing" is perhaps the correct word—with no project in view. I climbed to the top of the ridge, stopping on the way to make snowballs out of a patch of old snow lying beneath the pine trees, and looked at the January version of the view Rosemary and I had first seen that August afternoon. The limbs of the trees before me were stiff and stark and the hills that lifted against the horizon were a cold blue. In between, the landscape was a light brown, touched here and there with patches of white snow and edged on every side with the green of the evergreens.

I walked then down through the woods, noting the brown oak leaves hanging tenaciously to the trees and remembering the old tale in my fourth grade reader about the king who promised the hand of the princess to his evil conqueror when the last oak leaf fell. Like the oak leaves in my woods, the last oak leaf in the story did not fall before spring brought new leaves to the tree. When I reached the edge of the stream, I walked down along it and watched the clear water moving crisply over the sandy bottom. Here and there a bush had dabbled a branch in the water and had collected a knob of ice on the end of it. Now and then, several slate-blue birds flew ahead of me with a flash of white underwings. I was ruminating with some woodland thoughts and my nose and ears were just beginning to feel the sharp nip of the January air when my eye fell on a newly-cut, newly-driven, and newly-marked stake. The survey!

I walked rapidly up along the bank of the other stream, the one that separates my meadow from Mort's hillside, and found a succession of stakes. Each one bore some cryptic inscription in blue crayon. I examined them all with care, but neither their position nor the markings on the sides told me anything. But one thing was certain: after all the months of half-promises and equivocation and *surely-do-my-bests* the surveyors had actually been over the ground, had sighted through their instruments, and had driven stakes.

Next morning I called the surveyor's office. Yes, they had been out all right. Had a little trouble locating them corner stakes but finally did and everything went all right. Just drawing up the plot then and ought to have it all done up in another day or so. I was just to be patient because they were surely doing their best.

"But you remember," I said, "you remember that I've got to make a decision about where to draw the line."

"What's that?"

"The line. I've got to figure out where I'm going to draw the line between my property and his. And I can't do that until I know how much land there is there in that whole piece."

The silence on the other end of the telephone was not

quite complete but it was undeniably profound. I could faintly hear the click of a typewriter and the murmur of some voices, thinned and strained by the miles of telephone wire. Finally, my correspondent said, "Well, how are you going to do that?"

"Well, when you get it laid out on paper, can't you tell me how big such and such a part of it is?"

"Yeah, I guess we could do that."

"Fine. I'll just come out to your office and sit down and go over it with you. What day should I come?"

"Wednesday be okay?"

"Sure. Wednesday."

On Wednesday I presented myself at the surveyor's office. His desk was a litter of instruments and drawings. Two young men sat at draughtsman's tables nearby, working on large sheets of drawing paper with rules and pen. The surveyor worked out who I was after a brief delay and set out to find the plot for my land. I waited nervously, tense with the decision I was about to make, while he rummaged through rolls of paper and looked under piles of packages.

"Here it is." He brought back an impressive roll of white paper, cleared some space on his desk, and spread the plot before me. There it was, an irregularly-shaped rectangle, looking white and bare and not a bit like its varied and lovely self.

"Do you have any topographical notes so we can figure out where these various points are?"

"Just the streams and a few points in the description."

"Well, okay. Maybe we can make those do." I scanned the rectangle, looking for places to draw a line.

"First of all, how big is the whole piece you surveyed?"

"Well, the whole thing—from the country road over to that ravine—is just over sixteen acres."

Sixteen acres! Well, that was that. I could no more think of buying sixteen acres than I could fly. Mort and I had thought it was ten or, at the most, twelve.

"I see." A pause of some length while I tried to fix another point on the plot and relate it to the land itself. "Where's this, this crook in the stream. Is this just the other side of the crest of the hill? Right there where I've made a small gate between the forks of the tree? Right at the edge of Freligh's property?"

"Yeah. That's it."

"How much is that?" This called for the slide rule and a certain amount of figuring. Minutes passed and a large white-faced clock, the kind I associate with schoolrooms, marked each and every second with a tick or a tock.

"Well, let's see. I figure that at about twelve acres."

"Twelve acres!" My mind put on a feeble imitation of a calculating machine as I remembered the lawyer's stipulation that I must produce one-third cash of the total purchase price. Twelve acres would amount to that much and one-third of *that* was *that* much. Should I extend myself to that degree? After all, every foot was lovely land and potentially very valuable. As I calculated, my eye was moving over the plot before me, and I suddenly recognized that the wriggly line I was following was the little stream beside which we had built our campsite, the stream that had cooled my beer and whose banks had sheltered the white-winged birds. "What's it to here?" I asked on sudden impulse.

Again the slide rule and the muttered calculations and the pencilled figuring. "Well, I reckon that's seven or seven-and-a-half acres.

Seven acres or twelve acres, that was my choice. There was no suitable place on the terrain, as I knew better than anyone else, for drawing a line between them. Twelve acres would mean extending my credit facilities to the uttermost, if not beyond. As a matter of fact, I could not at that moment see where the requisite one-third cash of the amount required to buy twelve acres would be coming from. But there were relatives or.. well, something. On the other hand, seven acres was within the range of our visible assets. Only just barely, but nonetheless within. What should I do? I figured and figured, and I wavered, shuttling between shoot-the-works recklessness and cool, businesslike caution. And then finally, while the large white-faced clock ticked and tocked in solemn deliberation, I chose caution and elected for seven or so acres. It may be that my heirs and assigns for generations to come will think ill of me for that decision. I can only reply that to a relatively honest man, possessed at that moment of extremely modest resources and sitting as I was in a small surveyor's office, surrounded by confusion and disorder and the ticking of a clock that sounded like eternity itself, it seemed like the best possible decision.

"Let's draw it here along this stream," I said. "At about seven acres."

"Okay, if that is the way you want it."

It would have been idle to have tried to explain to the surveyor how I *really* wanted it, so I swallowed the words that started to come and said, "That's it."

"Well, I guess we ought to have this ready for you by Friday."

On Friday, I picked up the plot, done up in three copies and rolled into an impressive cylinder, and carried it down the street to the lawyer's office. He looked at it casually, extraordinarily casually it seemed to me, and turned to the typewritten description of the boundaries that was attached. "This is what is most important," he said. "The deed will be written around this." He looked it over for a moment or two. "Comes to 6.974 acres, doesn't it." He looked at it for another moment. "Okay, come back next Friday, and I'll have it ready for you. Bring your wife along so she can sign the papers at the same time."

During the ensuing week, Rosemary and I had several tries at assembling enough ready cash to make the necessary one-third payment. We would start out briskly enough: three hundred dollars here; two hundred and fifty here; one hundred fifty here; and one hundred and—oh, let's say—fifty there. Then we would total: five, ten, fifteen, carry the one; four, six, ,seven, eight. Eight, five, oh. Eight hundred and fifty dollars. In some respects, an imposing sum: more money than I had before assembled in my life. Nonetheless and regrettably, it was not enough. And so we would go back over the figures again. But no matter how we figured it up, we always came out well over a hundred dollars short. Where could we find more money? It was Rosemary who finally came up with the solution. If we let one or more of the bills go for a month—a remarkable suggestion coming from cautious, prudent Rosemary— then we would have enough cash to swing the deal. There was a minute or two of stunned silence while we thought about this daring idea. After all, we *could* get caught up again on the bills in the months to come after we had got over this critical point. And then we decided we had found the answer. We could buy the land.

Several times later during the long experience of obtaining a house on land of my own the image of the trapeze performer came to mind as it did on this occasion. We were like the white-stockinged figures high up against the top of the tent, and we had left the certainty of one swinging bar and were passing through the insubstantial air toward the other. Could we reach it? Could we make it? And then, straining with every resource, our arms outstretched and our hands rigid with reaching, we touched the bar with our fingertips and caught it and held it. We had made it! We had passed across the open space and had reached the new certainty.

On Saturday morning we drove to the county seat and in the lawyer's office, almost as mutually excited as when we had gone into the office of the marriage license clerk.

The transfer of title to the woods passed from the Freligh's to Rosemary and me with only the scratching of the pen for fanfare. I could not help thinking that the beauty and intricate variety of that meadow and woodland deserved a flaring brass choir to mark the passage of its ownership. But the trees themselves and the bushes and shrubs beneath them, their branches and bare twigs stiff in the January cold, and even the warm-blooded little animals who made their home in those 6.974 acres, were, I feel confident in saying, quite unaware they had acquired a new owner.

I experienced one sharp jolt during this brief and unceremonial occasion. The lawyer handed me a slip of paper bearing the figure of the amount of cash I was expected to produce, and it was over sixty dollars higher than I had expected. I realized in a moment that I had not included in my figure the tax on the transaction, the stamp and registration fees, and the other items an industrious bureaucracy had decreed. But there was no turning back at this point, so I manfully grasped my pen and wrote a check for the amount he gave me. After I had finished, heart beating fast, I essayed a little hearty jocularity. "Now the next thing," I said, chuckling as though the humor were too good to hold back, "will be to borrow more money and build a house."

If I had succeeded in being funny, the lawyer appeared to be unaware of it. He looked up at me, his long and somewhat horsey face serious and businesslike. "Buildin' money is pretty scarce right now." He looked down again at the check I had just handed him. "Anyway, you won't be needing it right away soon because the next thing you've got to do is to get the land paid for. Won't nobody lend you money to build a house until your land is free and clear."

Six

January and the elation of new ownership passed into the dreariness and slush of February. And then came March and the mud. We fell out of the habit of having our Sunday lunch in the woods, and as the temperature slowly rose through the early spring the need for fireplace wood grew less and less. Weeks passed without my setting foot on the land, and the vigor of my early enthusiasm waned from neglect. There was even one awful period when I took to reading the Sunday real estate advertisements, speculating as I read whether it would not be better in the long run to buy a house already built in some suburb like Bethesda or Falls Church.

But then came April and greenness began to run subtly under the dried grass of the meadow and the tips of the trees began to glisten and prink. And as the succeeding days of April and then of May wrought the evergreen miracle of springtime, I again discovered that time spent in my woods made other time seem misspent. Mostly I did little more than sit or stand, watching a procession of clouds move across the sky or a flight of migrant birds make a ceremonious arrival in one of my large trees. One time I was looking aimlessly at the bark of an enormous oak when I suddenly found myself gazing into the eyes of a lizard no more than eighteen inches away. We both pretended riot to be startled by this chance encounter and immediately fell into that somewhat adolescent gambit of attempting to stare each other down. In terms of size I had him greatly at a disadvantage because he measured about four inches from snout to tail. But as the seconds passed and my eyelids began to itch from the strain of staring I realized that he had an even greater advantage in his lidless eyes. The whole procedure began to verge on the ridiculous when good sense finally asserted itself in both of us and, as though by common assent, we simultaneously turned away to other considerations.

May came and all the dogwood trees took on a blooming white splendor in honor of the arrival. The long margin of the woods, where the trees stopped and the meadow began, was edged in billows of white. Even trees standing some distance away from the meadow stretched their limbs gaudy with blossoms toward the edge. The abundance of dazzling whiteness took me by surprise, and I realized that during the previous fall and winter I had looked many times at these very trees and had failed to realize that within the nondescript branches the white effulgence lay quiescent. I had probably even—and I winced at the thought—chopped down more, than one dogwood tree in my zest for clearing paths and open places. This thought caused me to make certain I could identify dogwoods in the future, and I looked narrowly and determinedly at the heart shaped leaves and the crenellated gray bark with the red skin visible here and there beneath it.

June arrived and carpeted the hillside with wild strawberries. Not small and pointed bright red beads with the harsh tastelessness I had always associated with wild strawberries, but maturely rounded fruits the size of a man's thumbnail and sweet in an artless and winsome way. And again, the abundance was extraordinary. At first, we foraged over the field with our baskets, picking a strawberry or two and walking a step or so before picking another. But soon we found large areas of the hillside where we could sit in one place for several minutes and pick dozens of the red berries without moving. As we plucked the strawberries from amongst the green leaves the wild juice stained our fingers red, and now and then we heard from the hillside across the little valley the bright whistle of the mating quail: "bob *white*! bob-bob *white*!" We took home quarts of wild strawberries, and for several weeks we had them daily, sometimes strewn over corn flakes, once or twice in pie, and toward the end of the season, Rosemary made them into strawberry jelly. There was great satisfaction in this. I was harvesting a crop from my own land, a crop which I had not sown and which had grown to fuition without cultivation or bidding.

But strawberries notwithstanding, as the lovely months of spring passed by I found myself growing more and more restless about the land. The reason was not hard to find. The hours I spent idling about in the meadow and wandering through the woods brought me great delight and gave me an intimate knowledge of the contours and lineaments of my land, but there was no mistaking the fact that I was making no progress toward a house. I did take advantage of the first dry weekend to make a gate where Mort and I had brought the mower through—sinking two large posts ten feet apart and cutting fourteen-foot pine poles for bars which were put up or lowered separately—and thereafter we drove the car in through the meadow alongside the stream. But this assuaged my longing for progress only temporarily.

It was not that I expected to begin construction of a house at once. The parting advice of the lawyer to get the land paid for before I began thinking about borrowing money to build a house had removed all thoughts of that. Far from getting the principal paid up, we were still struggling to pay back the several small loans which had made the down payment possible, and we would still be doing so for months to come. Looked at in that perspective, we could not hope to start our house for at least a year and possibly much longer.

Still, I needed some sense of progress. I had found it during the autumn in clearing and mowing the meadow for the first time and in cutting paths through the woods. But now those projects required only maintenance and this, though time-consuming and immediately rewarding, gave me no feeling of forward movement. What I needed, I finally decided was to make some permanent mark on the land. All that I had done thus far would, if left untended for two or three years, become overgrown and obliterated. I wanted to put up something more durable, perhaps a structure of some sort which would later become one of the outbuildings on the place. My conversation with Bud about a shed came to mind and suddenly it seemed just the right thing. After all, a place in the country needs more than just a house. It needs outbuildings of assorted sizes and uses, and the more the better. A shed would be a permanent beginning, and it would have usefulness immediately.

I had no very clear idea what kind of shed I wanted. As I thought about it somewhat dreamily I invested it with all the qualities of Thoreau's house at Walden, a storage place for tools, a potential garage, and a small stable for a pony. It would be snug in the winter with a little potbelly stove and cool under the trees in the summer. We could spend weekends there, sleeping on air mattresses and cooking our breakfast in the early morning coolness, the fragrance of coffee and bacon mingling with the smell of pine trees. And it would be immeasurably more convenient to leave my tools neatly stacked in a corner there or hung symmetrically along the walls on nails.

These reveries were brought to earth when I began to look around for pre-fabricated sheds and garages. After consulting the yellow section of the telephone book, I spent several lunch hours talking with salesmen of pre-fabricated buildings. These conversations disclosed that the smallest of these structures cost $600 and not even the keenest of the salesmen would pretend that they were any more than strictly utilitarian in appearance. I found it hard to imagine one of those raw and ungainly metal garages standing under the lovely trees of my woods.

But then advertisements began to appear in the daily newspapers for "a weekend cottage" which "any lot owner" could erect himself. All necessary materials were provided, so the advertisement declared, and full, detailed instructions told one how. Size: ten feet by fourteen feet. Cost: $299.75. This advertisement excited my imagination, and I returned to fancies involving the potbelly stove, the smell of bacon and coffee in the morning air, and all the rest. My daydreams orbited happily around this unassembled *weekend cottage* for a week or more until I went to the lumber yard where a sample *weekend cottage* had been erected. My reveries ground to a sudden stop. The *cottage* was a structure of no beauty with three meanly small windows and a narrow door. The scrawny studs and rafters within looked flimsy, and daylight was visible through innumerable cracks in the siding.

But though I rejected this packaged building, it had altered my approach to the problem of a shed in a slight but significant way. I had begun by looking for a pre-fabricated building but I had been led, by the seductions of the advertisement, to consider and eventually accept the idea of doing the assembling myself. At the time,

I was not aware of this shift in approach, let alone perceive its significance, but I later came to realize that my daydreams about the *weekend cottage* had carried me through an extremely important transition.

Meanwhile, the problem of the shed was laid aside while Rosemary and I dealt with an urgent but familiar problem. Somehow, we were not saving the quantities of money we had envisioned when we had moved to a guest house deep in the country the previous autumn. It was true that we had reduced the monthly rent by some thirty dollars but we seemed at the same time to have taken on new and unforeseen expenses. The extra distance we travelled to and from town doubled our monthly gasoline bill. For reasons which were anything but clear our telephone bill also doubled. Our heating bill and our electricity bill seemed to have grown inexplicably. These new expenses quickly gobbled up our saving in rent, and then punched large holes in what remained of our monthly income. In short, we were far from saving money; we were losing it steadily. And so long as this continued, our dream of a house on our land would dwindle and recede.

It is remarkable that we did not at this point turn to the possibility of giving up that arduous dream for something more easily attainable. We did not even consider it. By this time, the land had become an integral part of our life and the essential element in our plans for the future. And so, our only thought was how to reduce our monthly budget and begin saving the money we needed to pay for the land and build the house.

The obvious first step was to move to another and cheaper house. Rosemary set out on this quest, reading the rental advertisements in the morning newspaper, telephoning real estate agents, and trekking around to see prospective houses.

Rosemary looked at some very depressing places before

we heard of a vacancy in a development of small modern houses only a few miles from the *woods*. We were a little uncertain about moving into a housing development, deep country folk as we were, but the houses were new, compact, and attractive, and the rent within our bracket. Actually, we had made a very good choice, as we were soon to discover, one which turned out to be highly instrumental in furthering our progress toward building our own house.

Meanwhile, the months of spring were followed by the months of summer, and the grass of the meadow grew long and needed mowing and the leaves of the trees of the woods grew thick and dark green. But still with the exertions and expense of moving, I got no closer to a shed, and I again became depressed about my lack of progress. Only the mowing of the meadow, which Bud did with his tractor with a 9-foot blade lifted our spirits momentarily. We drove up to inspect the mowing one early evening in July. As the car moved in through the gate, the long shadows of the woods were reaching down the hillside across the meadow almost as far as the stream. The new-mown grass gave off a mild hay-like fragrance in the cool, moist air, and a robin caroled from a treetop. The meadow looked unbelievably serene; the grass lay calm, green, and ordered; and the sweep from stream to woods was rich in shadow and line.

Another month went by before I got well acquainted with Dick Mote, the development's general handyman, goodwill ambassador, and unofficial mayor. Dick, it developed, was building a shed in the backyard of his house. My interest in sheds being what it was, I hurried up to Dick's as soon as I heard this news. I found him wearing a carpenter's apron, a hammer in one hand and a can of beer in the other. Large and expansive, his speech and manner, a living manifestation of the Pacific Northwest, he was modest to the extreme about his undertaking and his talents. "Shucks, I'm no carpenter. I'm just slappin' a few boards together so I'll have some kind of a workshed."

Despite this disclaimer, it was obvious even to my inexperienced eye that the shed Dick was building was strong and well-made. I stepped inside and examined the intricacy of framework and studding.

"You know, I'm looking for a shed to put on a piece of land I own about three miles from here," I said over my shoulder to Dick. "I've been thinking of getting a pre-fab or one of those kits you see advertised in the papers."

"Oh, you don't wanta do that. Why don't you build yourself one? You can do it a lot cheaper and better."

I was reminded of my conversation with Bud up in the woods. "I couldn't build one," I said, smiling at the thought, "I couldn't even build a decent set of bookends in school."

"Well, building a shed is a lot easier than making book ends. That is precision stuff. This is just rough carpentry."

"Why, I wouldn't even know how to begin! Just for example, how did you know how to set these corner posts in this way?"

"Oh," he said, "I got all that kind of stuff out of a book."

A book! The word bounced around in my head like a ping pong ball, and I felt like Cortez with the blue sweep of the Pacific opening before him. A book! There would be no doubt that I was not a carpenter, either by training or by temperament, but no one had ever spoken derogatorily of my ability to read. If the way to build a shed was written down somewhere in a book, then I for one was pretty certain that I could work it out.

"What kind of a book is that? Where do you get it?"

"Oh, there are several of them. One of the best is the Army technical manual on carpentry. You get it at the Government Printing Office for 75 cents or so. Then I've got another one called *Building Your Dream House* or something like that. It's got very good pictures and diagrams. Here, I'll show it to you."

We walked into the house. "The best thing about that book," said Dick, handing me a thick volume, "is that it tells you how to do everything connected with building a house."

"Can I borrow it?"

"Sure."

That night I read how to choose a site for a "dream house", how to dig an excavation, to lay a footing, erect a foundation, and perform the other manifold operations involved in building a house. There was a lot of talk about plates and sills and joists that I found hard to visualize but the diagrams were helpful, and somehow the conviction grew on me that with this book in one hand and a hammer in the other I too could become a builder. The pictures of joists and braces, precise and neat in their blue and white drawings like an architectural plate, persuaded me against my better judgment and past unhappy experiences that my joists and braces would also be precise and neat. In fact, the entire process of building a house appeared, in print, beguilingly easy, and I said to Rosemary with the confidence momentarily created by the persuasive words and the precise drawings, "I think I will build myself a shed."

"What's that, dear?"

"I said, I think I will build a shed. Myself. This book tells me how to do it."

She looked at me for a moment, wavering between saying what she really thought and being the dutiful wife. "Do you really think you could do it? Saw all the boards straight, I mean, and make it good and strong?"

That did it! No man could be impervious to the chalnit-wit!" I declared, looking fiercely capable.

Seven

During my lunch hour next day I went to the sales room of the Government Printing Office and asked for the Army technical manual on carpentry. The clerk handed me a tan-covered booklet, and I riffled its pages. Sketches, diagrams, and photographs aplenty passed swiftly before my eyes, but what really clinched the sale was a passage my eye fell on which ran: *"To drive a nail.—* (a) Hold the nail in place with the thumb and the first two fingers of one hand. (b) Grasp hammer handle as shown in figure 71 [photograph of a hand grasping a hammer]. (c) Tap the head of the nail lightly to start it into the wood and remove the guiding hand. (d) Drive the nail." With a book like this I did not see how I could fail. Not only was there precise information in that set of instructions but there was inspiration and lift in the commanding tone of that final admonition: "Drive the nail." I paid the clerk seventy-five cents and walked out with my purchase.

It made fascinating reading during the course of the week. I read sections on timber, tools, joints-splices–and connections, bridges, and wharves -docks -and-piers. When the weekend arrived, I was ready to begin the project. My first assignment was fully contained in the single sentence: "When the location and alignment of a building has been determined, it should be staked out." The location, Rosemary and I decided, was to be on the southern side of the logging road, just at the point where the little road emerged from the woods into the meadow. The alignment? East and west with the doorway to the east. Now all that remained was to clear the site so that I could stake it out.

As I got out of the car on the nigh side of eight o'clock one Saturday morning in early September and confronted that luxuriant tangle of poison ivy, oak shrubs, and Virginia creeper, I realized that my first weekend would consist largely of clearing. I fell to with a great lusty and swinging zest. I was back to my old love, clearing, and I was clearing with an immediate and constructive purpose. On this site was to be built a shed—well, call it a cabin, if you like—and in that cabin I would put a little pot-bellied stove—or maybe even an open-fronted Franklin stove—and on the stove would sit a pot of coffee and in one corner of the cabin would be a table and a kerosene lantern by which to read and write at night. As a matter of fact, you might call this shed—uh, cabin—a studio, and I could pursue all manner of long-delayed scholarly and writing projects.

Sustained by reveries such as these, as well as by a packet of sandwiches, an apple, a thermos of coffee, and the companionship of our black poodle, Jocko, the clearing job passed quickly and by noon on Sunday I was consulting the carpentry manual for the next step. This was *staking out*—driving stakes in at the four corners of the planned building—and was easy. Using the tape I had bought at the neighborhood hardware store on Friday night, I drove a stake at the approximate point where I imagined the southwest corner of the building would be and then measured sixteen feet from it one direction and ten feet from it another. There was some juggling necessary on the fourth stake in order to assure that the sides were both sixteen feet and the ends both ten feet. There was also considerable time spent in anxious consulting of the manual, trying to wring more information out of the spare, dry sentences, and in wondering whether the way I was going about it was the right way.

The next step, according to my preceptor, the army manual, was to excavate. Translated into my modest terms, this meant to dig a number of holes in which I would place cinder block piers as the supports for the corners and centers of my shed. But before I had really begun to dig I found myself confronted with a baffling problem of heights and depths—how high should the piers rise and how deep should they sink? As I look back on it, I find it extraordinary that I became so mixed up over so simple a problem, but at that stage I was a neolithic man in the realms of carpentry and building. Each process required me to force my mind into strange and pathless areas. Each problem presented itself raw and unformed and had to be hand-hewn into some solution. At every new phase of the building operation, I was like prehistoric man trying to make a wheel without ever having seen one.

I began bravely and optimistically. Cinder block piers at the four corners and at three points in the center. Very simple. Now how far down into the ground do the piers go? Below the frost line which in northern Virginia is about eighteen to twenty-four inches. Again, simple. Now, how far do they rise above ground? Oh, anywhere between ten and twenty inches—high enough to give you enough light and ventilation to deter termites and rot; low enough so that it does not look as though your building is wearing stilts. Well, let's see: two feet below ground plus one foot above ground gives you a three-foot pier and a two-foot excavation. Extremely simple.

I scratched away the heavy matting of dead leaves and

twigs surrounding a corner stake and began to dig earnestly. My spade struck innumerable roots lying just below the surface and made it hard to get started, but an even greater deterrent to progress was the doubt, uncertainty, and finally bewilderment that grew over me and finally forced me to lay my spade down. The difficulty was simply this: the surface of the ground where the shed was to stand was uneven. If I merely dug holes two feet deep at all points and placed three-foot piers in them, my shed would have a foundation as uneven as the ground. Obviously, this would be less than satisfactory. The floor of my shed ought to be level—level, that is, with the horizon, not the ground—and to accomplish this it was essential that the tops of the foundation piers all rise to the same altitude above sea level.

But how? Did you dig one hole deeper than another so that the three-foot piers all rose to the same height? And if so, how did you know how deep to dig at the various points? Or did you dig the holes all the same depth and make the piers different heights? And if you did this another obstacle lay in your way. Cinder blocks are eight inches thick. Suppose you wanted one pier to rise two or four inches higher than another. With cinder blocks, you are tied to multiples of eight. Did you therefore slice a cinder block like a hunk of cheese two or four inches thick in order to give you the required height?

I sat down on a nearby stump and opened the carpentry manual. Around me were the subdued sounds of the woods on an October afternoon, and Jocko walked over beside me and rubbed his head against my knee. I read and re-read the few brief sentences describing excavations and foundations but found no answer to my questions. As I learned from subsequent experience, these are the kinds of questions the books never do answer, probably because their authors cannot conceive the imbecilities their readers are capable of. Well, what books cannot answer experienced men sometimes can, and I decided to go talk to Dick Mote who had met and solved this problem.

It was not easy for the pragmatic mind of Dick, as I discovered when I posed my questions to him, to understand what it was that baffled me. But part way through a can of beer clarification seemed to descend upon us, and the answers were gradually assembled and laid out. Yes, you do dig the holes all the same depth and vary the height of the piers. When the holes are dug you experiment by laying the cinder blocks in dry. If the height of the pier is going to be several inches off, dig that particular hole several inches deeper. The rest of the difference you make up by varying the thickness of mortar between the cinder blocks as you build it.

"Wonderful," I said. "That solves my problem."

"Have another beer," said Dick.

" Love to. By the way, where did you buy your cinder blocks?"

"Oh, I got them down at the cinder block factory in Arlington. I bought 'seconds' or rejects and picked them up ten cents apiece."

Next weekend I paid a visit to the cinder block factory and then to my neighborhood hardware store where I bought some prepared cement mix. In the fresh morning air I finished off the excavating, jabbing and gouging twenty-four inch holes out of the clay hardpan I encountered only eight or ten inches below the surface. In the afternoon, I mixed the prepared cement mix in a rusty iron tray I had found, using water I dipped out of the stream with a bucket. The directions on the bag were explicit, but I was as nervous as a bride mixing her first cake. Would I get too much water in it and make the cement too runny? Then again, leaves dropping from the trees overhead and landing in the gray ooze. Would the chemical interaction of leaves and cement weaken it? Finally, with much uncertainty, I finished mixing and began ladling the cement into the holes. My object was to lay down a pad of cement about four inches thick to serve as a base, or footing, for the cinder blocks. With much lifting and heaving of heavy mix and running back and forth from one hole to another, testing the depth of the semi-fluid with a stick, I finally finished the job. And then, as advised by Dick, I spread pieces of burlap and heavy paper over the holes and weighted them down with stones.

Next morning, I jumped out of the car almost before the engine stopped and ran to the holes. Jocko caught my excitement and ran with me, poking his nose under the paper covers in hopes of finding a chipmunk or some other fascinating quarry. Unfortunately for Jocko, the only game he found was one misguided toad who, luckily for both him and me, had fallen into the hole sometime after the cement had become fairly hard. But most important, each of the holes contained a solid footing for my piers. My building had in fact begun.

During the course of the day I tried to become a mason and put up the cinder block piers. There was much mixing of cement, running back and forth from the stream with buckets of water, and sighting along levels and tapping on cinder blocks to bring them into line. Most of the time I was in a fury of frustration and ineptitude, and even my best friend, Jocko, would have admitted, if the question had been put to him, that it was a sloppy and botched-up job. But when the day came to an end, and the straining and the fury subsided, I had seven fairly sturdy piers whose tops were all within a half inch or so of being level with one another. I did not realize it till much later, that at that moment I was over the worst. From then on, it all came easier.

When I reported to Dick with a sort of wan satisfaction

that the foundations were in, he said, "Fine. Did you put the bolts in?"

"Bolts? What bolts?"

"The bolts to hold your shed down onto the foundation. If you don't bolt it down, wind and vibration will eventually push it off the piers. You fill the center void of the cinder block with cement and stick the heads of the bolts down in it."

Bolts! Back to the carpentry manual. Yes, there they were in a sketch on page 119: "anchor bolts." No directions on how to put them in but it looked very simple. Well, I could put them in next weekend. It meant buying another bag of prepared cement mix, so I would have to wring another dollar thirty-five out of the week's allowance.

When I had bought the bolts and the bag of cement mix, I made a notation on the back cover of the carpentry manual of the money spent thus far:

Cinderblock	3.68
Prepared cement mix	5.40
Bolts	1.04
Additional cement mix	1.35
Total to date	$ 11.47

Not bad, I thought to myself, and showed it to Rose. "Look at this. Building a shed isn't going to be so expensive that I can't handle it out of current funds."

"Ummm. But isn't it going to be more expensive when you start buying lumber?"

"Well. . . Yes."

And so it turned out to be. Buying lumber was the next stage, and as before I turned to Dick for advice. "Well, I bought second-hand lumber at that place there near the Pentagon, but I don't think that I'd do it that way again if I had it to do over. Time I fiddled around with these odd sizes and all, I'd probably been better off just to buy new stuff. Taken a lot less time anyway."

"Well, time is what I've got more of than anything else. Is it good strong lumber? Are the nails all taken out of it?"

"Oh, sure, it's all cleaned up. And it's probably stronger than new lumber which may be green and full of knots. No.. if you don't mind taking the trouble to work with it, it's all right."

The evening newspaper carried half a column of classified advertisements for used lumber and other building material. I studied them with care every night, comparing prices and the kind of lumber offered. What I needed to start was two-by-six lumber for joists. I telephoned several places asking for two-by-sixes. The first one did not have any, but then I struck one that did. "How much are they?"

"Ten cents a foot. And ten per cent off for cash and carry."

That discount decided me and on Saturday morning I pulled up at the yard of The Ace Wrecking Company in one of Washington's less distinguished districts. I was driving the used station wagon I had bought when the old Plymouth gave out. A fat man with a three-day growth of beard, his pants held to about a half-mast position on his belly by sagging suspenders, stood in the doorway. "Do anything fer ya?"

"Yes, I guess so. Do you have any two-by-sixes?"

"Yep. How much you need?"

I consulted my slip of paper. "One hundred and ninety feet. That's lineal feet," I added for greater accuracy.

"Huh?"

"Lineal feet. Not board feet." This was a distinction Dick Mote had taught me, a board foot being an abstract measure representing as much lumber as is contained in a board twelve inches wide, one inch thick, and one foot long; a lineal foot being a twelve-inch length of any specific board, whether two-by-four or four-by-eight. It makes considerable difference in the amount of lumber you are describing.

The fat man, his blue eyes blurry, grunted. "You mean runnin' feet," he said. "C'mon back here." He led me back through the cluttered yard, rusty nails and bits of glass underfoot and lengths of pipe and derelict plumbing facilities lying around. As we went around the first corner and were out of sight of the office, he stopped and pulled a pint whisky bottle out of his pocket. He took a long pull. "Lumbago's so goddammed bad this mornin' I tole the wife I didn't think I could get through the day." He walked on a little farther. "There's your two-by-sixes," he said pointing. "Good, dry stuff."

I looked at the top boards in the pile in a casual, expert sort of way. "They look okay."

"You goin' to haul 'em yourself or you want 'em delivered?"

"I'll take them myself in the station wagon. Can I back it in here?"

"Sure. One of these fellas here will help you load. Charley!" A black man about fifty who was stacking short sticks of firewood looked up and walked over. "Help him load."

With Charley's help I had slightly less than two dozen pieces of two-by-six lumber loaded in the station wagon in fifteen minutes. The fat man returned and estimated the amount I had. "Call that hundred eighty-six feet," he said, and went back in the office to write up a slip. "Eighteen dollars and sixty cents less ten percent cash-and-carry comes sixteen dollars and eighty-six cents.

"Okay" I got out my billfold and began counting money. The fat man burped amiably. "Whatcha buildin'?" he asked. "A shed."

He took my money and made change. "Well, we got lots of good framin' and sidin' out there. C'mon back."

"Okay." I started out the door and then looked back and said, "Hope your lumbago gets better."

"What?" Then he grinned. "Oh, yeah. Thanks."

I tipped Charley a quarter for his help and then eased the car out of the yard and into the heavy stream of Saturday morning traffic. In half an hour I was crossing the Potomac at Chain Bridge and moving out into the Virginia countryside. Fifteen minutes later the car was nosing in through the gate to our field and shortly afterward I was unloading the lumber beside the cinder block piers. It was raining or misting lightly but I was too happily engaged to mind it much.

Next day I started to saw and nail the two-by-sixes into sills and joists. Sills are the wooden understructure which rest on the foundation and support the walls and the floor; joists are the supports which run crosswise from sill to sill and support the floor across the building. The manual admonished me, "When piers are used in the foundation, heavier sills are used. These sills are of single heavy timbers or are built of two or more pieces of timber. " My two-by-sixes were full measure, and I decided that doubling them and standing them on edge, thus giving me a sill four by six inches, would be adequate. I set to work making a wooden outline of the shed floor, ten-feet-by sixteen feet, four inches thick. Remembering poignantly my failure of the past, I measured with very great care—usually checking each measurement two or three times—and sawed with deliberation. I realized that the most efficient procedure would have been to do all the sawing at one time and then nail the pieces together. But I was too impatient to see how it was going to look and besides I enjoyed shifting from one kind of activity to another so I sawed each piece and then nailed it. By the time the light began to fail and I was forced to stop, I had completed the wooden outline, the sill to which the joists would be nailed.

I could not help thinking, as I loaded the tools into the car in the rapidly dropping dusk, that it was already beginning to look like a shed.

When I began the job of nailing the joists to the sills, I experienced ,really for the first time, the disadvantages of working alone. Sawing and nailing the sills together had been fairly easy. But joining the joists to the sills already standing in place was not so easy. The joists, each nine feet, four inches long, were to be nailed at either end to the two sills that ran lengthwise of the building. My problem was to hold these joists in place while nailing them fast.

The obvious solution, aside from holding the nails with my teeth, was a helper. But Rosemary was at this time engaged in an intimate and intricate construction project of her own (we named him Scott when he was born in January), and Stephen's interest, like any young boy's, was as sporadic as a puppy's. Besides, the year was moving into late autumn and I did not want to expose Stephen to the raw and sometimes rainy weather. So I had to solve the problem alone.

At first, I tried propping one end of the two-by-six up on cinder blocks and pieces of scrap wood. Then I held the other end with my left hand while I hammered. If the wood I was using had been new and perhaps slightly green, this method might have worked. But my lumber was old and well seasoned yellow pine and it was extraordinarily hard. Each blow of my hammer made the joist bounce and after about the third bounce it wobbled off the cinder blocks and scraps of wood and fell to the ground.

Next I tried nailing one end of the joint fast—propping the other end in place as I did so—and then nailing the other end. This method worked after a fashion, but it had several disadvantages. For one thing, the propped-up end kept bouncing and falling off and I had to run around to the other side and put it back. For another, I had to hold the joist with my left hand while hammering with my right. The strain of holding the joist precisely in place caused me to swing the hammer inaccurately, and my average of bent-over nails was high.

Finally, I found the solution. After measuring where the joists were to come, I drew a line at that point down the outside of the sill. Then I drive two spikes in at top and bottom, driving them just far enough in that their points came through the other side by a quarter of an inch or so. Having done this on both sides, I carefully placed the joist so that it was held in position by the points of the spikes. Sometimes this required some tapping to drop the joist in place. Sometimes I had to hammer the points back a bit to give the joist room to slide into place. But by and large it worked very well. Once the joist was in position I gave the top nail on each side a resounding clout and the piece was then held firmly in place for the remaining pounding. This discovery, tantamount in my terms, to the invention of the wheel, gave my progress a mightily shove and my spirits a boost. Despite the raw weather and the stark atmosphere of the surrounding woods—bare dripping branches and soggy matting of leaves underfoot—I sang and whistled as I worked, and my hammer blows rang out crisply in the damp air.

With the underpinning of the shed complete, the next task was to creosote the timbers. November unexpectedly gave me a mild, sunny day, and I set to work painting the dark brown liquid on with the large whitewash brush I had bought at the hardware store that morning. At first it was fun, transforming the mixed yellows and tans into an even dark brown while the sun shone warmly through the remaining brown leaves and the birds twittered and fluttered. Over the hill I could hear the sounds of the black children playing in the sunshine. Jocko sat patiently beside me, a large wooly, black object, occasionally dashing off to investigate the excited flutterings of some quarreling birds in nearby bushes. After a while, doing the creosoting and the innumerable little frustrations that accompanied it—the brush snagging in the rough wood, and the spots that would not cover and needed repeated daubs of the dark brown stain—began to seem a lot less attractive. It was a dirty job. My gloves dripped with the pungent-smelling liquid and my face was flecked with brown spots flipped onto it by the brush as it dragged across the rough surface.

I was close to chucking the job for the rest of the day even though it would mean cleaning myself up twice, when Bud came ambling up on Blackberry. "I knew what you were doing from way back over the hill," he said. "I could smell the creosote almost as soon as Blackberry and I left the barn. Man, you're really smelling up the countryside!"

I grinned at him through my brown spots. "Gotta be done. Have to protect the wood from termites."

"Yeah, I guess it helps. But some people say it doesn't do any good to paint it on. You have to soak the wood in it. Still, I would do what you're doing if it was mine."

"Sure is a messy job," I said.

Blackberry snorted and stamped his foot. "Yeah," said Bud. He sat quietly on the big horse for a moment, looking quizzically at my handiwork. Then he began to grin as he shook his head either in wonderment or admiration. "Boy, that's some foundation you got there! What are you going to put on that foundation—an apartment house?" He shook his head again.

I looked at him closely, uncertain whether I was being criticized or praised. "What's the matter with it? Something wrong?"

"No, not a thing. Question is whether it isn't too good. Looks strong enough to hold up a railroad bridge."

"Well, that's what it calls for in the book. Two-by-sixes doubled for sills and two-by-six joists. Of course, this is used lumber and these are full two-by-sixes, not nominal two-by-sixes."

Bud shook his head again. "All I can say is it looks strong enough to hold up a freight train."

It was only later, quite a while after Bud had gone, that I realized I had drawn my first compliment on my building prowess.

Eight

After the underpinning comes the floor, or at least the subfloor. I found this a very hard concept to master, and I gave Dick rather a hard time explaining it to me. To my somewhat categorical mind, the connection between the sills and joists and the upright frame of the building ought to be very direct. The floor, let alone the subfloor, was surely incidental to the main bones of the structure and ought properly to be put in after all the framing was done. But no, the carpentry manual was firm, if not explicit, on this point. You put the subfloor down, as Dick explained it to me, and then you lay the 2-by-4 sole of the frame over that and nail down through the subfloor to the sill and joists beneath. Perhaps, the best reason for doing it this way is that it gives you a solid surface to stand on while doing the framing.

Subfloors in houses are usually one-by-six boards, laid diagonally across the joists. But new one-by-sixes turned out to be fairly expensive, at least in terms of the amount which could be squeezed out of my weekly luncheon al-lowance, and used one-by-sixes appeared to be non-existent. Back I went to the classified section of the evening newspaper, and there I found used tongue -and-groove flooring advertised for anywhere between seven and fourteen cents a square foot. Used flooring, though slow and difficult to lay, would give me a tight, strong floor. And I could not hope to get lumber cheaper than seven cents a foot. The seven cent price was offered, as it turned out, by the used lumberyard where I had bought my handsome and over-size two-by-sixes.

The next Saturday morning I was on hand at eight o'clock, and the fat man with the half-mast pants looked, if anything, more bleary than he had several weeks previously. "Good morning," I said cheerily. " How's that lumbago?"

He looked at me dispassionately. "What'll you have?"

"I came to look at that flooring you advertised for seven cents."

"Yeah."

"How is it? Pretty clean stuff?"

He leaned over and emitted a long, dark stream of tobacco juice. "C'mon back and see for yourself." He walked out the door, and I followed him as he trudged, heavy and silent, back through the mud and debris of the used lumberyard. "Wife's sick," he said suddenly, still walking along and not looking back. "Real sick. I'm worried about her."

"I'm very sorry. What seems to be the matter?"

"Stomick. Can't seem to keep anything down. Hasn't had a square meal in three weeks."

"That's bad," I offered. "Real bad. You had a doctor for her?"

"Naw." He spat out another dollop of Juice. "If she ain't better by next week, we'll get a doctor around." He stopped walking and pointed to an irregular, misshapen pile fifteen feet high. "Here's your flooring. Some's pretty good and some ain't. Pick it out y'self and Charley'll help you load it."

"Okay, thanks." I looked up at the enormous pile of flooring, pulled tentatively at a piece or two, and decided that I would have to climb to the top to get at it. I did so, scrambling a little to get up the precariously stacked pile, and then began sorting through the pieces under my feet. It took me a while to establish the criteria of what to look for. Did it matter if the tongue was almost entirely missing or the groove broken on the bottom side? Did I want to get all pine, all the same width, or did I want to go in for random width and an occasional piece of oak which presented itself? I soon found that almost any criteria I established only resulted in my laying hands on more pieces of flooring that would not do than those that would. I finally decided that the important thing was to be certain only that the piece was sound. Not partially rotten, as some were, or split or cracked somewhere in its length. Even so, I found it extraordinarily slow work. I was in quest of approximately two hundred square feet of flooring (ten by fifteen equalling one hundred and fifty feet, the square footage of the shed, plus approximately twenty-five percent for wastage). Two hundred square feet, divided into standard flooring widths of three and three-quarters inches results in an unbelievable number of pieces.

Old Charley and I labored for nearly an hour, turning pieces over, turning them back, searching deeper and deeper into the pile, hoping to strike a vein of sound, splendid flooring. After a very long time, I paused and asked, "How much you think we got now, Charley?"

He looked at the fruit of our efforts, stacked neatly on the ground waiting to be loaded into the station wagon. "Oh," he said carelessly, almost disdainfully, "'bout a hundred feet."

"Is that all?" I cried. "Well, here, let's get busy." And back I went to the pile with a fury, selecting pieces I had previously rejected three times over, and soon we had another pile as large as the first.

Charley volunteered that he thought we had about

enough, so I walked out to the front of the lumberyard to get the car and back it in to be loaded. On the way, I stopped to tell the fat man, and he walked back to our selected pile of flooring and began figuring. I had just finished backing the station wagon into place when he announced the results of his estimating. "Call that one hundred and ninety-eight feet," he said with extraordinary precision. "Stop by the office when you get her loaded."

Charley loaded the flooring in through the tailgate of the station wagon. It varied greatly in length and in color, some of it bright red, some mottled green, other pieces a sort of disgusting brown, and some natural wood tones. Moreover, it was extraordinarily dirty, and along the upper edge of each tongue was caked the filth of several decades of human habitation, the precise chemical content of the residue being determined, no doubt, by the nature of the room where the flooring previously lay, whether bedroom, kitchen, hallway, or bathroom. One section of the flooring, as I later discovered while nailing it down, had been saturated by a pungent, musky perfume, a fact which sent my imagination scampering off in all sorts of fascinating pursuits. But nonetheless, however romantic or sordid or commonplace had been the previous history of that used flooring, it was dry, sound, and wonderfully cheap. It would serve admirably as the floor for a shed in my Virginia woods.

As I entered the office of the lumberyard, a man who gave off a managerial aura approached me wearing a commercial smile. I nodded in the direction of the fat man who was peering through a pair of spectacles at some writing before him. The manager-type said, "Oh, George will take care of you."

George looked up over the top of his glasses as I approached. He took the glasses off and put them in the pocket of his blue shirt. "That will be $13.86," he said, pushing the sheet of paper toward me. I looked at the figuring on it, checked it with my own multiplication, and fished out of my pocket fourteen dollars, ten of which had come from a secret hoard Rosemary had produced to supplement the savings I had made from sparse luncheons. He rang it up on the cash register and handed me my change as he walked toward the door with me. "Ya got some real good stuff there," he said, gazing sadly at the station wagon, its rear springs depressed so that the body almost covered the wheels. "Make you a good floor." There was a moment's silence while I groped for some remark to make an exit on.

"God damn!" he said suddenly. "I sure hope my ole lady gets better." His unshaven face with the red capillary streaks showing through the irregular stubble wore a scowl. "That ole woman has been awful good to me. Do anything for me. Never no complainin' about my drinkin' or anything. I'd sure miss her if anything happened."

"She'll get better," I said reassuringly and fatuously. "She'll be all right. But you better get her to a doctor and see what's wrong."

"Guess I will," he said morosely. "Guess I will." He turned around suddenly and went back into the office. "Be seein' ya," he said as his shapeless form moved in through the doorway.

I got in the car and moved it carefully out into the traffic. As I piloted my heavily-laden wagon, high in the bow and sluggish to move, across southwest Washington and into Virginia I mused about the domestic life of George and his ailing wife. I found it almost too much for my imagination to construct images of what their life was like.

Laying used flooring is exacting, tricky, and alternately satisfying and frustrating, but above all, it is slow. Flooring gets worn in almost direct proportion to the amount of traffic it bears. Pieces which run into a closet or into a corner beneath a bureau are worn considerably less by shuffling or hurrying human feet than those which run down a hallway or through the doorway to the bathroom. This caused used flooring to vary considerably in thickness. Also, some develop bow-like shape pieces as time has caused the floor to sag or warp. These characteristics of used flooring make it necessary to pound it, coax it, bend it, or slam it into place. Like most aspects of carpentry and building, this is better done with four hands than two.

But as before, I found there are little tricks which make the job easier. A short piece of flooring, 18 inches or so, serves admirably as a pounding block. One merely fits it over the tongue or groove of the recalcitrant pieces and gives it a whack. This saves the good piece of flooring from considerable punishment and does the job faster than any amount of gentle tapping. Also, after having spent hours over measuring and sawing the pieces to just the right length, but invariably missing it by a half inch one way or the other, I discovered that it was a lot easier to lay the flooring with the boards extending over the edge and then saw them all off at once.

During the two weekends I was laying the floor of the shed, the muscles of my hands became stiff and sore from the strain of twisting the pieces into place, and my legs got cramped and achey from sitting in the cold with them curled under me. But when I finished the job, I had a strong, hard floor, looking like a small bandstand or dance platform standing incomprehensibly in the November woods. Rosemary and Stephen came to inspect it, and the three of us jumped up and down on its rigid surface while Jocko ran round and round barking.

Nearly all the time I was putting together the foundation of the building and laying the floor I was impatient to get on to the more form-creating phases. It seemed that an unreasonable amount of time was involved in establishing what was really no more than the base of the structure.

This feeling was strongest while I was creosoting, with the messy brown liquid all over me, but it was also present during the tedium of laying the flooring diagonally across the joists. I yearned to get on to framing and raftering and other more glamorous phases. When the time came, I was so eager to get started with it that no amount of bad weather could have kept me from it.

By this time, I had fairly well sketched out the plan and details of the shed. Ten-by-fifteen feet, it was to have two four-foot barn doors at one end, two small windows along the sides, and a window at the opposite end. The roof was to have a medium amount of pitch and a foot-and-a-half or two-foot overhang. The siding was to be upright planking with a batten nailed over the crack where the boards met, the board-and-batten style which is commonly used for farm buildings in Virginia.

Before starting the framing operation, I had another session with Dick over several cans of beer. "I put my studs on eighteen-inch centers," said Dick after a long pull at his beer, "but I don't think it's really necessary. You can get by with twenty-four inches if you want."

My hours of poring over the carpentry manual and other literary works devoted to the mysteries of building had enabled me to field such remarks with one hand, so to speak. Studs are the upright pieces of two-by-fours that are the essential elements in the walls of any wooden house; the exterior siding and the interior finishing material merely put skin over them. They stand roughly fourteen to eighteen inches apart in most houses, this distance being determined by the amount of load the wall has to carry in supporting the roof and upper floors. Because two-by-fours are rough and vary somewhat in thickness, their spacing would be uneven if the measuring were done by their outside edges. Instead, therefore, you measure points sixteen or eighteen inches apart and *center* the studs on those points. "Eighteen inches on center"means the centers of the studs are eighteen inches apart.

"Oh, I'm sure I can put them on twenty-four inch centers," I said.

"It says so here in the book." And I got out my manual, my inseparable and oracular companion, and turned to the back where there was a sketch of a standard army field building. "See, it shows these studs two feet apart."

"Well, but what kind of siding is that? Oh, yeah, says here 'corrugated steel'. You say you're going to use vertical siding. I guess that would be all right."

"I know it would. Look what it says here." I flipped the pages until I found the permissive sentence: "Where vertical siding is used, studs are set wider apart since the horizontal girts between them afford nailing surface."

"Well," said Dick in his large, expansive way, as though he were granting me permission to begin construction of another Boulder Dam,"I guess you're all set to go ahead."

"Guess so," and in my momentary pride as a knowledgeable builder who could talk on even terms with another established builder, I took a long, manly swig of my beer. As I lowered my glass, I found Rosemary across the room smiling at me with that extraordinary mingling of affection and detached amusement that only wives can master.

Unfortunately for my building operations, funds were extremely tight about this time with Christmas approaching and a new baby nearly with us, and I had only slightly more than six dollars in my pocket when I set out for the used lumberyard. That would buy less than a hundred feet of two-by-fours, but I was determined to get started with the framing and I hoped to buy enough lumber to keep me going one weekend. As a variation of my previous routine, I stopped around at my favorite used lumberyard on Friday afternoon. I expected to conduct my business with George then and get an early morning start up in the woods on Saturday. Incidentally, I also hoped to get an up-to-date bulletin on Mrs. George's health.

To my disappointment, though, George was not there. Instead, I found the managerial type, his smile revealing dollar signs instead of teeth, who directed me to the two-by-fours department. "Seven cents a running foot," he said. "Can't beat that."

Closer inspection proved him to be right. The two-by-fours were all full-size, nut brown in color, and straight and dry and clean as a man could wish. I would willingly have bought the whole pile he showed me, but I was carrying less than seven dollars in my pocket and business was transacted at the used lumberyard on a strict cash-and-carry basis. So I loaded nine eight-foot lengths and two ten-foot lengths. I paid the commercial type $6. 44 and hurried on my way. We were going out to dinner way out in Maryland near Rockville, and I had many miles to go.

I had planned to hurry on out to the woods and unload my newly-purchased lumber, but the ho ur was so late I went straight home instead and off-loaded it in our front yard. Even so, Rosemary and I were definitely late when we pulled up at our dinner destination, and as my host, Osborn Webb, placed a carefully contrived martini in my hand I launched into an explanation of our tardiness which included the building of the shed and the purchasing of the lumber at the used lumberyard where George normally held sway.

"Well," said Obbie, "have you got all the lumber you need?"

"Hell, no," I said, having already had a sip of my host's high octane-count martini, "I need all kinds of lumber yet—more framing, siding, roof sheathing, and God knows what all."

"Well," he said, "I've got an old paddock here I want to dismantle. Mostly oak, I think, and you're welcome to it if you want to take it away."

"I'll be out tomorrow morning," I said and took a long draw at the liquid fire he was serving for martinis.

My enthusiasm next morning was considerably less than had been the night before but free lumber was not to be refused, so I undertook the long trek down across Chain Bridge and up along the north bank of the Potomac past Glen Echo and on past Rockville. I arrived at the Webb's paddock bout 8:30 on a raw morning, equipped with bow saw, axe, and crowbar. Osborn met me in front of the old dairy barn, then no longer operative but once the main building in the farm he had taken over. We looked through the gray, morning light at the paddock, the pens and corridors demarcated in the half-frozen black mud by rows of oak fencing covered with ancient and decrepit whitewash.

"There it is," Obbie said. "Help yourself to whatever you want."

I climbed the fence and waded through the mud out to the nearest piece of fencing. It was oak, all right, about one inch thick, six inches wide, and anywhere from ten to sixteen feet long. Some of it was bowed and some was bent, but on the whole it was straight and sound. I applied the bow saw to it, and thick, red grains of oak sawdust came out of the cut with the rasping teeth of the saw. When I had finished the cut, the new-sawn edge was dry and sound all the way across.

"I'll take it all, if that's okay."

"Help yourself."

For the rest of the day, I sawed across the oak boards, chopped the posts off even with the dark, oozy mud, and pried nailed boards apart with my crowbar. It was slow, exasperating work, and the air grew more raw and biting and the smell of the rich, fermented mud became more and more offensive. But by noon I had one load ready to drive the twenty miles back to my woods, and by five o'clock I had another. and by noon of the following day, I had the old, whitewashed paddock taken down, sawed and stacked in the Virginia woods beside the platform which was to become the floor of my Shed.

The ensuing week at the office was a prolonged wait. Whenever I lifted my eyes from the work before me, I saw a vision of those stacked two-by-fours and the rough, oak planking standing alongside my Shed in the dank woods. Meanwhile, the weather was wintry to the point of being uncharitable and the point was put to the climax when it began to snow in a steady, businesslike fashion on Friday night. There was great consternation in the household when I announced that, weather not withstanding, I intended to go out early in the morning and begin erecting the framing.

When morning came, the light was somber and grey, and the snow stood four inches deep on the sidewalks. Besides, my regular complement of tools, I put the kitchen broom in the car, and my first job upon arrival was to sweep the platform completely free of snow. Then I addressed myself to the task of putting up the framing for the north wall of my Shed.

If I had had a clearer idea of what I was doing, I could have put up the frame for the north wall in two hours' time. The difficulty was that I did not really know, and I kept finding it impossible to believe that it was really as simple as it seemed to be. The manual was slightly less than clear on the whole matter, and it seemed, from my somewhat befuddled point of view, to fall into the trap of dwelling upon the parts to the exclusion of the whole. There were individual paragraphs on posts, girts, top plates and sole plates, and braces, but there was no paragraph on how to assemble a wall and set it in place. I finally decided that for greater strength and unity the wall ought to be nailed

together and then set up. So with many a hesitant beginning and dubious advance, I began to measure and saw
the two-by-four pieces into six-foot, eight-inch lengths.

I measured the first two-by-four with a precision that
would have been admirable in a watchmaker, and then
sawed the piece off in a gingerly fashion. I repeated this
process with a second piece, and then, feeling somewhat
more sure of myself, attacked the third piece with greater
abandon. I had no sooner finished cutting it than I discovered I had made an extremely neat and precise cut just
eight inches short of the required length. I had cut it off at
the six-foot mark.

Even with this setback, I made considerable progress
that day, and when the weekend drew to a close I had a
ten-foot section of the framing for the side wall set in place
and braced by two pieces of the old paddock. This accom-
plishment meant that my Shed was no longer merely a
platform, standing inexplicably in the Virginia woods. It
was now clearly a partially finished building, and in this
knowledge I abandoned all further construction effort for
the year. The weather was spectacularly bad during the
rest of December and the month of January 1952, and I
was unable to resume working on the Shed until mid
February.

The time was not entirely lost, however, because I spent
many hours during that house-bound period poring over
the Montgomery Ward catalogue in search of materials to
order. Like many farmers with the catalogue propped up
on kitchen tables in farmhouses far and wide across the
North American continent, and like many a small land-
owner anticipating a surge of constructive activity with the
thawing of the creeks and the rising of the sap, I was
making out my mail order so that it would arrive before
I needed it.

Let's see now, building paper. Says here: "Excellent for

walls of cabins, summer houses, etc. One roll covers average room 14x14 feet , 8 1/2 ft. high." One roll should be plenty. Price, $2.45.

Windows, windows. Here they are: "All-purpose utility sash. Use for cottages, porch enclosures, cellars, garages, poultry houses, dairy barns, etc. Made of kiln-dried Ponderosa Pine, chemically treated to resist dry rot, blue stain and termites." Imagine! All that for $2.10 a window, twenty-by-twenty-five inches. I need three of those.

What about paint? I plan to paint it barn red. Yes, here it is: "Super barn paint, made with the best pigments and oils. Stays bright. Resists action of rain, snow, burning sun, freezing cold." Who could resist paint of such courage and such doughtiness? How much will I need? "Gal. covers up to 400 sq. ft., 2 coats." Okay, call it one gallon, $2.49.

I found it a great and wonderful game, playing with the Montgomery Ward catalogue. The detailed descriptions, dwelling on merits and virtues I had never known were possessed by such ordinary objects as window sash and building paper; the intricacies of shipping arrangements, whether by road or by rail, and the table of freight rates ranging from adding machines to woodworking tools; and best of all the fine pictures of equipment and materials, all of it gleaming and handsome and looking either incredibly easy to use or extraordinarily simple to install. It was not for nothing that the mail order catalogues were called the "Wishing Book" in rural areas throughout the United States before the advent of good roads and automobiles for everyone. And one need not be a benighted farmer to succumb to their lure now. I found that a slightly less than middle-aged Washington bureaucrat, relatively sound of wind and limb but somewhat moth-eaten on top, to be extremely susceptible.

Nine

The new year, 1952, had moved well into February and the major league baseball teams had begun to gather at their Florida and California training camps before I resumed construction activity on The Shed. Spring had not yet begun to manifest itself on the land, but the memory of man— particularly commercial man—was actively reminding me and my fellow citizens of Washington, Maryland, and Virginia that after February comes March and after March comes April, the month which epitomizes the coming of Spring. On every side I was being urged to buy seeds and new tools for a garden, rose trellises and children's swings for my backyard, and a new car for my forthcoming summer vacation. All these enticements were alluring but I decided that my shopping in preparation for the coming of Spring would consist solely of used two-by-four lumber for framing. And on this decision I set off once again for the used lumber yard and my fat acquaintance, George.

The passage of time and the coming of another new year had not seemed to have improved his personal grooming or augmented his beauty a bit. He stood before me, unshaven, with a small driblet of tobacco juice marking the corner of his mouth. "Haven't seen you in a long time," I said cheerily.

"Guess not," he said. "What'll you have?"

"Some more two-by-four framing. Got any left?"

"Hell, yes. All you can use." He set off for the two-by four stack."It's back here," he said and sloshed his way through the mud, the rusted nails, the bits of glass and metal.

"How's your wife?" I asked while picking my way with some care around a particularly large and, for all I knew, bottomless puddle.

"What's that?" he said, obviously surprised and made suspicious by this personal question. Apparently, all recollection of our previous intimacy on this subject had departed his mind.

"Is she feeling all right again?" As I asked it, I suddenly realized that I had ventured onto dangerous ground. For all I knew she might be dead.

"Her!" His tone was vehement and well-nigh scornful. "Hell, yes. You couldn't kill that old woman. Tougher'n a goddammed mule." He spat a glop of tobacco juice in cold exasperation. "Drivin' me crazy right now, pickin' at me to 'let her go out to Kentucky to visit her sister. Cost too damn much money. Sister's no goddammed good, anyway. She'll fill her full of ideas 'bout how to spend *more* money." He shook his head, filled with the angry sorrow of a plain man trying to understand the foibles and fripperies of womankind. He stopped then beside a large stack of two-by-fours. "Here Y'are. How much you gonna take?"

"About 150 feet."

"Pick it out," he said, sweeping his arm toward the pile in a large gesture. "Oh, Charley. C'mon over here n'help this man load some lumber."

When I had transported my load of two-by-fours to the

woods and resumed the job of framing, I found it went up very quickly. I had a clearer notion of what I was doing or, more important, how relatively simple a task it is to put up two-by-four framing: square cuts, accurate measurements, two tenpenny nails top and bottom to each stud, and there you have it. It all seemed to fall in place suddenly, and by Sunday evening I had the framing for the walls all standing, braced firmly in place by long pieces from the old paddock. I felt it made an impressive sight but unfortunately, because of the inclemency of the weather, no one was there to share it with me.

Mid-February weather in northern Virginia can be, and was, rough. The temperature was not really low: it fell just below freezing at night and got up to 40 or so during the day. But the days were sunless and damp, and the cold, wet ground seemed almost to suck warmth out of the human body. The road that went past my gate had become a rutted, bemired track, and even with snow-and-mud tires it sometimes took several tries to get up the steep hill that led to the hard-surfaced road. Since I was still driving across the meadow without benefit of gravel or any other surfacing, I regarded each passage in and out with my station wagon as something like a perilous voyage. "Made it again," I thought each time I reached a point beside The Shed or slithered out onto the dirt road at the gate.

Confidence in my ability to traverse a roadless meadow with a Ford station wagon in February was considerably bolstered one Saturday morning. It had snowed lightly the night before, and as I came in about eight o'clock across the new-fallen snow I made fresh tire tracks, enlivened here and there by certain slurring curves and other departures from straightness. I was diligently sawing and hammering away in the late morning when I heard the roar of a jeep motor coming closer and closer. Visitors were extremely rare at that time, so I looked up with more than usual pleasure in time to see Bud and Bob, skidding and yawing violently as they approached the Shed.

"How the hell did you get back in here with that station wagon?"

"Just drove in. No trouble at all."

"Well, it must have gotten worse since you came in. We had quite a bit a trouble just now with the jeep in four-wheel drive."

"Maybe so," I said politely, hoping my skepticism was not showing.

"We just thought we'd stop by and see how you're coming. We wondered whether you're all right."

This neighborly concern over my progress and my welfare warmed me and made my skepticism seem uncharitable. "Well, here it is," I said, waving my hand at my workings. "Gonna have a shed someday."

"Yeah. That's all right." They gazed at it several minutes longer and tried to summon additional polite or funny remarks. They did indifferently well in both fields. "Well, if you're okay, guess we better get back to our fencing."

It suddenly occurred to me that I was possibly being foolhardy. "Wait. Why don't you let me try driving the wagon out while you're still here. If I get stuck, you can tow me with the jeep."

"Okay. We'll go on out and wait for you at the gate."

I watched them making their way out across the meadow while I sat warming the engine of the Ford. The jeep swerved and thrashed and at one point came to a halt while Bud shifted into low-low. When I was sure they had had sufficient time to get out the gate, I started the station wagon across the meadow in second gear. I carefully avoided their track, making a new set in the melting, heavy snow, and kept my foot steady on the throttle. The wagon faltered slightly as we went through the one low spot, but the rest of the way it sailed straight and steady as a yacht in a fair breeze. I swung her handsomely through the gate and out onto the roadway.

"Boy, you must have awful good snow tires on that thing."

"Guess I do. They're brand-new retreads; paid $10. 95 for them." We grinned at each other for a moment or two, and I said, "Thanks a lot for coming by. " Then I pointed the nose of the Ford back in through the gate and high-tailed it for The Shed.

Actually, the problem of keeping warm proved to be no greater than that of crossing the meadow. The big problem was the feet. I solved that by wearing two pairs of socks, one light pair beneath woolen ones, an old pair of shoes, and galoshes. Topside, I wore several layers, reading from inside out: tee-shirt, old broadcloth shirt, woolen shirt, old hunting jacket, and short-length gabardine raincoat. Below the belt, in the same order, I wore: shorts, pajama pants, and blue jeans. In really cold weather, I replaced the blue jeans with old flannel trousers. The other anti-cold weather equipment I employed consisted of a thermos bottle of hot coffee and a half-pint bottle of sherry. And then if things got really bad, I could sit in the car, as I sometimes did to rest, with the engine and the heater running.

I usually started in the early morning in full regalia, all buttons buttoned and the raincoat zipped up to my chin. Within the first forty minutes or so, I began to move the zipper down and before long it was wide open. Then the coat came off and the collar of the hunting jacket opened. Not infrequently, the jacket came off too, and I worked in mid-February in my shirtsleeves I discovered that the process of sawing through a two-by-four causes the human engine to develop a considerable quantity of heat. And belting away at a ten-penny nail with a hammer has a similar effect. Under these circumstances, only two or three light layers of cloth are required to retain enough heat to keep a man extremely comfortable. More than that puts him into a sweat, and this creates a new set of dangers.

I discovered that my few hardy friends who made excursions out to see me did not always understand the thermal qualities of heavy carpentry. One Sunday in early March—a really cold day with the wind a searching cold blade and the ground frozen into rocky hardness—two of our Georgetown friends Ted and Barbara Lockard, drove out to cheer me up. They were both warmly dressed, she in a full-length mink coat and he in an alpaca-lined greatcoat. They had the heater on in the car; and when they opened the door and stepped out, the wind thrust at them with icy directness and explored the openings of their coats at the sleeves and the collars. I was putting on the corner braces that day, one-by-four inch pieces about eight feet long that run from a point high on the corner post diagonally down across the studs to the floor sill. In good solid construction, these braces are set into the studs so that they are flush with the outside edge of the two-by-four. This required a great deal of precise cutting in the edge of the two-by-four with hammer and chisel. My face was red, both from the wind and my exertions, but I was as warm as though I were sitting in my living room, and I had taken off the raincoat and was wearing the hunting jacket wide open.

Ted and Barbara, when they had recovered their breath from the onslaughts of the keen wind, were lavish in their admiration of my fortitude. "How on earth can you stand to work all day like this?" they said.

I tried to explain how it was that I was warmer in my hunting jacket than they were in their mink and alpaca, but before I could get the point across they were climbing back in their car, not to return until April had come to

Virginia and the air was soft and caressing. I have no doubt that if they had grasped a hammer and chisel and had undertaken to notch two-by-four studs alongside me, the long mink coat and the alpaca greatcoat would soon have been open at the neck.

Having surmounted the difficulties of framing, I turned with fair confidence to putting up rafters. I soon discovered that I had encountered quite a different sort of problem, one that required a slightly more geometrical approach. This was first brought home to me when I tried to figure out how long the rafters should be so I could buy the lumber. Now, let's see. The Shed is 10 feet wide, and I am planning to give it a peaked roof with about a foot and a half overhang. Half of ten feet is five feet. Then you add one and a half for overhang, making it six and a half. But wait a minute. That doesn't allow anything for the slope of the roof. Obviously, the rafter has to be longer if it angles up into the sky than it does if it merely extends flat halfway across The Shed. Okay, longer then. How much? That, dear friend, depends upon the angle. The steeper the slope, the longer the rafter. Sure, that figures. But how on earth do you figure out an abstraction like that?

As usual when I was stuck, I turned to my Army Manual, its tan cover by this time bearing such honorable battle scars as three creosote blotches and a touch of mortar. The manual turned out to be less than customarily communicative on roof-slopes but I did latch on to this sentence which seemed to be trying to tell me something: "The usual way to express roof pitch is by means of number, for example: 8 and 12, 8 being 'the rise and 12 the run." It took more head-scratching than I care to tell figuring out what this meant, but finally it came to this. If a roof has a pitch of 8 and 12, that means it rises upward 8 inches for every 12 inches it extends horizontally. To put it another way, if it was just 12 feet from the center of your building to the side wall, then a roof with a pitch of 8 and 12 would rise 8 feet from the wall to the peak. This would be a steep roof. A more shallow roof would be 5 and 12 or 4 and 12. I discovered from my researches in scholarly publications like *Better Homes and Gardens, and Good Housekeeping* that modern architects go in for very shallow slopes, like 2½ and 12 and even 1½ in 12. I settled on a conservative 4 and 12 for no particular reason and passed on to the next phase, namely, how long should the rafter be.

I found a passage in the manual which began,"To de-termine the rafter length" but then immediately dropped off into some unintelligible hocus pocus in which a carpenter's square seemed to figure prominently. I did not own a carpenter's square so I made a lunch hour trip to Sear's one day and bought one for $2.29. Fortunately, a booklet of instructions came with it and by playing the booklet off against the manual I made a little more progress. Turned out that you work the thing out by pragmatic demonstration, so to speak. You take your carpenter square and lay it on your two-by-four in such a way that the 4-inch mark on the inside of one blade of the square touches the edge of the two-by-four and the 12-inch mark on the other inside blade touches the edge also. You make pencil marks at these two points and then measure the distance between them. It turns out to be 12⅝ inches. In other words, if you follow me, it takes a rafter 12⅝ inches long to rise upward 4 inches while extending 12 inches horizontally. Having established that fact, you proceed—for reasons only slightly clearer to me now than they were then—to multiply this number by half the width of your building. This meant, for me and my Shed, multiplying five feet by 12⅝, and when all the dust had settled and I had added 18 inches for overhang it developed my rafters should be seven feet, one and one-half inches long.

I received this news almost as though it had come from

a Greek oracle or had been determined by the machina-
tions of a ouija board. I don't believe I ever fully understood it, and whenever I tried to think about it analytically
the whole thing grew as intangible as moonbeams. But by
that time I had the figure for the rafter lengths written
down, and it mattered little how I got it.

I next discovered that the carpenter's square possessed
other extraordinary talents: it could determine the angle
you saw across the rafter to make it flush with the ridge
pole and also the angle and depth of the notch you make
where the rafter crosses the top of the side walls. This again
involved laying the square on the two-by-four in such a
way that the 4-inch mark and the 12-inch mark touched at
the edge. But though I discovered to my astonishment that
it works, I understood this even less than the business of
the length. Moreover, I kept losing the knack of doing it
and would stand for minutes at a time laying the square
on the wood in one way or another until suddenly it
worked again. But it never ceased to amaze me. I always
referred to the process, when thinking about it to myself,
as that "4 and 12 magic", and I looked at my carpenter's
square with almost superstitious respect. Despite the tenu-
ous grasp I had of the technique of measuring rafter lengths
and determining the angles of saw cuts, I say with pardon-
able pride that I cut the sixteen rafters for The Shed without making a single mistake or ruining a piece of lumber.
Or maybe I should say, in whispers, That Square did it.

When all the rafters were in place, the outline of the
little building was complete. In fact, to my ever-loving eye,
the sheathing that was to go on the sides and over the
rafters seemed almost superfluous. You could *see* what the
building looked like. Why be crass about it, and underline
its outlines with sheathing? But though I indulged myself
with these fancies, I was more anxious than any one else
to have the walls and roof covered. Moreover, I got unex-

pected help from a friend, Henry MacLean, who suddenly returned from Greece. He took a very keen interest in my project—though never to the point of swinging a hammer in anger—and he immediately suggested that the enormous wooden van, or packing crate,in which his household goods had been shipped across the Atlantic would serve admirably for sheathing lumber. I used it to sheathe the roof from eave to peak to eave. Also, my friend had the good fortune to rent a house which had a termite infested porch, and he persuaded the owner it needed replacing. While the entire porch was being dismantled, he persuaded the 'workmen to stack the relatively sound lumber to one side. Then I appeared with my station wagon on the following Sunday and made off with the pile. To this day, it covers the north wall of the shed.

By the time I had laid hands on all this free lumber and had got it fastened at some point or other to the framing of The Shed, springtime had come once again to my woods and my hillside. Many times in the past I had had the experience of first observing the coming of spring and becoming determined to note each new phase individually and in detail as spring unfolded. And each time, I suddenly became aware that spring had arrived, in full leaf and flower, and somehow I had failed to notice the precise moment of its coming. Somehow it seemed, spring began deliberately and slowly, in steps that were easily distinguishable and separate, and then suddenly, everything seemed to happen at once and spring was not coming—it came. This year, though, I was determined to establish and announce to the world the exact time that spring had come.

What I discovered was probably no news to any farmer or country dweller but was certainly previously unknown to me. And that was that there is no exact moment when spring arrives in any given locality. The fact is that it arrives in a steady series of succeeding moments, and these moments are determined by terrain, prevailing winds, and accessibility to sunshine. Thus, at one moment in mid-April, spring had arrived on my land and was in full possession of the banks of the stream and the broad expanse of the meadow, while at the edges of the woods it was still standing on tiptoe, undetermined whether or not the time had come to make an entrance. Within the woods only ten feet or so, the new season was still sleeping soundly, unaware of the rejuvenation and excitement taking place so short a distance away. One little dogwood tree that my eager axe had spared in the middle of the field, shot forth tightly furled little leaves, spread them forth luxuriantly in the young sunshine, and went on to produce some amateurish and adolescent-appearing blossoms before the larger and more knowledgeable trees in the margin of the woods became aware that the time had come for the annual demonstration of their blossom-making skills. And within the woods, dogwood trees continued to hold themselves in the same attitude of mute suspension they had maintained since the previous November.

As a consequence of this phased advance of springtime, the woods surrounding The Shed was still deeply entrapped in winter dormancy as I was nailing the sheathing to the rafters while a mere twenty feet away the meadow was dancing in the April sunshine. The lumber I acquired from Mac, my friend who had newly returned from Greece, was presumably Greek in origin. At least, it had somehow found its way to Athens where it had been assembled into a packing van. What it was, I never discovered. It was mostly quite green in color, sometimes fairly sticky with resin or a similar substance, but in general it had a consistency not unlike celery and it was highly susceptible to splitting. I began by using eight-penny common nails, as I understood the manual to suggest, but changed to six penny common when I split more pieces than not. When the six-pennies continued to cause splitting, I changed to six-penny box nails (slender nails with broad, thin heads) and thereafter had little trouble.

Spring had advanced several yards into the woods by the time I finished the roof sheathing and turned to putting on siding. The dogwoods at the verge had become aware that an upstart in the middle of the field was stealing the show and had hastily begun hanging out fresh blossoms. Meanwhile, a mountain laurel bush at the very doorway of The Shed had begun to try on tiny, new leaves for size. At this point, I was deeply and happily engrossed in putting on vertical siding. I began with the termite-tainted porch material which came in ten-foot lengths, ten or 12 inches wide. It was soft pine, and it went on with great ease and dispatch. Beneath it I put the building paper I had bought from Wards ("ideal for a cottage, etc."), and I worked down along the north wall nearly to the northwest corner before the easily worked porch material gave out. Then I turned to the old oak paddock and things took on a different complexion.

It was not merely that the oak was hard, which it was, so incredibly hard that at times it approached imperviousness. But also, it was warped in eccentric ways, and I found it necessary to match one piece against the edge of another, and at times to pull and haul the new piece over closer to the one already nailed. this pulling and straining spoiled the accuracy of my nailing, with the result that I bent over many more nails than I drove home. Not even Ivory soap helped too much. Moreover, my arm grew tired and sore from the strenuous and unabashed slugging necessary to drive the nails home. I wondered many times whether the time consumed in tearing down that paddock, moving it the twenty miles to The Shed, and applying it to the framing was justified economically. Each time, however, I quickly came to the same conclusion: time was something I had more of than money. Also, whatever difficulty I had in putting it on, that oak siding had wearing qualities approaching those of steel.

Spring had arrived even within the woods when it came time to put the roofing on over the roof sheathing, but I somehow managed to pick a weekend when the temperature was sub-fifty to lay on the roofing. At any time, the long, heavy rolls of asphalt and mica are enormously clumsy and difficult to manage, but in cold weather (colder, that is, than fifty degrees) it becomes fiendishly difficult to apply. Stephen came out to help me and was very effective at nailing down the edges of the roll roofing at four-inch intervals, but even so I remember it as a difficult session. We had great difficulty in heating the cans of tar compound sufficiently so that we could seal the edges where two rows overlapped, and at one point I fell off the ladder while carrying a hundred-pound roll up it. Fortunately for me, the roll took another route to the ground and left me unscathed. We spent a long, hard weekend at it, but when we sat down to our baked beans dinner on Sunday night—I having prepared myself with two bourbon old fashioneds beforehand—we had the pleasure of knowing The Shed was completely roofed and snug. Little then remained to do to the building except to put battens on over the joints of the vertical siding, install the windows, and build two four-foot barn doors for the east end.

Ten

When I was in college, my English professor frequently referred to one of the classics of literary research, a book *The Road to Xanadu* by John Livingston Lowes. In this book, Professor Lowes located all the elements, bits of imagery and names in Coleridge's poem, *Kublai Khan*, and demonstrated how they were introduced into Coleridge's mind by things he had read and heard. Well, if one were so minded, and not troubled by the absurdity of the exercise, a similar piece of research could be done on the way The Playhouse, the house I built which we later named "The Little Red House," was introduced into Rosemary's mind and mine, how it gradually took shape as an idea, and finally found form and substance as a board-and-batten structure on our hillside.

It must have been some early spring evening after we had got the children to bed and were having one of our rare, uninterrupted conversations that Rosemary first gave voice to the idea. We had been going round and round on the perennial topic: rent. We were paying out approximately fifteen hundred dollars a year in rent. If there were only some way that those fifteen hundred dollars could be channeled into a building investment of our own instead of someone else's (I remember that the phrase "down the drain" figured prominently in this familiar discussion), then it would be a relatively short time until it became a substantial accumulation. In ten years it would become fifteen thousand dollars; in twenty years, thirty thousand dollars. In the short time we had lived in Virginia, we had paid various landlords between seven and eight thousand dollars. For that we had received only the transitory benefits of *quiet tenancy* and relatively snug shelter. We had nothing material and substantial to show for the expenditure of that sizeable lump of money, merely the memory of several hundred nights of sheltered sleeping. And as I had discovered, seven or eight thousand dollars would buy stacks and stacks of lumber, innumerable window frames, and dozens of rolls of roofing. There *must* be some way to break out of that closed circle in which we were helplessly orbiting: unable to build because of no money/unable to save money spent on rent/unable to build because no money.

It was against this background that Rosemary said on this memorable evening, "Why couldn't we build a very simple place, just one large room, and move into that? That way, we could stop paying rent and after a year or so we could start building our house."

It would perhaps be more telling and dramatic if I could report that I leaped into the air at that moment and yelled, "You've got it! We will start tomorrow!" I did not. Actually, 1 was quite dubious. One large room, however large and cleverly divided by screens and furniture, could become terribly confining in the course of a year. Moreover, the Shed was the model my mind inevitably turned to, and proud as I was of that structure I did not find it easy to imagine my comfort-loving wife and my children living in a rudimentary building like an expanded shed. "Would you really be willing to live in a one-room house with a — well, a tar-paper roof ?"

"Of course I would. After all, it wouldn't be forever, and we are going to have to do something. We can't go on paying rent the rest of our lives. Besides, it doesn't have to look like a tar-paper shack. It could be made quite attractive."

"Well, what would we use it for after we had built our house? Would we tear it down or what?"

"No, we wouldn't tear it down. We could use it for lots of things. Storage and so on. You can always use extra storage space in the country. We could—" Rosemary paused for a moment while excitement gathered in her face. "I'll tell you what we could do! We could use it as a square dance barn, like Bob and Lucy Housel's. It could be our entertainment place, like a rumpus room, only separate from the house. It would be our Playhouse!"

At the mention of Bob and Lucy's square dance barn, my mind turned a corner, as it were, and before me now lay an entirely new set of possibilities. A square dance barn—or better yet, Rosemary's word for it, a Playhouse —offered possibilities as a model which were more intriguing than The Shed. Moreover, Rose's excitement was infectious and if she was willing to endure the relative discomfort of living in a square dance barn—sorry, Playhouse--for a year or so, then perhaps this really was an idea to get excited about.

"By golly, I think you've got something! Why don't we do it?"

"Oh, honey, do you really think you could build a place we could move into?"

When Rosemary had last questioned me about my building capabilities, just before I had begun building The Shed, 1 had answered with slightly more bravado than sense. But since that time I had spent several hundred hours putting up a small building with my own hands, and I had some understanding of the problems of the work involved. Moreover, I knew that constructing a shed for storing tools was child's play compared with building a structure to shelter human beings, and there were immense areas of building practice—such as wiring electricity and installing plumbing—which were totally unknown to me. Still, the basic problems of framing, raftering, and siding were the same, and I still had confidence in my ability to wrest out of books or the conversations of my acquaintances sufficient understanding to deal with the unknown problems. Besides, I had read just the previous Sunday a long account by a fellow Virginian who had built his own house over several years' time (I remember he described with passion the hours he spent digging by hand in the Virginia hardpan), and this example spurred my imagination onward.

"Yes," I said somewhat soberly, "I think I could do it."

It was about this same time that one of the glossy magazines, *House Beautiful* or some other, devoted an issues to what they called, *The Retirement House*. I have great sympathy for the editors of monthly magazines who are obliged, year in and year out, to turn out twelve issues crammed with *new* ideas. But this particular idea struck especially responsive chords in Rosemary and me. We were thoroughly intrigued and the ideas presented in that issue provided the last few ounces of impulse we required. The main theme of the issue was that most families require a large house of three or four bedrooms only for a period of relatively few years while the children are growing up. After that a large house is an unnecessary burden. What is then required, the magazine argued, is a small house of one or two bedrooms, easily managed, into which the parents could retire. Before retirement, the small house could serve as a guest house or an entertainment house (Playhouse?). After retirement, the large house could be rented and thereby provide additional income for the retired couple. Viewed in these terms, the magazine contended, a small house built somewhere on the ground adjacent to your main house was a sound economic enterprise.

This was all we needed. It did not matter that we intended to build the *retirement house* first and the main house subsequently. This merely provided additional economic justification. Moreover, we could add to the arguments in favor. Both of us had parents who would someday want to spend a month or more at a time living with us. How better to deal with the age-old *in-law* problem than to have them live with us in an adjacent, small guest house? Moreover, we could probably rent the small house during those first, difficult years after we had built the main house, thereby reducing our financial burden. So there we were. Building a small house on our land turned out not only to be a means of breaking our financial impasse—the necessity to pay rent—but it also provided good economic returns over the long term. As one who has always had a profligate tendency to do what he wanted, regardless of the long term implications, this last consideration had a particular appeal. Here was an opportunity to do what I wanted to do while savoring to the full the realization that I was doing the *right* thing, the forward-looking, provident, prudent thing. This I could not resist.

But if I were going to launch a new and more grandiose building project, what was clearly required was that I finish The Shed in the shortest time possible. I could use The Shed then to store tools and materials. I turned to the task of putting in windows with brisk enthusiasm. The three small casement windows I had bought from Montgomery Ward went into place on the north and west walls with no difficulty except a powerful amount of planing. Along the south wall I tried a modest experiment. I bought some material called Cel-o-glass, or something like that, which is really only translucent plastic sprayed over window screen. I had read about its being used in chicken houses and similar places where light is wanted but cold air is not. I made an opening about ten feet long and two-and-a-half feet high along the south wall, and stretched the Cel-o-glass across it. For $3.69 I obtained a window-wall which now lights up the interior of The Shed so long as there is light in the sky. It was my first experiment in the modern architectural use of large windows, complete with southern exposure and all the solar, thermal benefits derived thereby.

For battens over the cracks of the vertical board siding, I bought three or four bundles of used lath from my favorite used-lumber dealer. It is customary to use wider battens, but the lath turned out to be in perfect scale with the six-inch oak planking and the building's small size. Besides, it is easy to overlook small imperfections of size and scale with any building material that comes so cheaply as fifty cents per large bundle.

The barn doors could not be built out of used lath, however, or any other used lumber that I could discover. This brought me to a new crisis: the necessity to buy new lumber for the first time. I consulted the nearest sage and oracle at hand, Bud Bradley. "I've always bought my fencing and two-by-fours from old Mister Rose up there past Forestville. Don't you know old Rose?" I had to confess I did not. "Why, man, you've missed one of the real characters of these parts. He's an old fella, way past sixty, and he wears a sort of chauffuer's cap and when he talks his eyebrows move up and down and the cap moves with it. He's kept the same price on his lumber for the past fifteen years-seven cents a board foot. He's as honest as the day is long. Only trouble is, he loves to talk, and when you go up there to his sawmill you want to plan on spending a half day, or at least a couple of hours."

When I set out for the Rose sawmill, I carefully followed Bud's directions and counted the number of side roads until I came to the right one. I went about a quarter of a mile down a muddy road until I came to a ramshackle farmhouse on the left. turned in and stopped. A young man, no more than twenty, came shambling out from the house, naked from the waist up. "Is your old man around?" I asked.

"If you mean my daddy," the young man replied, "he's back at the mill. Just follow the lane on back. He is back there supervisin' the sawin'."

The lane leading to the sawmill cut across a meadow. On either side of the fences handsome Hereford cattle grazed in the knee-deep grass. An occasional curious animal lifted its head at the sound of the car, its black muzzle glistening wet and its soft eyes blandly inquisitive. Then the lane curved to the left and passed through a handsome stand of oak trees as it went down the hill to a stream. There stood a casually assembled log bridge and across it was the sawmill itself, looking like a Civil War relic with its tarpaper sheds and belt-driven saw. I hesitated to trust my station wagon to that obviously inadequate bridge, but across on the other side, standing near a mound of reddish sawdust, was a good-sized stake truck, and I decided that the bridge which could support the truck could also support the wagon. 1 crossed without difficulty and snaked my way past the truck and a pile of logs to a relatively open space.

As I got out of the car, the high-pitched whine of the big saw sounded in the morning air. Standing near the saw were two men: one about thirty and bare-armed, the other much older and wearing a dark blue chauffeur's cap. From Bud's description, I knew that the second man must be old

Mister Rose. He seemed to be directing the younger man, probably his son, as he guided the whining saw up the length of a big log.

I walked slowly over and watched the operation for several minutes. If old Rose saw me, he gave no sign, and after a few more minutes I walked away toward the stacks of lumber standing off to one side. I had got myself straightened out as to which was poplar and I had just located the oak one-by-sixes when the old man walked up. Apparently his curiosity had overcome his reluctance to forego the supervising of the sawing.

"Do anything fer ya?" he asked.

"I want to pick up some one-by-sixes. Oak," I replied.

"Looks like there's plenty right here," he said. "How much do you need?" As he talked, his chauffeur's cap moved up and down in an indescribably comic way—just as Bud said it would—and his red eyebrows raised and lowered with remarkable abruptness.

"Not very much. About 70 feet."

"How do you want it? Eights, tens, or twelves?" Again the remarkable movement of the cap bill and the reddish orange eyebrows.

"Well, eights, I guess, if I can get it."

"I guess you can have anything here you see. Call it nine eights." He paused and the bill of his cap reached a new altitude. "or ten?"

"Ten."

"Ten." He turned around and began flipping over pieces of red oak with unexpected vigor. He pulled one out. "Here's a good one. Got that knot down on the left side though. That's the trouble with all the oak around here these days—it's all wormy. Poplar's better for most things. It's just as strong after it gets seasoned. What are you going to use these one-by-sixes for?"

"Doors on a shed. The shed has oak siding".

"Well, I guess you want oak then. Let's see what we can find." And he set to work, flipping boards with experienced skill and great agility. Now and then he lifted one up by the end and sighted along its length to check its straightness. "Here's one," he would say and slip it off the stack for me to load into the station wagon. In a very short time, we had ten eight-foot lengths of red oak loaded. "That do you?" he asked. Then he said, "If you don't mind, I'll ride up to the house with you."

"Fine, get in." I got in myself and eased the wagon out through the ruts, around the deep chuck-holes, and across the crude bridge.

"How long you been livin' here in Virginia?" he asked as I took the hill in second gear, up through the handsome stand of oaks.

It was a simple question; one with a perfectly simple answer, such as three years or four and a half years. But I was keenly aware of the discrepancy between the length of my tenure in Virginia and old man Rose's and I hesitated to expose my newcomer's status to him. My concern was needless, however, because the old man began talking again before I could possibly have answered him.

"I been here now on this place for forty-three year," he aid. "My daddy bought this farm and I moved here with him when I was just nineteen. I sure seen a lots of changes since then." He paused a minute to lean his head over the side of my station wagon and spit out a stream of tobacco juice.

"When me and my daddy first started this mill, there was all kinds of good lumber right around here close. Good oak, plenty of nice clear poplar, and lots of pine—big stuff. Now they ain't nothing around here except some wormy old oak and a little poplar, mostly small stuff, and now and then a big one some fella's been keeping in his yard or something like that. Why, last winter we hadda go fifty

miles into Maryland to get some poplar. One of these builders wanted ten thousand feet for sub-siding and we couldn't
fill it with the stuff we had on hand." He shook his head
in simple sorrow over the degeneracy of the age. And
besides that, I'm having trouble getting help. My oldest
son—he's the fella running the saw down there now—is
the best sawyer I ever knew. He can get more good, straight
boards out of one log than anybody, including my old
daddy. But he don't like the lumber business. Wants to quit
and take a job in Herndon where he can make twice as
much money." Again, the sorrowing shake of the head.

I expressed the hope that he was going to keep the
sawmill running for quite a while because I was hoping to
get some more lumber from him later on.

"Oh, we'll keep on sawing as long as we can get the
logs. And we'll keep on charging seven cents a foot for it.
Been my price for fifteen years now. Seems like a fair price
to me."

By this time we had reached his doorway and had been
sitting there for several moments, the idling engine serving
as background to the rural Virginia voice, the vowels as
soft as red mud and the consonants slurred and worn. Bud
had warned me that old man Rose's garrulity knew no
bounds, so I was prepared to have this monologue to go
on at length. But to my surprise he got out of the car with
some alacrity and said, "Well, come on back when you need
some more lumber."

"I will. But I haven't paid you for the lumber I just got."

"No hurry. Pay me next time you come back or pay me
now. Makes no difference."

"Well, I'd just as soon pay you now."

"All right then. Just let me get a piece of paper to
give you a receipt." He was back in a moment with paper, pencil, and a little booklet. He thumbed through this,
wetting his thumb in his mouth, muttering something about

two-by-sixes, eight. He puzzled and studied for a moment and then declared, "That'll be two dollars and eighty cents."

I gave him three one dollar bills, and he pulled a small leather pouch out of his hip pocket—its throat closed by a string with little metal beads on the ends—and fished out change. "And three," he said. "And I thank you."

I hesitated a moment, the engine of the station wagon idling gently, and then said, "I'm thinking of building a small house. What kind of siding do you think I ought to use?"

"Poplar. Best thing you can get."

"But isn't it awfully soft?"

"Soft? Sure it is when it's green. But when it gets seasoned up it's so hard you can't get a nail into it."

"Well, what do you do? Season it before you put it up?"

"Naw." He paused a moment and then continued, all seriousness now, his chauffeur's cap bobbing up and down earnestly as he talked, and his adam's apple fluttering in his red-skinned neck. "No, you lay it on green. It's the only way you can handle it. Then, the way a lot of them does is to put battens over the edges of the boards. When they draw up then it don't make no difference." He paused again; then pointed to one of his outbuildings. "See that barn over there? That is poplar siding. Been standing now for twenty-three years and every board on her is sound. No, you can't beat poplar for siding."

"Well, I'll be back to get some someday. Thank you."

"Yours truly." And he turned and walked into the house, a curiously engaging figure.

I drove the five miles back to the woods with my newly-bought lumber giving off a pungent smell of raw oak. 1 turned in at the gate leading back to the nearly finished shed and drove across the meadow on the track I had worn on the early June grass. It was almost noon and the sun stood high over my woods, casting deep shadows at the edges of the sun-washed meadow. I spent the rest of that day and the next putting together two four-foot doors. This was not a complicated task but hard. The unseasoned oak was monstrously heavy and, when assembled, one of the doors was all I could handle alone. When it came time to hang it, I wrestled it into place, propped it there with a two-by-four, and drove wedges into the sides and bottom to give the door clearance as it swung on its hinges. By conservative estimate, one door weighed two hundred and fifty pounds.

But in other respects the lumber was surprisingly easy to work. It sawed as easily as pine and the nails went in easily and straight. The wood was surprisingly green. Drops of moisture gathered around the nail heads as I drove them home. The acid in the oak sap turned the nail heads purple and where my hammer head struck the wood round purple stains spread like ugly bruises in flesh.

The unabashed greenness of the lumber troubled me, upsetting as it did all the folk wisdom I had accumulated over the years about the necessity for building lumber to be dry and seasoned. I asked Bud about it. "Was it all right? Could I consider using it for The Playhouse I was going to build?"

"Sure, I'd go ahead and use it. Matter of fact, I'm going to build a horsebarn with it this summer."

"But is it as strong?"

"I don't know, but it seems to be strong enough. Farmers around here been building with it for a couple of centuries."

"Yeah, I guess that's right."

The doors hung, it only remained to paint The Shed. There was no problem about what color to paint it. What color other than barn red would be appropriate? And white trimmed, Rosemary insisted. White on the window frames, around the doors, and on the fascias. I set myself firmly

against this prettifying of my functional and honest building, and mailed off my order for two gallons of the red
paint to Montgomery Ward. I found a sunny, dry weekend
toward the end of June and set to painting with zest and
joy. The birds chittered and fluttered in the woods around
me; the paint fell in drops of burning scarlet onto the dark
green leaves of the bushes and weeds around the shed;
and the clean smell of new paint mingled and contended
with the odor of greenness and the acrid scent of the rotting leaves on the moist ground. My paint brush snagged
and caught in the rough texture of the oak siding and then
released suddenly, flipping little specks of red paint onto
my face and my clothes. But with all these distractions and
minor hindrances I got The Shed painted in the two days
of the weekend, and by Sunday afternoon it was sitting
amidst the mature June greenness a glowing red shape. To
my eye, the vivid contrast of the primary colors sharpened
the definiteness of the little building's outline and somehow heightened its reality. It helped to persuade me that
I had actually accomplished what I set out to do several
months before—to build a shed.

In the exhilaration of this achievement, I was on fire to
press on with The Playhouse. But before I really got started
on it, Stephen and I celebrated the completion of The Shed
by spending the night in it. It was quite an adventure. We
ate supper at home and then set out in the early evening
for the woods. It had been a warm day but as we turned
into the meadow at the gate the air was cool and fragrant
with the dampness of green grass. The meadow was tran-
quil in the evening light, and the woods gathered shadows
slowly and transformed them into darkness. By the time
Stephen and I had unpacked the car and made up our
beds—mine a G.1. Cot and Steve's a sleeping bag—it was
dark. We finished by the light of an electric lantern, and
then went out for a brief stroll before turning in.

The woods loomed high and silent over The Shed, the trees rising to mysterious heights and forming huge, indefinite shapes in the darkness. When we stepped out into the meadow, the stars leaped out of the blackness and the sky became a shimmering sweep of innumerable pricks and points of light. The brilliance and incredible profusion of the stars astonished me, and I realized that not for many years had I looked at the sky at a place where nearby lights of houses or cars did not diminish their intensity. We stood for a moment at the edge of the meadow, the ten-year-old boy and I gazing up at the dazzling spectacle. Then we walked slowly out on our improvised lane toward the gate, and I watched over my shoulder as the Big Dipper lifted itself from the topmost branches of the trees and moved up into the sky above the woods as I walked. Midway down the meadow, we stopped for a moment. Ahead of us on a hill to the left shone a yellow light, an oil lamp shining through the windows of my black neighbor, Mr. Alvin Brown. Up to the right, the dark mass of our woods loomed in the blackness. Off in the distance, a dog barked—not urgently but conversationally, as it were. I turned around, and there hanging over the end of the meadow was the Great Dipper fully revealed, the two stars of its outer edge pointing to the North Star. I checked the direction of my lane and found it ran almost true north and south, as did the brook marking the eastern edge of my land. It was good to know that my land sat somehow four-square to the world.

This was the first time I had ever walked on my land at night. It seemed to me it possessed even greater beauty than I had realized, and I felt a greater sense of completeness of possession than ever before. My desire to build The Playhouse and move onto the land and live there all the days and nights grew fiercer and more compelling than ever before. Stephen and I walked slowly back to The Shed. By the light of a candle—the rafters clean and bare above us and the windows black against the night—we undressed for bed, talking of the fun we were having. Outside the night was loud with katydids and crickets, and off in the distance a whipporwill chanted his monotonous insistence in urgent cadences. We slept somewhat unevenly and woke by first light. We stepped outside and found the woods a miracle of damp freshness. We cooked our breakfast in Stephen's camping utensils and then went home to tell Rosemary how we had fared.

Eleven

The next Saturday at eight on a handsome mid-June morning I made the first step toward building The Playhouse: I chose the site. Rosemary and I had discussed where in general it was to be. If we were someday going to build a pond where the meadow was low and marshy, then The Playhouse ought to sit slightly up the hillside over-looking it. As we talked about it we conjured up some highly appealing images of ourselves sitting on a porch or deck of The Playhouse, sipping placidly at something long and cool, while our youngsters disported themselves on the pond, fishing from a boat, perhaps, or splashing in the shallow edges.

My task was to locate the precise place on the hillside where The Playhouse would nestle most attractively. I also was seeking a spot where the slope was at a minimum in order to reduce the problems of the foundation. I picked my way laboriously through the dense pine grove on the hillside in quest of the right place. Brambles tore at my blue Jeans, honeysuckle vines stubbornly opposed my passage, spider webs added their, puny resistance, and the dew of' the early morning turned my trouser legs a deeper blue half-way tip my shins. I felt as though I were invading the deep jungles of Africa as pine boughs raked across my face and my feet caught in the close vines. It was extraordinarily difficult to see the ground clearly enough to discern the slope and equally difficult to look out through the pine branches and see the view. I finally decided, after much thrashing around and swearing, where I thought the best place was, a spot roughly thirty feet up the hillside and facing slightly north of east.

And on that, I began clearing the hillside from the bottom up. It was slow, exhausting work. A stupendous' number of pine trees had infested that hillside, and I got increasingly hot and sweaty as the sun climbed the eastern sky and smote my laboring back. I felled and dragged out roughly a hundred young trees and I slashed and slew a million vines. And by the end of the weekend, I stood in a raw clearing and said, "Here. This is where The Playhouse will stand."

It was to be 16 feet x 40 feet. I could not truthfully say how those dimensions were arrived at. I had learned that, most small, modern houses were 16 feet wide, and it seemed to me within my capabilities—untested though they were— to build a structure 40 feet long. Well, there you are, 16 by 40. So, my clearing was slightly more than 40 feet long and it cut a swathe into the pine grove approximately 45 feet deep.

The next weekend I staked out an area sixteen by forty. I had the same momentary difficulty as I had with The Shed, juggling the fourth stake a little this way and a little that in order to make certain the two sides and two ends were the same length. But this time I had the assurance of knowing I had done it before, and I knew that there were no unexplored mysteries lying ready to trap the inexperienced. Once the corner stakes were in, I stretched a length of carpenter's twine on the forty-foot uphill side, and then, firmly grasping my shiny new mattock, began to dig a foundation trench.

I had only a general idea of what I was digging. I knew that I wanted a continuous-wall foundation for The Playhouse, not the pier arrangement I had used for The Shed. A wall would prevent winter winds from whistling under the floor. But the construction of a foundation wall on a sloping hillside gave me problems not easy to solve. How deep into the ground must I dig for the foundations, and is this depth the same on the uphill side as the downhill side? In other words, was it possible to have the uphill foundation several feet higher than the downhill? I decided, though without any great conviction, it was possible, and in order to reduce the difference, planned to dig the uphill foundation deeper than the downhill. For the uphill trench, I chose a depth of thirty inches, bringing to bear a slight degree of rational calculation and a large admixture of arbitrary decision. The trenches had to be twenty inches wide according to the county building code.

And so, my immediate task was to dig a trench forty feet long, thirty inches deep, and twenty inches wide. I began with considerable zest. After all, I was taking the first steps toward building my own house, and this is a solemn and joyous task with rich traditional meaning. My ritualistic joy was somewhat dashed by some ten-year-old pragmatism from my son whom I had persuaded to work with me. He was extending the clearing farther up the hillside above the site. I looked up from my trench, the sweat rolling down my forehead into my eyes and dropping off my chin in fat salty drops, and asked in what I hoped was a tone of hearty camaraderie, "Isn't this fun, Steve, working together to build our house?"

Stephen glanced up from the three-inch trunk of the pine tree he was sawing and said, without haste or rancor, "But we aren't building anything. We're just tearing things down."

True, but disinspiring. And what this flatly objective

remark had begun, the rock-like hardness of the red clay soil and the gruelling late June and early July heat completed. The sun had come over the eastern ridge at six o'clock and by eight was smiting the slope where I worked with ferocity. Sweat streamed off me, and my heart beat with heavy, throbbing blows until I grew light-headed and apprehensive. And all this time, the gnats or midges, call them what you will, hung in a black mist before my face and got in my eyes and up my nose if I bent over quickly. Subjected to this harsh treatment, my enthusiasm wilted, and the job became an extended endurance contest. I hacked and struck at the ground with my mattock, each blow flaking off a small portion of red material, the steel tool leaving a dark, shiny mark on the clay. Then I gathered up these flakes and crusts with my shovel and loaded them into the wheelbarrow. When it was full I threw down my shovel with gratitude and staggered off down the slope behind the erratic wheelbarrow, given to sudden lunges and unexpected swerves. Then I trudged back up the slope, drawing in great gulps of air and lifting my head high to ease my aching back muscles. And then, with great reluctance but a fierce determination to finish the bitter task, I picked up the mattock and began to hack and pick.

Part way through this ordeal, I went over to the county seat and got my building permit. My father, who was visiting me at the time, went along. I was grateful for this break in my ditch-digging routine, and Dad and I talked aimlessly as we drove through the green countryside. My mind was only partly on the conversation because I knew that I faced a slight problem in getting a permit. Applications for permits to build dwellings were supposed to be accompanied by several sets of blueprints. I was so far from having a blueprint for my projected Playhouse that the very thought was laughable, and I was not quite certain how my interview with the building inspector would turn out.

I presented myself at the reception desk at the county office and a brisk young lady began asking me questions. The first one I stumbled badly over: "Are you building a house, a garage, or a barn?" Correct but unspoken answer: "None of those. Got any more choices?" The second one, however, I hit on the nose: "Dimensions ?" Proud answer: "Sixteen by forty." The third one threw me for a total loss: "Approximate cost of construction?" Honest but silent answer: "Haven't the faintest idea. See me in about a year."

The brisk young lady decided that I was too hard a case for her and turned me over to her superior, a white-haired man who looked as though he customarily turned a pleasant face toward the world but at the moment was bored.

"What are you building?" he asked.

I paused for a moment, decided that a direct answer was best, and plunged. "Well, my wife and I call it The Playhouse."

He looked at me blankly, it being perfectly apparent from his expression that neither in his mind or on the form on the desk before him was there a category known as "Playhouse". He frowned slightly and tried again. "Well, what are you going to use it for?"

This was considerably easier. All the numerous and manifold uses I intended for the Playhouse came tumbling into my mind, and I said, "Oh, we'll use it for storage, and entertain—

"Storage," he said, his face registering greater certainty and assurance. "Storage. It's a storage shed?"

"Well, yes," I said hesitantly. "But it's also to be used for other things."

"But mostly storage?" he asked hopefully, almost plead-ingly.

I hesitated again. It was clear he was perfectly happy with "storage" as a category, and there was no telling where we would end up if I rejected "storage" and sought a more precisely accurate term. I gave in. "Yes, storage."

"Fine. Dimensions? Oh, yeah, I see you've got it here already: sixteen by forty. Approximate cost of construction?" He looked up, expecting a simple, direct answer.

I paused, badgered by complete uncertainty. "Well, I don't know exactly. I guess it would be—"

He cut me off briskly and took charge. "Well, let's see, sixteen by forty, that's six hundred forty square feet. Barn construction, I suppose. Well, what shall we say. Do you think a thousand dollars will cover you?"

To a man whose only building experience consisted of constructing a ten by fifteen shed out of scrounged materials and used lumber bought with left-over lunch money, a thousand dollars mentioned in one breath seemed like a lot of money, and I promptly answered, "Yes."

The rest came easier. I breezed through such questions as location, rural or suburban, and similar queries without wrinkling my brow. When we had filled out the form, the man said, "That'll be nine dollars."

I gulped, in the knowledge that I had only three dollars with me. (Who would have thought a building permit would be more than three dollars?) I said, "Wait just a minute. I'll be right back."

Dad, who was waiting outside, promptly produced the needed six dollars, but I could see from his expression what he thought about a man who was setting out to build a house and had to borrow money to pay for the building permit. It was to him another instance of the unerring impracticality I had displayed since my younger days, still unblemished despite his lifelong campaign to instill pragmatic and businesslike concepts in my dreamy head. He was undoubtedly right but what mattered to me at the moment was that I had got my building permit despite all my forebodings of difficulty. I was officially blessed in my undertaking to build The Playhouse—oops, sorry, Storage Shed.

Back to the trenches. I was taking a vacation from the office at the time, and I had the whole day to spend at ditchdigging. The trouble was that I could not stand a whole day of hacking and digging. What with the heat and the grim hardness of the red clay, I became exhausted after four or five hours. But at the same time, there was nothing else I wanted to do except to go on digging and finish that godawful job. I experimented with getting up very early in the morning and starting to dig around six o'clock. No good. In that year of gruelling heat throughout June and July, the sun came over the edge of the world looking cruelly red and hot. By eight o'clock the heat was shimmering on that eastern slope where I worked.

I tried working after three in the afternoon when the shade from the woods was creeping down over the clearing. It was little better. It was the hottest part of the day, the shade notwithstanding, and the gnats were at their most numerous and most persistent. They danced in front of my eyes, flew in my nose and gasping mouth, and whined maddeningly in my ears.

Since it was obvious that the digging was as brutally exhausting during one part of the day as another, the only thing to do was to get it over as quickly as possible. So I drove myself in almost a frenzy, swinging the heavy mattock which rang like an anvil as it struck the rock-like clay, scraping the red flakes off the bottom of the trench with my shovel and careening down the slope with a hard-won wheelbarrow load. My leather gloves got sodden and squishy with sweat, and my heart pounded until my vision got blurred. Now and then I would retreat on trembling legs to the densely-shaded woods where the contrast in temperature was so great I quickly got chilled. And while I sat in the doorway of The Shed waiting for those great waves of fatigue to subside, I wished with bitter vehemence that I could soon get the ugly job of digging footings finished.

After many more hours of passionate labor, I got the long back trench finished and was nearly completing the south end trench when Bud drove up on his tractor. He had been mowing in a nearby field and was passing my gate on his way home when he decided to turn in and check on my activities. As always, his expression quizzical and amused as he sat slouching on the gray metal seat of his tractor.

"They tell me you're building yourself a house to move into."

"Yeah. A Playhouse, we call it. It'll be a square dance barn later, like Bob and Lucy's."

"Yeah." There was a long pause while the engine of the tractor idled gently. After so long a silence that I was about ready to turn back to digging, Bud said, "Well, what are you doing now?"

"Digging footing. It's a mean and nasty job. I'll be mighty glad to get it finished."

"Aren't you going to excavate it so you'll have a cellar underneath?"

"Nope. I'm going to put up a foundation wall to build the house on and I'll just have some crawl space underneath."

"But don't you want to have a cellar and add all that space?"

"Nope. It'll cost too much money. And besides, this is just a Playhouse. You don't want a cellar under a square dance barn."

Bud looked at me as though he found it hard to speak. Finally, he shook his head and said definitively, "Man, you're crazy. One of these days, about five years from now, you'll be crawling in here with a bucket and shovel trying

to excavate a cellar. I've seen it happen to other people."
He paused and looked up the hill at the trench I had so
painfully scratched out. "It would be a crime not to put a
cellar under there. You get twice as much space for just a
little more money. Way you're going at it, you're just wrap-
ping that space up in cinder block and keeping it useless."

I should have been shaken by Bud's eloquence but
actually I was firmer than before in my resolution to proceed as I had planned. "No, Bud," I said. "The big thing
I've got to avoid is to get too much money tied up in this
thing. If I do, I won't be able to go on and build the real
house later. I've just got to keep all the building costs down
to a minimum. I admit, though, it would be a fine thing to
have a cellar."

"It wouldn't cost very much either. Why, you could
probably get it excavated for practically nothing. Being on
the side of the hill like that, there is not very much to dig."

I shook my head sadly. "No matter what it would cost,
it would be too much."

Bud looked up the hill again and the expression on his
face was more determined than I had ever seen it. "Look,"
he said, "I'll excavate the darned thing myself with this
tractor. I really think you ought to put a cellar under there,
and I'll do it myself."

"Have you ever done any excavating with a tractor?"

"No, but there wouldn't be any trick to it. I'll bet I
could do the whole thing in four or five hours." He pursed
his lips and his face again wore its habitual quizzical look.
"I'll tell you what I'll do. I'll excavate it with my tractor at
six dollars an hour. I'll probably get it done in under a
day. But if I don't, I'll just charge you for one day's work.
The most it could cost you is eight hour's worth, forty-
eight dollars. And it probably will cost you only thirty
dollars."

I looked at him unbelievingly. "Are you serious?"

"Sure. I'll do it on that arrangement. I *know* I can do it in four or five hours."

"Well, okay," I said weakly. "It's a deal. When can you do it?"

"Next week maybe." Bud climbed up on the metal bucket seat and dropped the tractor into gear. "I may end up regretting that I talked you into it but I still think it's what you ought to do."

"I guess you're right," I said meekly. And as he swung the tractor around and drove off, I walked slowly up the hill and picked up my tools. There was no sense in going on with my scratching and scraping when the whole thing was going to be excavated by tractor. I was a little at a loss to know just what I could do with my time while I was waiting but it was clear I was through digging, at least temporarily. Footings would have to be dug by hand later, after the excavation was finished. Failing all else, I could return to my old love, clearing trees and brush. For the time being, I was uncertain whether I ought to be feeling regret over the enormous waste of energy expended in digging the trenches which were soon to be ripped up by Bud's tractor or merely relief that for the moment at least I was through digging. Relief finally won.

After slightly more than a week, Bud telephoned me that he was ready to start excavating, and I met him at the meadow the next morning at eight o'clock. The day was bright and already growing hot. The grass surrounding Bud's grey tractor was drying in the warmth of the climbing sun, and the birds in the woods behind us were making more subdued sounds than they had when I first arrived a half hour earlier. Bud and I discussed for several minutes what he was to do: in essence, merely to pull a wedge of dirt shaped like a piece of cake on its side out of the hill. My trenches and some stakes would serve as guides. The dirt he moved could be pushed out in front of the sixteen by forty foot rectangle in order to provide flat ground in front of The Playhouse.

"What about this pine tree right here in the middle? You want to take that out?"

"Well, Rosemary and I were hoping we could leave it in. We thought it would be nice to have it just outside our living room window."

"I was afraid you'd say that. Well, we'll see what we can do."

With that, Bud pointed his tractor up the hill and climbed to a place just below my painfully hacked out trench. He swung around downhill and then backed up until the rear of the tractor hung over the trench. He dropped the harrow and pulled slowly forward downhill. The steel teeth raked through the hard clay crust and opened six-inch deep wounds in the ground. It looked ridiculously easy. After twenty minutes work with the harrow, Bud unbolted the hitch and put on the scraper blade. Again, backing into position just below my hand-hewn trench, Bud dropped the blade and pulled forward. A six-inch deep slice of earth curled up on the steel face as the tractor moved slowly down the hill. As I watched the blade scraping a strip off the hillside with so little physical exertion on Bud's part and only a mild murmur from the tractor engine, my back and shoulder muscles twinged in memory of past strains and aches.

But however easily it went at first, the difficulty, at least from Bud's point of view, was that it went rather slowly. At the end of the day, he had dug down three or four feet at the back of the excavation, but he was far from finished. As we judged it by eye, the back wall would need to be eight or nine feet deep in the ground before we could make a flat space sixteen feet broad on the hillside. Bud shook his head, grinning ruefully, and said he would come back next day. Another full day went into the job, backing the tractor into place and dropping the blade and pulling another slice of earth forward, and still Bud was not finished. But he had moved an impressive amount of earth and packed it flat beneath the wheels of his tractor. The third day he brought along his hired man, Irving Honesty, and another tractor, and the two of them set to work with a fury. The two tractor engines, straining by this time as the rear blades dipped deep into the softer earth, roared impressively, and the shouts of the two men as they exchanged signals in order to keep out of each other's way made my modest little project seem bustling and important. After well over half a day, "chasing ourselves around that damned pine tree" as Bud described it, the job was done as well as could be by tractor. "I quit," said Bud. "That's best I can do for you."

I looked at the back wall of the excavation, standing at least eight and a half feet high, and at the flat expanse of freshly dug, hard-packed earth that extended twenty-five feet out from the back wall like a shelf in the hillside, and I realized that a terrific amount of work had been accomplished. "You've done a hell of a lot," I said. "I don't see how I can ever repay you."

"Think nothing of it. Just call it 'Bud's Folly'." He sat motionless on the tractor a moment, a slight blue-shirted figure with a quizzical expression on his tanned, loose-skinned face, "Boy, I sure misjudged how long that job would take. But I'll tell you one thing, I could do it a lot quicker next time. There's a knack to it. Just let me know anytime you want any cheap excavating done." He grinned at me and turned to his hired man on the other tractor, "Well, Irving, let's get started on that fencing." He dropped the tractor into gear and led the way as the two tractors rambled across the field to the road.

After they had left, I examined the excavation more carefully, and I discovered that a great deal of hand digging remained to be done. Bud had done an extremely precise job—far neater than a bulldozer could do—but even so the sides and back walls sloped considerably and the corners were round instead of square. Also, one corner contained a deposit of red rock nearly ten feet across, soft enough to be broken up with mattock and shovel but too hard to yield to the tractor blade. And after the excavation was squared up, I would once again have to dig the trenches for the footings, twenty inches wide and twelve inches deep. I groaned inwardly at the thought of swinging that mattock again and pushing that awkward, laden wheelbarrow, but there was no avoiding it. And so, even though it was after three o'clock on a hot July day, I walked slowly back to The Shed and got out the tools. After all, the sooner I started the sooner I would be finished.

By the time I had swung the mattock three times down through the swarm of ever-present gnats and into the clay earth I was once again fully immersed in the agony of digging. The air hung close and damp in the excavation, undisturbed by the light movement of the breeze that feathered the pine trees gently over my head. And the dirt, though softer and therefore easier to break up with the mattock, was heavy and lumpy. And always those gnats! I tried to distract my mind by wondering where that particular crowd of gnats had been hanging out during my absence from digging. And how, by what invisible telegraph, had the glad tidings been passed about in the gnat world, that I was back at the old stand, available for observation or heckling or for whatever purpose it was they gathered before my eyes in a dancing, maddening cloud? But it was no use. I was engaged in a miserably unpleasant, but entirely necessary, job, and no amount of distraction would let me forget that fact before it was finished.

The only thing to be said in its favor, aside from the fact it had to be done, was that it was a job with definite and easily discerned limits. It was easy to see what had to be done and how much progress I had made. I was back on a weekend basis by this time, and I spent three laborious weekends squaring off the edges and corners. Aside from the painful and mind-dulling slogging, nothing eventful occurred except a major cave-in of the back wall after a very heavy rainstorm. So depressed was my morale that it seemed at the time a major catastrophe. Actually, it took me somewhat over two hours and approximately thirty wheelbarrow loads to clean it up. I also encountered some very heavy going in the rock at the northwest corner, but that in time yielded to a few thousand blows of my mattock.

When I laid out the lines by which to dig the trenches for the footings, I made an important discovery. My building was not going to be sixteen by forty as I originally intended, not unless I was willing to hack out another four feet at one end of the excavation. During the digging, the length of the excavation had shrunk without my noticing, as a result of Bud's gradually moving in his tractor at the beginning of each cut. The longest I now could get was thirty-six feet. Well, I reflected, my original plan was to have a building sixteen by forty providing a square footage of 640 feet. Now I was going to have a building only thirty-six feet long. How wide should it be in order to approximate 640 square feet? No great mathematical effort was required to establish that if it were eighteen feet wide the square footage would be 648. Done! The new dimensions of my Playhouse were to be eighteen by thirty-six, a pair of figures arrived at by entirely pragmatic means. And I set the stakes, strung the lines, and dug the trenches--at the cost of another weekend or so. When I finished with the last wheelbarrow load, laid down my shovel, and stood back to admire my neat rectangle of trenching, my relief was monumental. I was strongly tempted to buy a bottle of champagne and break it over my mattock. Instead, I hung up my soggy leather gloves in The Shed and drove home to tell Rosemary I had finished that miserable job.

By this time, the leaves had begun to turn and some were starting to fall, and I realized I must make haste if I was to get all the cement and mortar work done before freezing weather would delay me. The first problem was to get the concrete footings poured, and I set about finding out who to call and how to proceed. It was my first dealing with the concrete fraternity and my first effort at sub contracting. I went at it with all the assurance of a blind man trying to thread a needle. Some of my knowledgeable acquaintances—a circle that grew steadily as I got further involved and met more people who knew something about building—told me you buy concrete by the cubic yard and the cost per yard is determined by the distance the concrete must be hauled. They also gave me the names of two concrete dealers in nearby Virginia. All that remained for me to do was to figure out how many square yards I would need and call the company I chose.

After some elementary arithmetic, which I checked and re-checked, I came up with the answer six and a half cubic yards. Armed with this, I went to a nearby dealer. "Six and a half," he said. "Better make it seven. When do you want it?"

"Saturday morning, I guess, if you can make it. About 10:30."

"Okay. We'll be there. Where'd you say your place was on this map?"

I pointed to it, pridefully.

"Now let's see. That'll be $13.25 a yard."

I nodded my head and started toward the door. I stopped and turned back, feeling as awkward as a new boy at school having to ask where the toilet was, ''By the way, I've never poured any footings before. What do I have to do when the truck comes?"

If this display of ignorance regarding his chosen field

of endeavor caused any pain, the concrete dealer did not reveal it. "Well," he said, "you want to have plenty of people on hand to shovel it around into place as it comes off the truck. Can't let it set. Another thing, unless the truck can get right up in there where he can pour it in off the spout you'll need some wheelbarrows."

"Okay. That's what I wanted to know. Thanks a lot."

As I drove home, I mulled over the information I had acquired. At $13.25 a yard, seven yards of concrete were going to cost me $92.75. That was undeniably a lot of money but a footing for a building was something you bought only once, as you might say, and besides there did not seem to be any way to get one cheaper. The treasury would have to disburse $92.75. Next my mind moved on to the phrase "plenty of people on hand." The thing to do, I thought, was to gather some friends around for a few hours and make it an occasion for fun rather than work. I could get a case of beer and put it in a tub of ice and maybe get some wieners to roast over an open fire. That sounded like fun, and I thought of Hal Ford down at the office and Don Chase and Doug Douglas at the housing development. They would probably enjoy a Saturday morning in the open air, and they certainly would enjoy the beer.

It was a crisp fall morning when we gathered in my meadow awaiting the concrete mixer truck. I had been up since before 6, so excited by the event I had been almost unable to sleep. I had the beer in the tub, the green bottles glimmering through the ice, and some kindling wood gathered for a fire when the others arrived.

"What do we do?" they asked.

"I don't know anything we can do until the truck arrives except to lay out the shovels." They gathered around the excavation and looked at the carefully cut trench. One of them noticed the little wooden stakes set at frequent intervals along the bottom of the trench.

"What are those?"

"Grade stakes. You have to put those in to measure the depth of the trench so you can see whether you have poured enough concrete or not. Also, they're there to give the building inspector a measure of the depth of your footings."

"Building inspector? Does he have to come and inspect it?"

"Supposed to. I notified his office last week. He's supposed to inspect before and after the footings are poured. Maybe he came last week when I wasn't here. It's sort of like the Easter bunny or something."

Shortly we heard the sound of a heavy truck coming down the hill, and in a moment a big cream and red truck lumbered over my meadow. It stopped near us, and a man with an excessively Irish-looking face leaned out. "Where do you want it?"

"Right here," I answered.

"Can I back up on that fill there?"

"Far as I'm concerned. Just don't damage that pine tree."

With a mighty roaring of the engine, the truck backed up the fairly steep slope of the new fill, the big double tires -keeping the heavy truck from sinking down. Once in place, the driver jumped down from his cab and unlimbered a long spout clamped on the side of the truck and hooked it on the back; then he turned some large valves near the mixer and made some other adjustments. With everything ready, he asked "You all set?"

"Sure," I said and glanced nervously around at my plucky little band. One of them was scowling and the others were grinning foolishly. "Let her rip."

He proceeded to do just that. None of us had even seen concrete footings poured before, let alone do anything constructive about the process, and we all stood clutching our shovels, feeling there was something we ought to be doing but not having the slightest notion what it might be. Before things got out of hand, the driver jumped down, grabbed a shovel, began using it like a canoe paddle. "You got to keep it mowing," he said. "Spread it around."

On the strength of his example, we all began paddling away at the thick concrete mix. We filled the back trench first, then the south side, and we had got part way down the north side when the concrete suddenly ceased to flow. The whole operation up to this point had taken no more than fifteen minutes. "That all?" I asked, dismayed.

"No, that's just four. Have to go back and get the other three. Take about a half hour." He fastened his spout back on the side of the truck. Before he drove off, he turned to me and said, "Tell you what you might do while I'm gone. Push that short handle shovel up and down in the mix. You're supposed to work all the air bubbles out of it."

"Okay, thanks, I will." And all four of us began to jab our shovels in and out of the fresh concrete while the truck roared off down the meadow and up the hill.

The rest of the pouring went off without incident. The truck came back just as we were finishing our beers, and we went to work this time like hardened professionals. The job was finished in another half hour, and the only problem remaining was to dispose of approximately half a yard of concrete, the difference, as I later realized, between the six and a half yards my computations disclosed and the seven yards I was induced to buy. We disposed of the extra concrete on a particularly low point where I drove across the field.

When I had finished writing out a check, I said to the driver, "Have a beer."

"Thanks, I will. This is my last job today, being Saturday. I don't drink on the job." He took the beer I handed him and drained half of it on one draught. We all sat down in the golden autumn sunshine, drinking beer and talking.

The kindness the driver had displayed in helping clumsy amateurs had already won my admiration, and his conversation was further evidence that he was a man of good will. "Got a nice place here," he said, "real nice."

"Thanks. Have you lived in Virginia long?"

"All my life. In the same house, about five miles from here."

"Have another beer."

"Believe I will."

Part way through the next beer it dawned on all of us that we were an extraordinarily fine group of fellows, and moreover we were extremely fortunate to be alive and vigorous on a day when the sun streamed down like liquid gold and the air was winey with young autumn. On the strength of it, we started the fire within the circle of rough stones and cooked the hot dogs over it. That called for another beer and what with one thing and another it was well after three o'clock before we broke up. As they all departed, Pat the truck driver remarked it was the best pouring-of-the-footings he had ever attended, and the others agreed it was a memorable occasion. After they had gone, I walked up to the site and looked at the new footings, the concrete already greying as it dried. "Well, I thought to myself, "I have begun to build." I suddenly remembered Stephen's remark during the digging phase that we were not building but tearing things down, and I reflected on second thoughts that "begun to build" was slightly strong. Well, at least I had filled up the trenches I had dug so the minimum statement possible was that I had got back up to ground level. From here on, all progress would be constructive and upward.

Meanwhile at home, Rosemary had successfully brought another child into the world whom we named Christopher.

Twelve

L aying cinder block, I was assured by many people (some of whom had laid cinder block themselves and some had not), is very simple. It's like playing with children's blocks, they said. But something about the prospect of laying cinder blocks myself gave me pause. Sawing and nailing wood was something I had learned to understand, but masonry and mortar were totally alien, and I somehow could not imagine myself doing it. Moreover, cold weather was approaching, and I felt it was essential to get the job done quickly. It seemed to me, all things considered, I would be well-advised to pay to have the job done. In any event, I could not imagine it would cost very much.

In that frame of mind I obtained a personal loan from my bank for $500, an amount which I hoped would carry me a long way on the Playhouse, and then set out to find someone to lay the cinder block. First, I went to a man in our neighborhood who had done some building and who reportedly did very good work at a reasonable cost. His answer, after he had got the dimensions and specifications, was chilling. He would be very glad to do the job for $550. Next, I tried a mason from among a list I was given by a friend. His approach was very direct. "How many block you going to lay?" Fortunately, I had worked out that figure during my dealing with the neighborhood builder, and my answer was pat: "Between 650 and 700." There was slight pause and he said over the telephone, "Well, I'll tell what I'm going to do. I'll put those blocks in for you at 35 cents a block." "Thanks," I said, "I'll let you know." A little pencil work revealed that his charge would come approximately to $230, to which I would add the cost of the blocks, mortar, and sand. Still pretty steep.

I next tried my neighbor, Alvin Brown, who lived just down the road from my entrance. Alvin had a reputation in the neighborhood for being a good mason, general repairman, and all-round handyman but was regarded as frequently difficult in personal relations. A black man of Jamaican origin, he and his family owned large tracts of property nearby which had been in the family's possession since Civil War times. After several tries I finally found him at his house late one afternoon. A slender, brown-skinned man with a soft pleasing voice and accent, he came out on his porch, and we talked in the gathering autumn twilight. I told him my plans to build a small house, described the extent of the masonry work I wanted done, and asked him whether he was interested.

"Why yes," he said, "That would be real nice. I could come home early in the afternoon and work there for a couple of hours till I got it done."

"And there would be the weekends too," I said. "Saturday and Sunday."

"No, sir, I don't work Sunday. Sunday's my day of rest. But Saturday would be all right. Yes, sir, I'd like to do that."

"Fine. How much would you charge me to do the work?"

He pursed his lips and looked thoughtful for a moment. Up the hill at the next house on the road a dog barked meditatively in the gathering dusk. "Well, sir, I think I could lay them block for you at 12 cents a block. And then there'd be my helper, someone to mix the mortar for me and build the scaffolding and hand me the block. He oughta get a dollar a hour."

"How would it be if I was the helper? You'd have to show me what to do at first, but I could do it all right and I don't mind hard work. I'm trying to save as much money as I can on the job."

He looked at me thoughtfully for a moment and then said, "Why, yes, we could do it that way if you like. That would be all right."

"Fine. Twelve cents a block sounds good to me. Let's go ahead on that basis. When can you start?"

"Soon's you get the block."

"I'll have it here this week." And I stepped off his porch and walked in the near-darkness down the gravel road to the entrance to my field, elated with the bargain I had struck.

It took me only three queries by telephone to discover that the principles of shopping for cinder block are no different from shopping for anything else: don't take the first price you hear. I first called a local feed store that handled building materials on the side: 25 cents per block. I then called a trucker who hauled cinder block from a factory somewhere in Pennsylvania: 22 cents per block. I then tried the little plant where Dick sent me to get cinder block *seconds* when I was building The Shed. There was a short exchange involving the number of blocks I wished to buy and the volunteered information that I was, as a builder, entitled to a 10% discount. Then the quotation came: 18 3/4 cents per block. Sold! How was I fixed for mortar and sand? I was, in a word, unfixed. Also, I was elaborately uninformed as to how much I would need. How much? There was a pause during which I heard some muttering on the other end of the telephone line and then the professional opinion was offered that twenty bags of cement and four tons of sand ought to see me through.

I made it a point to be on hand when the cinder block was delivered the next afternoon because I had read somewhere during my scholastic preparation for this phase that building materials, particularly cinder block, are frequently damaged during unloading. Two heavily ladened trucks groaned across my meadow and backed up onto the flat space near the footings. Aboard was more cinder block than I had ever before seen in the unassembled state. Under my watchful eye, three men unloaded and stacked it with moderate care. The cement we put in The Shed.

After the trucks had departed I fussed around the enormous stacks of cinder blocks like a housewife dusting and straightening. I also counted the blocks and reached the unforgettable figure of 683. I admired the huge mound of reddish sand and thought to myself it would be nice if some were left over for a children's sandpile. Then I laid out the tools—a bucket, a shovel, and a hoe—and hauled near the sandpile a big mortar box a friend had gratefully given me in order to get it out of his front yard. I was just trundling from The Shed to the site with a bag of mortar in the wheelbarrow when I saw Alvin, a spare, brown-skinned figure, walking in across my meadow. He was whistling cheerily and walking crisply.

Alvin looked my site over professionally and turned an appreciative eye to the scenery surrounding. "Mighty pretty place you got here. You know, I've worked in this field many a time. Ever since I was a little boy helping my daddy."

This glimpse into the history of my meadow intrigued me. The land had assumed so much meaning to me over the past two years that it came almost as a surprise to realize it had a past extending back beyond my first acquaintance and probably a rich and varied history. It was a little like discovering that your girl had been in love before. "What did they used to grow in this field?"

"Just about everything. Beans, corn, wheat. Very rich soil here in this little valley. This was just about the best field on the whole farm."

Beaming over this deserved and well-informed compliment to my meadow, I said, "Well, what do we do first?"

"First we mix some mud. I see you got the mortar all ready. Next we gotta get some water."

"I'll get it." I grabbed the bucket and walked down to the stream, stepping proudly across the best field on the farm. I scooped a bucketful out of a little pool, just below a place where the water burbled and foamed over large black rocks, and walked back with it.

"Looks like a good footing you got here," Alvin said. "Good and level." He had already emptied a sack of cement into the mortar box, and he was throwing shovelsful of sand on top of the cement, counting as he shoveled. "Nine, ten. That ought to do it." Then he mixed the grey cement and the red sand with quick, deft movements. "Now the water." And he took the bucket and splashed a small amount into the box, shoveled some more, added another dollop of water, and shoveled again. At one point I went back to the stream for another bucket of water. After five or ten minutes of extremely thorough shoveling and mixing, the *mud* seemed to be of a texture pleasing to Alvin. He put a shovelful on a broad piece of board, walked over to a corner of the footing, and began trowelling mortar onto the footing. Then he placed a cinder block carefully atop the mortar and tapped it gently, laying his mason's level along the top to check it. After that he placed another cinder block at right angles to form a corner, and after that another block at each end to lengthen the two sides of the triangle.

In a little while, no more than fifteen or twenty minutes, Alvin had built a corner five or six cinder blocks high right before my eyes. For me, the building began to exist at that moment. As I stood there watching the man work in the fading October afternoon, I had a sudden and absurd realization that those dozen or more cinder blocks formed a real and authentic corner, no different from those I had seen in completed buildings. This was the reality, this was permanence. A corner is in some respects the very essence of a walled structure, and here before me was a corner that was mine, a structure behind which my family and I could seek shelter from sharp winds and pelting rains. I was now fully launched on a project that had suddenly assumed a reality as material and rough-textured as cinder block. My Playhouse had suddenly ceased to be a set of oral commitments and expressions of intent and had become the solid corner of a wall.

During the remainder of that afternoon, Alvin got the other back corner started. Then, as the darkness from the woods above us slipped slowly down the hillside, we agreed to stop for the day. "Well, we got ourselves a start," he said. "Now, maybe if we can get in a whole day, we can get quite a bit of it done."

"How about Saturday?"

"Saturday would be fine."

"Eight o'clock?"

"All right, sir. I'll be here."

Saturday was another fine October day, and we began promptly at eight and worked steadily until after five. Alvin put in the two front corners and then worked steadily filling in the space between the corners. When the walls rose as high as the corners, from which he had run a piece of twine to serve as a guide to straightness and levelness, he built up the corners again. And as he worked, it became increasingly apparent to me that I had made a very good bargain. Not only did he work with a deft economy of movement that was delightful to watch, but his work was neat and spare, like his person. He was thorough and painstaking, and the joints between the blocks were even and precise.

Most of the time I was too busy to watch very closely. I found the actual mixing of the mortar very heavy work, and my back and shoulders grew tired and began to ache. Alvin worked so fast, once he had got the corners set accurately, that I was kept busy nearly full time mixing *mud*. But in addition I had to run to the brook to get water, and I was supposed to keep Alvin supplied with cinder blocks. And on subsequent occasions, when the walls had risen higher than he could reach, I also had to build scaffolding for him to work on. All in all, I put in a very active day, and when Alvin said toward the end of a solid eight-hour day, "Now, if it was summertime, we could get in another two, three hours," I replied, "Maybe you could, but I'm ready to quit. I'm pretty tired."

He looked at me quickly and said, "Well, you've been working hard, no mistake about it. We usually have two helpers for each mason." At that I beamed, as gratified as though I had been awarded the Mason's Helper's Medal of Honor (Apprentice Class).

Alvin and I put in two more good sessions before finishing. In the last session, we put in the steel window frames, one at each end of the building. Then he went on alone one afternoon to put up a supporting column midway along the inside of each end wall. This, as my books quaintly called it, was a "pilaster", and was designed to hold the beam running lengthwise of the building. After that, he coated the outside of the cinder block with a thin layer of cement—"parging", the books called it—and he was done.

That weekend I stopped around at Alvin's house to pay

him. He had it all worked out on paper. There were 685½ cinder blocks in my foundation, as he had counted them, and at 12 cents a block that came to $82.25. In addition, he proposed to charge me $10 for the parging, making a grand total of $92.25. I paid him and shook hands on concluding the deal. As I walked down the road I made some mental comparisons. The first mason I had telephoned wanted approximately $230 for the job Alvin had done. He could not possibly have done it better. And the local builder had offered to do the whole thing for $550 whereas I had spent, adding Alvin's fee to $129 for cinder block and $33 for cement and sand, only $254.25. I felt there was a lesson for me in this episode of the foundation, and after some reflection I decided it was this. You can save the most money in building by doing your own contracting; next most can be saved by hiring yourself as helper to a professional workman. Subsequent experience bore this conclusion out.

Thirteen

By this time, I was completely immersed in building The Playhouse, and it occupied my mind at every moment I was not engaged in something requiring my full attention. It. was like being in love. Everything reminded me of The Playhouse. Thoughts about it waited always at the edge of my conscious mind, ready to rush in at the first opportunity. Details of construction fascinated me, and I looked at a house, any house, with all the rapt attention of one who had never seen a house before. As a matter of fact, I never *had* seen a house before, not as I was looking at one now. Although I had spent half a lifetime living in houses, I had never focused on moldings, door jambs, eaves, window frames, and all the rest. Each building detail was potentially a problem I would someday have to solve, and my eye restlessly worked over them all one after another, seeking to learn the secrets of their construction. Some of my friends and acquaintances found it disturbing to see me staring fixedly at their ceiling or running an inquisitive finger along the inside of their window frames. On every possible occasion, I persuaded my host to take me down into his basement or up into his attic, and there I happily examined the construction of his joists and his beams or his rafters and his trusses.

I also read everything I could find about houses and building. Advertisements in magazines confronted me with one potential decision after another. What kind of pump should I have for my well, piston or jet? What kind of heat, floor furnace, oil burner, or forced hot air? What kind of lighting fixtures? What kind of flooring? And on and on. But since the literature of house building is not large, I usually ended by reading my two *bibles*, the Army Technical Manual on Carpentry and the book Dick Mote had led me to, *How to build your Dream House for Less.* In fact, it became standard procedure for me on Friday night to read the chapters of these two books which dealt with the building phase that was going to occupy me next morning.

Somehow, it amused Rosemary a great deal to see me boning up on the next day's activity, and she always asked me on Friday nights whether I was doing my homework. I usually was.

Even more importantly, my preoccupation with The Playhouse led me to make innumerable drawings and sketches of it on long sheets of yellow paper. I used the spaces between the lines as two feet, and on that basis I drew and re-drew plans for The Playhouse. The basement plan was simple. The only unusual aspect was that purely for aesthetic harmony I had decided to build the front wall of the foundation only four blocks high above the ground and to bring the front wall up the remaining distance to the second floor with wooden framing. The front wall was to have a four-foot door in the middle and two six-foot windows on either side of the door. The second floor was somewhat more complicated. The living room was to be the width of the building, 18 feet, and 24 feet long. The remaining twelve feet on the second floor was to contain two bunk-rooms on the front part of the house and a kitchen *ell* and bathroom on the back. Mostly I concentrated, at this stage of the designing, on the outward appearance of the building. I decided, after innumerable drawings, to have a gable roof with very shallow slope and a three-foot overhang. I also decided on a 12-foot window across the front of the living room and two large rectangular windows at each of the two bunk-rooms. But the really important decision I made at this time, as far as the appearance of The Playhouse was concerned, was to run a four-foot-wide deck across the front of the house and to extend it four feet beyond the house on the northern end. I later realized, when the house was finished, that the projection of the deck out beyond the house was the most important architectural feature in its appearance. The extension of that line broke up the boxy appearance of the building itself, and bestowed a lift and a grace on an otherwise firmly planted little building.

Although my evenings and leisure hours of the day away from the building project were devoted to airy architectural projections, my hours spent actually working on The Playhouse were at this point exceedingly grubby. The first task that confronted me after Alvin had finished constructing the foundation walls was to coat the below-ground portions with asphalt waterproofing compound. This proved to be an exasperating and thoroughly messy business. When I got down between the cinder block and the dirt wall at the back of the foundation, the space was so narrow that all the asphalt I put on the wall came off on me. Besides, I quickly developed an acute sense of claustrophobia. Another difficulty arose from the fact it was late autumn by this time and the chilly weather made the asphalt very thick and sticky. I swore at it and labored at it and made very slow progress. Finally, with the aid of a sunny afternoon and Rosemary's brilliant invention of tying the swabbing brush to a long stick, thus enabling me to stand up above the narrow trench and reach down with the black, gooey brush, I finished waterproofing the foundation. My relief on this occasion was almost as great as it was when I finished digging the footings.

My next task was to fill the voids along the top row of the foundation with cement and to set bolts in at eight-foot intervals. Looking back on it, I find it difficult to understand why I undertook to fill all the voids—it was necessary only where the bolts were placed—but some perfectionist urge got me started and, once begun, a mixture of the same perfectionism and pride prevented me from stopping. I stuffed newspaper in the holes in order to keep the cement from falling all the way through to the bottom of the wall, but even so I used a prodigious amount of cement and mixed batch after batch of cement until my shoulders ached and I hated the sight of that mortar box. On two occasions, I finished working after dark by the headlights of my car.

It was on Thanksgiving Day that I made the transition from uncongenial cement and cinder block to the more familiar wooden framing. I had gone out the previous weekend to Rose's sawmill to get 2 by 8 pieces which were to become the wooden sills along the top of the foundation wall. I had laid them on trestles and had creosoted them. Somebody had told me it was modern building practice to put a metallic shield between the foundation and the wooden sill, so I consulted Bob Housel, the most knowledgeable of my friends regarding building construction. Bob, a brusk, sometimes abrupt man, who thoroughly enjoyed playing the role of a heretic, responded to my question with a snort, "What are you worrying about termites for? I have had termites in my house ever since I bought it. I go down in the basement once a year, spray my joists and beams, and kill off all the termites. They come back during the year but before they can do any damage

I kill them off again. No problem. Costs me $1.35 a gallon for the spray. People get all excited about termites but they're nothing to worry about."

I had gone to Bob for advice before, and I had learned to not be put off by his opening blast. Behind the heretical facade lay shrewd judgment and sound knowledge. Sometimes the methods he proposed for solving building problems appeared highly unorthodox but they always had the merit of simplicity and workability. "But, Bob," I said, "if you were building a new house, wouldn't you put some kind of a shield between the foundation and the sill? It's very easy to do at this stage. I understand most people use sisalkraft, that copper stuff."

"Yeah, I know they do. Sure, I guess I'd put a shield in there. Won't do any harm, might do some good. I can get the sisalkraft for you if you want it. But you know what I would use if it was mine?"

He paused a long time to give his answer maximum effect, his face screwed up in a wicked grin. "No, what," I said.

"I'd take some of that heavy aluminum foil your wife uses in the kitchen, and I'd lay that on there. As long as you don't tear it while putting it on, it'll make a perfect shield and cost about a third as much."

And that is how it came about that Rosemary, while doing her Thanksgiving shopping, bought four 20-foot rolls of heavy aluminum foil and brought them home together with the turkey, the cranberries, and the cans of pumpkin pie mix. On Thanksgiving morning, while the turkey was slowly roasting in the oven, Rosemary, Stephen, and I went over to the woods to lay on the sills. Stephen carried the aluminum foil.

It turned out to be a job involving a fair degree of coordination, and I was very glad to have four extra hands to help. First, we bored holes at exactly the right points in the wooden sills for the bolts which would secure the sills to the foundation. Then I mixed a batch of mortar and troweled a thin layer of mortar onto the top of the foundation wall to provide a tight seal between wall and sill. Next, we laid the aluminum foil carefully over the mortar, with holes neatly cut to fit over the bolts. Then the 2 by 8 was fitted over the bolts and down atop the foil. And finally, we put the washers and nuts on the bolts and tightened them with a wrench while the mortar was still soft and compressible. The whole job had to be done with some speed because the batch of mortar sitting in the mortar box was gradually hardening. Also, a fitful breeze fluttered the aluminum foil and threatened to blow it off the top of the wall before we could get the sill in place. But we evolved a system which solved the problem. Stephen and I trowelled the mortar along the top of the wall for approximately the length of one 2 by 8. Then Rosemary fitted the aluminum foil in place while I got the sill. As I tightened the bolts down with a wrench, Stephen began laying additional mortar. Then Rosemary put on the aluminum foil, and I was ready with another length of 2 by 8.

Perhaps the thoughts of our waiting Thanksgiving dinner spurred us on to extraordinary speed, but in any event we finished the job in less than three hours. When I tightened the last nut, the foundation was topped and the Playhouse ready to rise out of its cement and cinder block base. Later, as we gathered around the dining table, the golden brown turkey surrounded by the bright green parsley and the scarlet cranberries, we raised our wine glasses in a toast and said, "Here's to our Playhouse. Next year we'll have our Thanksgiving dinner there."

The Friday following was a holiday also, and I spent the whole of it putting in cement sills for the basement door and the two basement windows. Because the job was totally unfamiliar, I worried and fussed over making the forms. By the time I came to mixing and pouring the cement, the weather was lowering and the wind grew colder and colder by the minute. I carefully covered my work with burlap and paper bags when I finished, but my apprehension was great that night as I noticed about 10 o'clock that the temperature had dropped to 20 degrees. I was virtually certain that my cement work would be ruined by the freezing temperature but through some freak it was saved, and when I examined it next day it was sound and strong. Luck was with me.

I was ready then to put in the framing across the front, and this required another trip to the sawmill to get the lumber. It was a late November day of crystalline clarity, and the blueness of the sky was as icy hard as the frozen ground underfoot. There seemed to be no one around at the sawmill, so I selected my own 2 by 4's from the stacks lying on the open ground. I found, to my surprise and pleasure, a small cache of oak 2 by 4's. The framing across the front of the first floor would support the joists for the second floor, and I was pleased to have the added strength oak would provide. I spent the rest of that weekend putting in the framing. The oak was very clean and strong in appearance, and where I had doubled the 2 by 4's around the windows it looked extraordinarily massive and rugged.

By this time, I was growing very impatient to get past the underpinning of the building, and get on to the more rewarding work of framing and roofing the second floor. But first I had to solve the problem of the girder. During my hours of studying the Army Carpentry Manual, it had become clear I would need a girder running lengthwise of the building in order to break the long span across the 18-foot width. With a girder, the joists spanned a distance of only nine feet, and the stress tables I consulted indicated that with a nine-foot span, 2 by 8 joists would be adequate. Always to me in the past the word *girder* meant a steel beam, but my manual assured me that "the girder is a heavy timber... often built up by placing two or more joists side by side and nailing them together." On that basis, I decided to make my girder by nailing together three 2 by 8's. Two pieces would probably have been suf ficient, but I wanted my floor to be strong enough to support two sets of square dancers without vibrating.

One cold morning in early December I picked up twelve oak 2 by 8's of ten-foot length at the sawmill. I needed three columns to support the girder at nine-foot intervals, so I went back into my woods in search of a straight, young oak tree that would provide material for columns. It would have been better to have used steel columns under the girder, but steel would cost money and the young oak tree would cost me only the effort to cut and trim it. As I walked back through the woods with Jocko on my heels, the heavy matting of leaves underfoot rustling as we walked, I remembered Bob Housel's account of a similar decision he had made some years before. When he had bought his house in the country, his first act was to run electricity to his house. In those days, one had to pay for the poles to support the power line, and since the distance from the road to his house was almost a quarter of a mile, the cost would be considerable if Bob used the electric company's poles at $20 each. So he decided to use some of the big pine trees on his place, cutting and trimming them and dragging them into position himself. As Bob told the story, the young engineer in charge of the installation crew was horrified. "Why, sir," he said, "those pine poles will rot below ground in five years time and fall over. Then you'll have to do the job all over again. It will cost you a little more money now to put in the right poles but they will last indefinitely."

"Young man," said Bob, "what you say is true. But it just happens that right now I don't have the 'little more money' you mention. In five years time I expect I will. And when those pine poles fall over I will replace them with your cedar poles."

"And," Bob went on, leaning over and looking straight into my face to make sure his remarks were registering, "five years later almost to the day, the first of these pine poles keeled over. But by that time we were over the hump financially and I put in new cedar ones without too much strain."

It was on that basis that I was seeking a straight young oak tree for columns. After the familiar difficulty of locating a growing tree that was *really* straight, I finally picked one and felled it. I trimmed the branches with my axe and cut the tree into three 9-foot lengths. Then I drove the station wagon up into the woods along the little logging trail and dragged the 9-foot sections out one at a time with a rope. Even though I was using a modern station wagon instead of a team of mules, and the logs I dragged were small, I got a great deal of satisfaction out of putting the century-old road to its original use.

Constructing an oak girder was obviously not a one man job. So I cast about for a volunteer worker. One of my office acquaintances had shown keen interest in my building operations and had several times spoken about wanting to come and work on the weekends. "Let me know, anytime," he said. "I'd sure like to get some exercise." I let him know on this occasion and added, for good measure, that if I was any judge, putting up a 36-foot oak girder ought to provide a hell of a lot of exercise.

How right I was! Added to that, it was a raw, bitter day, and the cement and cinder block foundation around us seemed to suck the warmth out of our bodies. My friend, Bill, suffered a good deal from the cold, and when I put him to work with a saw on the theory exercise would warm his blood, he found the task of sawing through a 2 by 8 oak plank very heavy going. He got through the first one with difficulty, faltered badly on the second, and threw in the sponge on the third. I was startled by this development because I was sawing through the planks without great difficulty, although admittedly sawing oak is not like slicing butter. It made me realize that the work I had done over the past year or more had put my carpentry muscles into pretty good condition.

But however inept Bill was with the saw, he was invaluable when it came time to hoist the first section of the girder into place. The manual had informed me that I could either nail the several pieces forming the girder together before putting it up or I could build it in place. For the first section, I chose to put it together on the ground. When it came time to put it up, Bill and I found it was all we could do to lift it. We were dealing with a mass of green oak six inches thick, eight inches wide, and nine feet long. Finally, with much grunting, Bill lugged one end of the section up the step ladder and heaved it on top of the pilaster while I held the other end over my head. Then he pulled the ladder over beside me, relieved me of my end and heaved it onto the oak column which was held in place beside me by some 2 by 4 props. We both began to take a deep breath when the girder toppled off the column. There was a great deal of frantic scrambling on our part. Fortunately, the heavy oak thudded into the ground without smashing any legs or arms. We were shaken by this experience but after a moment of rest we tried again. This time it stayed up.

We decided to build the remaining sections in place. This went off straightforwardly, and only the nailing gave us difficulty. I was following the instructions in the Army manual to nail top and bottom every 18 inches with 30-penny spikes. I remembered my experience with the oak siding on The Shed, and I had brought along a fresh bar of Ivory soap. Even so, the oak was terribly hard and the slightly insecure footing on the ladder threw my aim off and caused me to bend over approximately one spike out of three. What with the slowness of our advance and the difficulty we had in pulling out the bent over spikes with a crowbar, we were only three-quarters finished when the cold and the darkness forced us to quit. Bill left without much ceremony. "Ask me again," he said. "Sometime when it's warmer."

The next day I went back and managed, with the use of some temporary props and a certain amount of luck, to put up the remaining section of the girder single-handedly. I then worked my way down one side of the girder and back up the other, driving in spikes at places we had left for later. By three o'clock I was exhausted, and I quit unashamedly. After I had packed up my tools, including the bar of soap, I stood back and looked at the girder for the first time. I had reason to know it was strong but I was surprised when I first really looked at it by the visual impression of strength and stability it conveyed. And the sections of the oak tree standing in place as columns, still bearing their coat of bark, looked as though they could support a bridge. I found enough satisfaction in that to make me forget the throbbing in my right arm.

During the course of the ensuing week I drove out to the sawmill on my way home from work. I wanted to talk with old man Rose and make certain he could deliver the lumber for my floor joists before the weekend. It was dark when I stopped my car alongside the little frame house. As I walked up to the door, several dogs barked cheerfully at my heels, and a cat arched and curvetted around my ankles. In response to my knock, the door opened and a round, motherly woman said, "C'mon in." I stepped in-side the low-ceilinged kitchen dominated by a black wood-burning range and permeated with rich cooking odors. "If you're looking for Dad, he's inside there. G'wan in."

I opened the door before me and walked into a room that seemed filled with people. It was a small room and a large dining table nearly filled it, but somehow tucked around the edges were three grown men, two women, two children, a baby, and—sitting serenely at the table in the middle—old Mr. Rose. Every one else's attention was unswervingly directed toward the television set at one end where a wild west movie was flickering and squawking, but old Rose was reading a newspaper, his spectacles resting almost on the end of his nose. He was not wearing his chauffeur's cap, and he looked remarkably younger, his reddish hair waving and soft like a baby's. My entrance did not deflect his attention from the printed page, but one of the younger women saw me. "Daddy," she said and put her hand on his arm.

He looked up over the top of his spectacles and said, "Oh, c'mon in, c'mon in! Have a seat." He waved his hand toward a chair. "I was just reading the evening paper here about the way they're carrying on in Washington." I took a chair beside him and he turned part way around toward me. "Spending more money, raising taxes, raising wages. They keep on that way, t'aint going to be worth my while keep on working. Things get any tighter, I'll just keep a few cows for milking, hens for eggs, grow a few vegetables, and close down the mill. What's the use to keep on working if you can't keep any of it? Can't get any help to do the work any way."

I nodded sympathetically as I sat down beside him, hoping to convey the impression that his problems and mine had much in common. I wanted to get down to the business of my lumber quickly, but at the moment my concern over floor joists seemed less fundamental somehow than his problems. I remembered also Bud's remark that part of the price of Rose's lumber, which was so incredibly cheap otherwise, lay in listening to his long conversations.

"Why, forty year ago when my daddy was running this mill, you could get all the help you wanted at two dollars a day. And I mean they put in a good day's work. Nowadays, all these young fellas think about is looking at television, buying a car, and chasing girls. Soon's they get a little money in their pocket, they disappear somewheres and you can't get them to work." And the old man rambled on and on, lamenting the passing of a better age when both men and lumber were of sounder quality. Meanwhile, the television set vibrated with gunfire and pounding hooves, and the low-ceilinged room seemed to grow closer and warmer.

After several minutes of decrying the times, during which I nodded at appropriate intervals, he suddenly asked, "What can 1 do for you?"

"Oh," I said, "I need some lumber for joists, and I thought I'd come by and see if I could get you to deliver it before Saturday."

"What size you need?"

"Well, I figure I can get by with 2 by 8's if they' re oak. That's what the building code calls for."

"Building code? What difference does it make what the building code says. It's your house you're building, isn't it? On your land. You going to let someone else tell you how to build your house? If it was mine, I'd go ahead and build it any way I liked. What can they do if they don't like it? It's a free country, isn't it? Huh, what can they do?" He looked at me intently over his spectacles, his blue eyes like round marbles. Before I could work out a reply, he answered his own question. "Can't do a thing. Not a thing.

I decided to try to get around the jurisdictional question by moving the matter onto a level of practical carpentry. "Well, anyway, I think 2 by 8's would be all right for joists on a nine-foot span, don't you? Wouldn't you use 2 by 8's?"

He looked at me solemnly for a moment. "Well, yes," he said, "I'd use 2 by 8's .That's what you *should* use, 2 by 8. But just because that's the right weight timber for that job, not because anybody's telling you you gotta use 2 by 8's." He nodded his head vigorously, having put the claims of bureaucracy to rout on practical grounds. "How many of them do you need?"

I got out my slip of paper. "Let's see, I need thirty-three 2 by 8's ten feet long and fifteen of them fourteen feet long."

He got a little notebook out of his pocket, tipped the pencil with his tongue, and made a note. "May have a little trouble finding that much good oak. But we'll see what we can do."

"And I'd like to have them delivered before next Saturday."

"Well, now where's your place? Can we get our truck in there all right?"

"Sure, no trouble." And I went on to describe my road and the entrance near the stream.

"Down there?" he asked incredulously. "Down in that pretty little valley there? But that's part of the old Oliver place, isn't it?"

"Yes, it is. I bought a small piece of it." Slowly, the incredulity on his face was replaced by a richer emotion, considerably more complex and difficult to read. He smiled thoughtfully. "Why," he said, shaking his head slowly, "I used to court on the Oliver girls before I met up with the missus." His smile grew warmed. "But that must have been almost fifty year ago. She's an old lady now." He paused, lost in ancient and nearly forgotten memories. "We used to go walking in the woods there on Sunday, probably right there where you're building your house." He shook his head and the look on his face transformed from nostalgic wonderment to a knowing grin. He glanced quickly behind him at the closed door to the kitchen. "And she wasn't an old lady then," he said with a quick nod of his head.

As I drove home through the December darkness, having finally got myself outside the house after protracted goodbyes and having refused an invitation to sit down and have a bite of supper with them, I thought about old man Rose, a slim, redheaded youth, strolling under my trees on a Sunday afternoon with an Oliver maiden. It was an appealing image which I was happy to add to the small stock of lore I had acquired about my land.

Fourteen

The next Saturday morning was heavy and dark, and it was drizzling dismally. There was no question in my mind, however, as to how I intended to spend the day, whether drizzle or blizzard. Along with some sandwiches for lunch I packed, as anti-damp precaution, a thermos of hot coffee and a half pint bottle of sherry. As I drove in across the meadow, the station wagon sloshing and slipping slightly in the wet, I saw the newly-delivered lumber lying on the ground before the foundation. It formed a misshapen pile, rather like an enormous jackstraw heap, and I decided as I got out of the car that the first task was to stack the lumber properly.

It was no easy job because the big oak pieces, already extremely heavy, had gained added weight by soaking up the falling rain. But after almost two hours of wrestling and straining with the raw oak lumber, its red and white grain vivid and glistening with moisture, I got it stacked with a piece of wood separating each piece from the other.

Then the question arose as to what to do next. It was absurd, I realized, to attempt to put floor joists on single handedly. Aside from the sheer weight of the lumber, it was a risky and awkward job. But I had no helper in sight, and I did not feel I could call on one of my friends. Not only was it raining and ugly, but it was the weekend before Christmas. The urge to make progress was strong, however, and I decided just to slide a few planks in place so I could see how it would look.

I squared off two of the 2 by 8's and nailed them together at right angles to form a corner. These were the *header joists*. They rested on their edges on the wooden sills and were nailed securely to them. Then I squared off another 2 by 8 and, with much cautious maneuvering, I angled and slid it into place. I put the step ladder up under the girder and, after making certain the joist was in position on the back wall, I ran down the hill, climbed the ladder, and shouldered the joist into position on the girder. Then I nailed it down at both points. This, I decided, was good clean fun. I picked out another 2 by 8 and repeated the process. And so it went throughout the rest of the day while the rain continued to fall drearily. I skidded and slipped in the mud while carrying the sodden oak planks, but somehow managed to escape a fall with the board landing on top. I rolled and slid the joists across the nine-foot gap between back wall and girder and dropped only one down in between—and that one without damage to the plank or to me. Dozens of times I trotted down the hill from behind the back wall, down around the end of the building, inside the foundation, and up and down the ladder. By nightfall, I was bone-weary and soaked to the skin but I had made an appreciable beginning. I also had learned another useful lesson about how much one can do alone, with a little ingenuity. A tubfull of hot water, a double bourbon on the rocks, and a sound night's sleep restored me to very nearly full strength, and next morning I returned to the job. By Sunday night, it was half done.

Christmas Day came during the course of the following

week, and there were a few words in the bosom of my family regarding the possibility that I might just get out in the afternoon after Christmas dinner and lay up a few more joists. Sentiment against my demaning the holiday with housing construction ran fairly strong. It was alleged that I did not give a single thought to anything but The Playhouse (absolutely and unquestionably true), that I never wanted to do anything but work on foundations and joists (entirely fair statement), and that I was becoming dull company for my family and my friends (indubitably accurate observation).

As a matter of fact, looking back on it I can see that I must have cast a heavy pall over the holiday merrymakin of a number of people. The truth was that I was like an athlete in training. On Friday and Saturday nights, just when the parties began to pick up and go and the hosts cheerily called for another round of drinks, I usually was working my way furtively toward the door or else I was harrassing and cajoling my poor wife—who was just beginning to feel relaxed after a hard day with the children—into going home. I did not want another drink because I wanted an entirely clear head next morning. I found the social conversation of my friends empty and superficial because problems of carpentry and housing construction so seldom surfaced in it. I begrudged every minute I had to spend having a good time after 10:30 or 11 o'clock because I wanted to be in bed, storing up strength and vigor for the morrow. And if my wife and social secretary was so unwise as to make social plans for Sunday evening, the result was inevitably a social disaster. After two ten-hour days spent slugging away on The Playhouse, gulping in deep draughts of cold and extraordinarily fresh air, I was a hollow husk of a man. Two old fashioneds and a solid Sunday night supper usually finished me off nicely. From then on my friends and family were treated to the sight of a well fed, thoroughly contented, and soundly sleeping man.

After Christmas I returned to the joists. I got unexpected aid in finishing the job from Greg Van Buskirk, a farmer friend of mine from upstate New York. This poor man, having just completed the harvest of 600 acres with only the help of his 19-year old son, was on his way to Florida for a brief vacation. He made the mistake of staying with us over a weekend and thereby fell into my clutches. The first day Greg stopped by, dressed in his best clothes, just to see what I was doing. The next day he insisted on borrowing some old shoes and pants from me so he could help. I went through the motions of protesting. "You don't want to spend a day working with me out there in the cold. You get plenty of that at home, and you're on vacation."

"Aw, hell," Greg said, "it's always more fun cleaning out somebody else's chicken coop. Besides, it looks to me like you need some help."

His last remark turned out to be completely true. Someone had suggested to me that the deck on the front of the house would be stronger if I were to extend the floor joists an additional four feet out from the wall of the house as the base for the deck. This I decided to do, but it meant using fourteen foot 2 by 8's across the front. I had got fairly adept at flipping and angling the ten foot oak planks into position but the fourteen foot pieces were quite a handful. With his help it went fairly quickly and several times more easily.

Greg was extremely impressed by the strength of the oak underpinning of The Playhouse. "My God," he said, "I never saw anything that looked so strong. You could put a department store on those joists and foundation. You don't need to worry about this building holding up. It will still be standing here long after you're gone and forgotten."

Even allowing for some friendly exaggeration, these were pleasing words, particularly coming from a working farmer who had done a fair amount of frame construction of one sort or another. And it was a soul-satisfying notion that my little building, constructed in desperation by an amateur whose carpentry derived from books, might stand solidly on that lovely hillside for a generation or more.

With the joists in place, I was ready to lay the subflooring. As before when I was building The Shed, I was not certain what lumber to use. Orthodox construction calls for 1 by 6 boards or, when time is an important consideration, 4 by 8 plywood sheets. Plywood was obviously too expensive, but I was tempted to buy I by 6 boards at Rose's sawmill. They would go on easily and quickly. The only difficulty was that his lumber was unseasoned, and the boards would shrink after they were laid down and leave gaps. Used flooring, as I had used in The Shed, was slow and hard to lay but it was seasoned and made a tight, sound subfloor. I decided to shop around for used flooring and to make my decision partly on price. After telephoning several places I found one which offered me flooring at $25 a thousand square feet, providing I would select, load, and haul it myself. At that price, my subflooring would cost 2½ cents a square foot, as compared with Rose's price of 7 cents. And since a thousand feet was just about what I would need, the difference was $25 against $70, or $45 saved. I decided that I could think of no better way of earning $45 than to load and haul flooring and to spend some extra time putting it down.

On the Friday before the first weekend in January 1953, I went by the used lumber yard and got a load of flooring. The large, irregularly stacked pile I was selecting from contained lots of unusuable stuff, but I was able to find more than enough that was sound. I stacked lumber through the tailgate until the station wagon was loaded to the gunwales—or to the buckboards if that is more appropriate-—and then called the manager of the yard to check my load. "I figure you've got a little over 300 feet there," he said. "Two more loads about that size and you'll have your thousand."

"I'll be back next weekend to get it." Saturday morning I unloaded and stacked my flooring. Then I began to lay it on, standing on the ladder at the northeast corner. Progress was slow but by noon I had a small triangle established on which I could stand and work. By nightfall, when Rosemary came to get me, I had a fair-sized corner of solid flooring. She climbed the ladder and stood beside me looking out across the meadow in the gathering dusk. We were standing on the floor of our living room and, since the floor was a good eight feet above ground level at that point, we were seeing the meadow, and the woods growing thick and dark in the falling light, from a perspective no man had ever viewed it from before.

By Sunday night I had laid on all the flooring I got on that first haul. The weather the following weekend was foul. I spent more of Saturday hauling flooring: standing in the steadily falling rain in the muck of the lumber yard selecting and loading lumber, driving slowly out into the country to my land, unloading and stacking the flooring in the unrelenting rain, and driving Back into town to the lumber yard to repeat the process. Sunday, I worked all day in the steady rain—the sawdust looking like red oatmeal as it came out of the cuts on the teeth of my saw, the wood spongy under the nail, its wet surface splatting under the driving hammer--and by nightfall I had half the floor laid.

The weather the following weekend, the third week in January, was nearly as bad but on Saturday afternoon the skies cleared temporarily. Rosemary was working with me for the first time, and the task of fitting together the irregular lengths of flooring appealed to her jigsaw puzzle instincts. "Isn't this fun?" she kept asking. "Isn't this fun?" It was fun, and it was also profitable. With Rosemary's help I made tremendous strides and by the end of the day the back of the job was broken. Next day, I defied some thoroughly unpleasant weather and finished the job before dark. After I drove the last nail in place, I stood up on cramped, aching legs and drank a small swig out of my bottle of sherry. Then I strolled up and down the length of my floor for several minutes while the dark and quiet of the night gathered in my meadow and the surrounding countryside

But before I moved on to the next job, I did some cost accounting. Money was getting short and I wanted to see where I stood. I sat down at my desk and listed all the items of expenditure:

9.00	building permit
92.75	7 cubic yards concrete for footings
48.00	excavation by Bud
131.47	698 cinder blocks
27.80	28 bags of mortar
13.60	4 tons of sand
3.26	2 basement window sash and screens
.36	36 steel tie-plates for pilaster
4.37	20 9" x 1/2" bolts for foundation
92.25	services of mason
16.29	233 board feet lumber, sills and framing
2.00	2 gallons creosote
3.75	3 bags of prepared cement for sills
4.00	7 gallons asphalt waterproofing
61.74	882 board feet lumber, oak joists, etc.
2.80	20 lbs ten-penny nails
.56	10 lbs thirty-penny nails
1.40	10 lbs eight-penny nails
1.40	10 lbs six-penny nails
25.00	1000 board feet used flooring
$ 551.80	Materials and labor for Playhouse foundation and subfloor

These figures confirmed what I already knew: that the $500 I had borrowed from the bank was used up, and I was then operating at a deficit. I was well satisfied with the progress I had made toward The Playhouse with an expenditure of only a little more than $500, but I knew I was going to need a great deal more money in the future. I decided to make the rounds of the money-lenders again to see what I could do.

My first stop was at the building and loan association in a nearby town, and the answer I got was the same as before. Their loan funds were fully committed, but I could make an application which would be considered at some indefinite date in the future.

Next I tried a new bank at another Virginia suburb. I had been told by a friend that this particular new bank had undertaken an expansion program and was seeking new business by granting loans. Business was humming when I called at the bank. A long line of applicants sat waiting their turn, and the loan manager they were waiting to interview was making loans over the telephone faster than he was by interview. When my turn came, he looked over my application.

"How much do you want to borrow?"

"Well, I'm building a house, and I'm probably going to need about $3000 eventually. But what I want right now is some ready cash to keep me going, say $500 or $1000."

He looked over my application again, checking off the assets and liabilities. "Well, the trouble is I can't give you a personal loan; you've already got one for $500. And you've already got your car pretty well tied up, although I might be able to do a little for you there. How far along are you on the house? "

"I've got a foundation and subfloor."

He nodded and looked thoughtful. I fidgeted slightly. I was by no means as desperate as I had been when I first went to the banks, but I was concerned. Unless I could get some money somehow the whole venture would fail. "Well, I'll tell you what I'll do," he said after several minutes reflection. "I'll re-finance your car and get you $300 in cash right now. Then, when you get to the point where your house can be lived in, I'll make you a loan of anything you need up to $2500."

"By 'lived in' do you mean complete with heat and plumbing?"

"No, just so it's a complete shelter. Your house becomes a genuine asset then, not just an incomplete construction project."

"Sounds pretty good to me. I don't know whether I can make it to that point on $300, but I'll give it a try."

As I walked out of the bank, smiling over the successful negotiation, it seemed to me I had made it to the next bar of the trapeze one more time. To be sure, the swinging bar I had caught would not take me far, but it might enable me to catch still another bar with a longer swing which might carry me to the landing platform. The important thing was that I was still swinging, still in the act. I had not gone crashing down into the net.

Fifteen

Flushed with new funds, I ordered 610 feet of 2 by 4 framing lumber from Rose's sawmill. When I had got the handsome yellow and brown lumber stacked, I set happily to work building the framing. The experience I had gained building The Shed freed me from the doubts and uncertainties I previously had felt. Moreover, the hours I had spent sketching and resketching The Playhouse on a long yellow pad paid off handsomely in that I knew each dimension of the house by heart. The distance from the corner to the edge of the big window that ran across the front of the living room? Six feet. The width of the window? Ten feet. I encountered no new problems, and I enjoyed thoroughly the experience of transforming pencil and paper sketches to nail and lumber outline. I finished the framing toward the end of January.

Rosemary worked with me a fair amount during this period. The fun she had experienced laying flooring whetted her appetite. Besides, the building was beginning to take form—the framing accurately delineated its shape, marked its doorways and windows—and I think she found it easier to believe in its existence. I put her to work setting in the 1 by 4 braces on the corners and either side of the doorways. It was work admirably suited to her strength and temperament. Great amounts of muscle were not required to notch the 2 by 4 studs so the braces would lie flush with their outside edges, but heaps of careful precision and patience were.

One cold January day, while the dry stiff grass in the meadow shivered in the wind, we worked together all day long. Rosemary suffered a fair amount from the cold and the wind made her face apple red. Even I, with my several layers of clothing and my collar buttoned close, found it cold and nippy. As the day drew to a close and I was standing on the ladder nailing on the top plate, Rosemary made a mock-up fireplace at the end of the living room with 2 by 4's. Then she got out a. thermos of hot tea laced with whisky, and we sat before our mock fireplace—the northwest wind slicing past the 2 by 4's—and drank a toast to our little house. It was beginning to come to life.

Another afternoon we had fun putting in posts which support the deck. I had taken advantage of a mild afternoon previously to put in little concrete footings for each post and lay four-inch high concrete pedestals, each with an upright thirty-penny spike embedded in it. My first move was to level the deck, jacking it up at low points by driving 2 by 4's underneath at an angle. If my carpenter's level indicated the deck was still low, I whacked the base of the 2 by 4 with an axe until the deck lifted into position. Then I measured very carefully the distance from the underside of the deck to each pedestal and cut 4 by 4 oak posts to fit. I bored a hole in the base of each post, smeared the butt with asphalt, and placed a small aluminum foil cap on the pedestal. After whacking the 2 by 4 again to lift the deck another half inch, I fitted the post over the upright spike and set it in position. I dropped the deck down onto the post by knocking out the 2 by 4 jack, and then, after tapping it once or twice until it was perfectly vertical, I nailed it in place. The result was highly gratifying. The deck had formerly been supported by odds and ends of scrap pieces set at odd angles. Now its support consisted solely of four oak posts, looking extremely neat, four-square, and capable.

My next task was to put in the beams that were to run across the width of the building. The function of these beams, which rest on the top of the side walls and are fastened securely to the top plate, is to tie the two sides of the building together and prevent the peaked roof from pushing the sides out. Once the beams were in place, I could take down the temporary braces that zig-zagged across the floor and made movement somewhat difficult. Also, I wanted to have the beams securely placed before putting on the rafters which would immediately impart considerable side thrust to the walls. The decision as to which lumber to use for the beams involved several considerations. No great strength would be required because such beams do not hold anything up; they hold things together. The pull on them is lengthwise. Actually, a strong rope or cable would do as well as a wooden beam. Planning as I was to leave these beams exposed, I remembered the handsome massiveness of the oak beam in the basement and decided to use oak. Since the 18-foot span would require several pieces of greater length than any of Rose's sawmill was likely to have, I decided to build up each beam by nailing several pieces together. After some experimentation, I settled upon three 1 by 6 pieces for each girder, and on a Sunday morning in early February I assembled the first beam and put it up eight feet from the south end of the building.

Normally, I would have gone ahead then to put up the rest of the beams, but I got involved in another problem. I had been negotiating with the electric power and light company for several weeks about having electricity run into my place. The chief advantage of having it installed as soon as possible was that I could use an electric saw and save myself hours of hand sawing. Probably as much as a quarter of my time had been devoted to laborious sawing by hand: squaring off each 2 by 8 oak plank for the joists, trimming the thousands of individual pieces in the subflooring, cutting each 2 by 4 in the framing, fitting each I by 6 oak piece in the beams. With the big 8-inch power saw I had bought from Montgomery Ward (which was still resting unused in its carton), what had been the work of hours would become the work of minutes. Furthermore, with the coming of spring and milder temperatures after dark, I could work at night with a floodlight. The immediate difficulty, however, was the power line did not run down the road past my property, and the company would be obliged to bring a line almost a third of a mile from another road. This made the installation of my place a major project, and it required approval by the Richmond office. The complicated negotiations took a lot of time and involved a number of trips to the company office at the county seat.

Another difficulty had to do with just where the power line would enter my property. The company engineer naturally assumed that the line would enter directly opposite The Playhouse and cross the meadow straight to the building. I had always envisioned the meadow as a free, open place with a broad sweep of green grass and the uncluttered rise of the hillside. A line of power poles and the heavy black cables between them scarcely fitted this vision.

I spoke to Bob Housel about it. "That line will run right across my view from the main house, and I'll be sitting there for the next thirty years looking at a power line."

"Hell," Bob said, "have them bring it in where you

want it. It's your property. They won't like the idea, but they'll do it if you insist. They may charge you some extra because you're not going in the most direct way."

"It would be worth it," I said, thinking of those thirty years to come and my spoiled view. I went back to the company office and talked to the company engineer. I pointed out, in addition to my objections to running the line across the otherwise clear meadow, that I planned to build another house on that hillside someday. By running the line to The Playhouse down through the woods, they would be placing it close to my future building site, thus saving themselves another major installation at some future date. This argument carried the day. "I should think we ought to be able to do that for you," the engineer said. "Next time I'm out your way we'll look it over, and you can show me where you would like to have the line run." Several days later we met at my woods, and I pointed out how I wanted the line to enter along the ridge of my land and run down a sort of natural alleyway through my woods to The Playhouse. He agreed to my proposal, saying, "We don't want to cut down any more trees than we have to." He looked down the hillside toward the framed outline of the building and said, "You know you're going to have to put up a tripod or some kind of temporary pole for us to hook the line onto."

"Yes, I know." I had studied the instruction form the power company had given me. It provided for two kinds of situations: installation of electric service on a temporary tripod beside the building project, or installation directly onto the building when it had risen to a point at least ten feet above ground. I was not looking forward to building the tripod because I regarded it as an expenditure of time and money not directly devoted to making progress on The Playhouse. Still, I wanted the power as quickly as I could get it, and building a tripod seemed the quickest way.

Meanwhile, a week or more went by while we awaited final approval from Richmond. I put off doing anything about the tripod and continued to push on with the framing. I had just got started building the beams when a postcard arrived saying that Richmond approved my installation and the service could begin whenever I indicated I was ready. At this point I had a sudden brainstorm. I had already got one beam up near the south end of the building. Why not put on the end rafters and run two pieces of siding up to them? Then the service could be permanently fastened onto the house, and I could dispense with the nonsense about the tripod. The inside of the two pieces of siding would provide an inside wall where the entrance switch and fuse box could be placed permanently also, and I would be spared the expense of hiring an electrician's service twice for the same job.

And so, it was on that basis I turned in a thoroughly unorthodox fashion to putting up the first rafters before I had built all the beams. The procedure, I quickly discovered, was not only unorthodox—it was very nearly impossible for a man possessed of only the usual number of hands. I had got through the brain-stretching process of learning all over again how to determine the length of rafters—and the angle of their cut (that old "4 and 12" magic with the carpenter's square), and I had sawed the two fourteen foot 2 by 6's into the proper shape. Then with a ten-foot piece of 1 by 6 for rooftree in one hand and the two rafters in the other, I manfully climbed the ladder and sought to do the impossible—hold all three pieces and nail them together at the same time. Wobbling around on the ladder, I tried laying one rafter down in order to nail the other rafter to the rooftree, in itself no mean feat. The trouble with this was that the other rafter was essential in forming the triangle which held both rafters up in position. Fiddling around, laying one piece down, picking another up, holding the nail in my teeth and the hammer between my knees, I got so exasperated I almost felt a third arm and hand would come sprouting out of my shoulders and relieve my frustration.

When this did not happen, I became convinced that nailing those three separate and ungainly pieces into a unified joint was not possible in one operation by one man. I reluctantly climbed down the ladder and laid the rafters and rooftree on the sawhorses. After nailing one rafter to the rooftree, I set a small 2 by 4 post on top of the framing just high enough to support the rafters as they rose to the peak. Then I nailed the rafters to the post and to each other. Except to get me by an otherwise impossible situation, the little post served no permanent function inasmuch as rafters hold themselves up by thrusting against each other and against the outside walls of a building. But it did no harm, and it did solve my immediate problem. I repeated the process in putting up rafters above the beam eight feet from the end.

Then I made a hurried trip out to the sawmill to get two pieces of poplar planking to put up for vertical siding. When I got back, I ferreted some left over building paper out of The Shed and tacked it over the studs. Then I trimmed the pieces of siding and put them on. By the time Rosemary came by to pick me up late in the afternoon, the job was done. We walked down into the meadow a little way to get a better perspective. To our prejudiced eyes, the addition of the two end rafters added the final grace to the outline of The Playhouse. They clearly delineated the low pitch of the roof and the long, low overhand. Although I had tested the harmony of the dimensions by drawing them repeatedly on my yellow pad, they were somewhat arbitrary and theoretical, and I was not certain what appearance they would give until I had actually seen the rafters rising into the evening sky. I was very pleased by what I saw in the waning light of a raw February afternoon. The proportions seemed to be handsome and right, the roof line appearing firm enough to keep the building from looking light-headed and yet light enough to give it grace and symmetry.

It was a little over a week before the power crew came to install my electricity and during that time I finished putting up the beams and made more progress with the rafters. On the following Sunday morning it rained in so unrelenting a fashion that even I was deterred from working, but by noon I was so restless I would have worked on The Playhouse if it had been under water. Stephen volunteered to help me and together we braved the nasty, wet weather. We set out to put up the end rafters on the north end of the building, the identical job I had developed such a massive frustration over a week before. To my surprise, it went like a breeze, and we were so pleased with our progress that we added another length to our ridge pole and put up several more rafters. Despite the steady cold rain, we were very gay and Stephen ran like a nimble squirrel here and there, saying, "Toot! toot!" I was amazed by the difference it made in the ease and celerity of my progress to have a ten-year old boy holding the other end of the rafter while I nailed it, handing me the hammer or a nail at the appropriate time, or running to get the one thing I needed but did not have when I got to the top of the ladder with my hands full of rafters and tools.

The power crew and I arrived simultaneously at my woods at 8 one frosty morning, they to do the work and I to keep them from ruining my woods in the process. As Alvin Brown, my neighbor and mason would say, it was a harsh day. The temperature never rose above 20 degrees and the wind came out of the northwest like a knife. The parchment-dry leaves of the oaks on my hillside rattled and rasped in the sharp, thrusting wind, and the ground underfoot was hard as stone. Notwithstanding, a remarkably large group of men assembled in my woods and set to work hooking my little Playhouse up with the power grid of northern Virginia. The tree-cutting, crew, whose job was to cut a thirty-foot swath down through the woods, numbered nine men: three operated gasoline-owered chain saws, the remaining six cut brush and trimmed the felled trees with axes. The line crew also numbered nine men: six of them dug holes for the poles with pick and shovel, the other three handled the power lines.

With this number of men, the activity was considerable and diverse, and I had some difficulty watching all of them at once. But within the first half hour I discovered something which made all the inconvenience and discomfort of being there worthwhile. I located the three men digging the hole for the first pole at approximately the place I had expected It to be, and then walked down into the woods to find the other three diggers. I found them considerably farther to the north than I had expected, and when I got to a place where I could sight between the two partly-dug holes I found that the line was going to run at least twenty feet off from the line the company engineer and I had agreed upon. It was, in fact, going to run right over the top of the tallest tree in the whole hillside. It took several minutes for me to locate the crew foreman and several minutes more to convince him he was putting the line in wrong. Finally, he agreed and reluctantly told the three diggers to stop and shift their digging to a spot twenty feet to the south. I expected some choice language, or the least some muttering and evil glances. To my surprise, they cheerfully accepted the decision and began to fill in the hole they had so laboriously dug. "If that's where the man wants it," one of them said, "That is where it will be!"

We had just got straightened out with the diggers when the chief of the tree cutters approached me. "How do you want them logs cut?" he asked. "Six-foot length be all right?"

I was surprised I had a choice in the matter. "Why, yes, I guess that will be all right. Sure."

The tree man turned and walked back up the hill. When he was out of range, one of the diggers said, "Say, mister, you know he has to cut those logs any size you say. Why don't you have them cut smaller so they'll fit in a fireplace? He has to do it if you ask for it."

"Is that right?" I thought a minute. "Then in that case I guess I will. Might as well have them cut to fireplace size." I walked up the hill and found the tree cutter. "How about cutting those logs to four-foot length so they'll go in my fireplace?"

He gave me a knowing grin. "Okay, if that's the way you want it." He turned to his cohorts and said, "Make them four."

I stayed around a while longer watching them work. They were a capable group of men, and I was particularly impressed with the way they moved their truck with its heavy equipment around through my woods with the aid of the power winch on the rear. When they had set the poles and stays, and the tree cutters had felled all the trees they intended to, I decided my supervision was no longer necessary, and I set off for town. My next task was to locate an electrician who could install an entrance switch and fuse box for me.

Sixteen

Several people, among them my old mentor Dick Mote, had urged me to do my own electrical work. "There's nothing to it," Dick said. "If you have ever played with electric trains you can wire a house." But something about the prospect of looking up the electrical connections intimidated me, just as the cinder block work had, and I decided to hire a professional. Rosemary preferred it that way also. "Then you will be sure it's right," she said. The problem was to find the man who would do it least expensively. I knew from my experience dealing with masons that the expense would vary enormously from one man to the next, so I decided, on the basis of the satisfactory way things had worked out with my mason, to seek Alvin Brown's advice on selecting an electrician.

"Why, yes, sir," he said when I finally located him at his house one late February afternoon as he came up from feeding the chickens, "I know a *good* man. Used to be with telephone company, but now he's retired and does electrical work. He'll do you a nice job and won't charge too much."

"Well, how can I get in touch with him ?"

"Well, sir. Suppose I have him come around here some

evening this week, and he can look at the job and you can talk with him."

"Fine."

"Only thing about this man, he's had a stroke. But he does real good work."

One evening later in the week, Rosemary and I drove out to the woods just about dusk. Alvin was there, together with a middle-aged man and woman, each of whom was driving a 1939 Packard. The woman was seated at the wheel of a seven-passenger sedan. Alvin and the man were standing alongside the building when I walked up. "This is Mr. Fones," said Alvin.

"Hello, Mr. Fones." I waved my hand toward The Playhouse. "Well, there it is. What I want done right now is to have the entrance switch and fuse box put in. Of course, the whole house will need to be wired later, and if we can work out a satisfactory deal now I might want you to do the whole job. Would you be interested in it?"

Mr. Fones nodded in the affirmative but though he struggled visibly no sound came from his mouth. He tried repeatedly but apparently could not speak. I was a little dismayed by this development and a little uncertain what to do next. I finally decided to push on.

"I understand, Mr. Fones. Well, how much would you want to put in the switch and fuse box?"

Again, Mr. Fones struggled painfully without audible success. Eventually, he fished a pencil out of his pocket and I handed him an old envelope I had in my pocket. He wrote on it, his pencil held in a hand twisted like a claw, "$2 a hour."

I was perplexed what to do. Certainly there was nothing wrong with his price, but his obvious infirmity troubled me. Could he do the work? I was also puzzled by the two enormous and obviously expensive, though ancient, cars. How did it happen that this man was willing to work for two dollars an hour? I turned away to consult Rosemary and the instant I did words came tumbling out of Mr. Fones' mouth.

"I can't talk very well because I've had this stroke. But I'm all right otherwise and I can do the work all right. I'm a licensed electrician."

I turned back immensely relieved. "Well, fine. That price sounds good to me. Why don't we go ahead on that basis?" Again Mr. Fones sought to speak but despite his obvious effort only one word came forth. "Permit," he said.

"All right, I'll get the permit." This answer did not appear to satisfy him completely so I repeated it in order to reassure him. "I'll get the permit."

With that he shrugged his shoulders. I nodded decisively as though to terminate the interview and turned away to walk to my car. The instant I did, he said, "Want you to meet my wife."

We walked over to the block-long Packard and, after the introductions were over, Mrs. Fones said, "We had a fifty-thousand dollar a year electrical contracting business until Ed had his stroke. He should stop working but he won't do it. Got to keep busy somehow."

I hated to talk about him as though he were not there, but I needed to be reassured on one point. "Well, Mrs. Fones, is the physical work too much for him? Can he work on a ladder and do the other work?"

"Oh, sure. He doesn't do anything of that, actually. He has boys like Alvin here to work with him. He tells them what to do and checks their work."

"I see." I turned to Mr. Fones. "Well, I guess we can go ahead on it. Can you do it sometime this week?" When he nodded his head in agreement, I said, "I'll get the permit tomorrow."

During my lunch hour the next day I drove out to the county seat and sought out the electrical inspector's office.

I encountered only one slight snag: the permit was to be applied for by the man who was going to do the work, either a licensed electrician or an owner who intended to do it himself. Since I had already told Mr. Fones I would get the permit, I decided to go ahead as though I intended to do my own work. After all, I reasoned, Mr. Fones was not exactly doing it himself either.

On the following Saturday morning, the last week in February, Mr. Fones put in my switch and fusebox. He had as his helpers Alvin and Irving Honesty, the hired man who had helped Bud with the excavation. It took them only three hours and when they finished I had as professional an appearing fuse box as I had ever seen. "But don't you connect it up with the power line?" I asked when I looked up and saw the two wires from the house sticking uselessly up into the sky.

"No, no. Power company does that." He paused and after a little effort, said, "Must get it inspected first."

I telephoned the electrical inspector's office the following Monday morning and made an appointment to have my work inspected. I went out late one afternoon and waited for him to arrive. The more I thought about it, the more nervous I became. Did it really matter that I had not done the work? Would he be sticky about it if he realized I had not? I tried to imagine what questions he might ask to trip me up. While I was worrying over the way this imaginary dialogue might develop, I noticed a car stop at my gate and sit there for some time. Finally, after a prolonged pause, it turned and came in. The car stopped before The Playhouse and the driver, a sour looking man with a turned-down felt hat, sat in the car writing something with his notebook propped against the steering wheel.

"Hi, there!" I said cheerily.

There was a long silence while the man continued to write and Jocko circled the car several times, inspecting the tires and making certain liquid annotations. At last, the man said without looking up, "I don't know whether I should answer you or not."

I gulped hard and said, "Why, what's the trouble?"

He finished whatever it was he was writing and started to get out of his car. "Been looking for your place for over two hours. Gave me bad directions."

"Gosh, I'm sorry." I looked around helplessly, seeking some way to make amends. If the interview with the electrical inspector began this badly, who could say how it would end? "Uh, well, how about having a beer for your trouble? I've got several cold bottles down there in the creek."

He slammed the door of his car. "I wouldn't touch it if you gave me fifty dollars!" At that, my alarm mounted to the sky and I was on the verge of confessing everything about the permit and explaining that I was only trying to save an old, enfeebled man some trouble, when he said, "I don't drink beer," and smiled a sort of crooked smile. He walked slowly up toward The Playhouse, looking it over as he came. "Nice place you got here," he said appreciatively. "Real pretty setting."

'Thanks," I said, taking a long, deep breath. "Come up and have a closer look." After that, everything was all right. The inspector checked the work, found it satisfactory, and turned an approving eye upon my carpentry.

"That beam looks mighty strong. You doing all the work yourself?"

"Yes."

"Looks mighty fine. You'll have yourself a snug little place here someday." And with that and a pat on Jocko's black woolly head he was off. I went home to Rosemary in a glow of triumph and we had a celebratory martini before dinner.

"We'll have the power connected in a day or two. Then I'll really make progress!"

Several nights later, word having come from the power and light company that my service was connected, Rosemary and I went out to the woods after dinner, taking with us an 150-watt portable flood lamp I had bought from the local hardward store. With the aid of a flashlight I located the socket and plugged in the flood lamp. A great explosion of light burst forth and flooded The Playhouse with white, wonderful illumination. I turned it up toward the woods and the pine trees sprang out of the blackness with etched clarity, each little pine cone distinct and delineated. "Isn't it wonderful!" Rosemary cried. "It looks like a picture or a stage setting." I turned the floodlight this way and that, admiring the extraordinary effect it made. Somewhere in the woods a bird chirped in alarm and I realized that not only Rosemary and I but the woods and all the unseen dwellers within it were having a unique experience. Never in all the centuries that had passed had a great, white electric light suddenly burst out of the blackness and made a large illumined room on that hillside. Aboriginal men may have crouched near a wood fire there, Indian hunters may have walked through the woods carrying torch flares, and oil lamps inside the cabins of colonial settlers may have cast a pale light across my meadow, but never had that place been flooded with illumination like this. "We should have several of these floodlights on The Playhouse," said Rosemary. "They make it look so wonderful!"

With the power installation completed, I was free to return to the rafters. Before I did, however, I had to correct a small difficulty that had developed in the meantime. I discovered that when the power wires were connected to my incomplete and inadequately braced building, they had pulled the end rafters a couple of inches out of line. I was puzzled how to get the building back in position single-handedly. I mentioned the problem to Collas Harris, one of my neighbors, at a cocktail party. "Shucks, that's no problem," he said. "I'll come over Sunday morning and help you put it back."

He was as good as his word and Sunday morning at 10 o'clock he drove into my meadow. It was the first week in March and there were the vaguest of intimations that spring would someday begin its annual pilgrimmage northward, but thus far the daily temperatures were anything but mild. As Collas stepped up on the subfloor, I handed him my half-pint bottle of bone-warming sherry and said, "Have a drink!"

He reached back to his hip pocket and pulled forth a half-pint bottle of bourbon, "Have a drink yourself," he said. "Got you topped." We drank his.

Then we turned to my problem. "If we can figure out some way to push the peak a few inches to the north," I said, "I can hold it there with these braces I've got set here."

"That ought to be easy. Just give me a good long pole, and I'll push it back for you. Here, just nail two of these twelve-foot 2 by 6's together." We did this in a moment and Collas took the twenty-four foot pole, holding it with his two hands down between his knees like a Scotsman heaving a log. He gave a mighty push and the peak moved a good three inches. I was not quick enough, though, and it slipped back before I could get my brace placed. Next time I was ready, and in a matter of minutes my building was once more four-square and vertical to the great revolving axle of the earth. "Boy, if my problems were all as simple as that," said Collas, "I wouldn't have a worry in the world." He offered me his half-pint bottle, "Have a drink."

"No, thanks," I said, pointing to my hitherto unused electric saw, looking powerful and menacing in its carton, "I've got to saw."

After Collas had gone back to his chores as a weekend farmer, I got the electric saw out of the carton and plugged it in. I had fifty feet of extension cord and could work with it anywhere on the building. As I squeezed the pistol grip the big saw jumped and revved up with an astonishing amount of noise. I held it in a gingerly fashion almost at arm's length. When I released the grip the high-pitched whine of the saw began slowly to descend, something like a miniature fire siren, and it took several seconds for the big toothed circular blade to stop turning. It seemed to me that all that power ought to make short work of the rafters I had left to do.

I laid out on the trestles a 2 by 6 piece of poplar (poplar because old man Rose had talked me out of using oak for rafters: ("You don't want all that weight up there. Poplar's the stuff for rafters"), and drew the lines for the angled cuts with carpenter's square and pencil. Then I took the electric saw and carefully set it on the piece. I squeezed the drip and again the saw jumped and began to turn up with astonishing speed and alarming noise. I guided it very carefully along the pencil lines, having some trouble at first seeing where the blade sawed in relation to the sole plate of the saw, and in three or four seconds I had completed the cut. Actually, it took longer for the blade to stop turning after I had released the switch than it did for me to make the cut. I went on then with greater assurance and greater efficiency, and I made all the cuts on that one rafter in less than 30 seconds.

When I made the last cut, I held the big nickel-metalled tool out at arm's length while the blade continued to whir as it slowly lost its terrifying momentum (4500 revolutions per minute). My feelings as I gazed at it were a compound of admiration, wholesome respect, and a quantity of fear. After the hundreds upon hundreds of hours I had spent laboriously sawing by hand, this brawny tool was a boon comparable, in terms of my immediate concerns, to the invention of the wheel or the discovery of fire. But profound as was my gratitude—and it continued to grow as

I used the saw and grew more proficient in exercising its capabilities—my regard never took on any aura of affection. I was too aware of the ghastly effect those spinning, slashing teeth would have on human flesh and bone if they accidentally came in contact.

With the aid of the electric saw, I put twelve rafters in place in two hours time. After lunch, Rosemary came over and together we made short work of the remaining rafters.

By late afternoon we were nailing the last one in place. We were performing before a small audience by that time. Barbara Donnelly, her children and her husband napping, found herself bored and came over to see how we were coming along. And Jim Victory, his wife housebound by an ailing child, was urged by the vague intimations of springtime to sally forth on the late Sunday afternoon and used our woods as a destination. "Wait," I said when Rosemary and I placed the last rafter and toe-nailed it securely, "We must have a little ceremony." I stepped up into the nearby woods in search of a pine sapling. I cut a little one about 18 inches high and brought it back and nailed it to the rooftree, as I had read builders do in Germany. Rosemary poured out my little bottle of sherry into four paper cups, and we all solemnly drank a toast to our rooftree. "Long may it bestow snug shelter and happy living!" I said, moved to eloquence by the occasion.

Later, as I picked up my tools and loaded them into the wheelbarrow, I found myself almost regretting the completion of the raftering. I was going to miss working on rafters. It is fine work. It is difficult enough to be steadily interesting and challenging but never tedious, as is notching studs for bracing and laying flooring. Each rafter makes an important contribution toward filling out the outline of the house and adding to its structural strength. Rafters are fine.

I had just finished locking The Shed when Bud came riding down the old logging road on Blackberry. "What are you doing, quitting early?" he called. "It's not even dark yet."

"I know," I said, feeling a little guilty about not taking advantage of every minute of daylight, "but I finished the rafters and it's too late to start another job."

"Well, I thought I'd just ride by and have a look at your progress. I haven't been over here since we finished the excavation."

"C'mon, I'd like to show you."

Bud dismounted and tied Blackberry to a nearby pine tree. We walked up inside the building and Bud began to inspect it. I was a little nervous, knowing his dry and sometimes sharp tongue, as he walked around looking at my joints and splices. A framed but unsheathed building is completely naked; its flaws and compromises are uncovered to every man's eye. No fakery with moldings and sheathing is possible at this stage. Finally, just when I began to suspect Bud was going to be kind and forebear saying anything, he said, "You're really doing a wonderful job. This place is going to have lots and lots of charm."

I was so taken aback by Bud's straightforward sincerity, in contrast to his usual quizzical badinage, that I was at a loss for something to say. "Thanks," I said. "Thank you."

He looked through the 10-foot window wall. "And that pine tree there is just right. I'm sure glad we left it in but it was an awful pain in the neck while we were excavating. I went round and round that pine tree until I got dizzy. Felt like one of those horses on a merry-go-round." He turned his attention upward at the rafters and something caught his eye. He craned his neck in order to see better and said, "Am I seeing things or are those rafters sticking up about an inch above the top of the rooftree?"

I almost squirmed with embarrassment. "No, that's right. The rooftree is dropped an inch below the top of the rafters."

"Well, I never saw anything like that before. Why did you do it that way?"

I felt like a high school girl who has been told her dress is nice but it looks home-made. "That's one of my own inventions. You see you ought to have some kind of ventilation underneath the roof between the roof sheathing and the insulation. That's what the book says anyway. Well, I plan to put vents under the eaves between each rafter but I couldn't figure any way to get the air to circulate over the top because the rooftree is solid. So I dropped the rooftree an inch and now the air can circulate all the way through."

Bud guffawed. "Boy, that's rich! That's the best solution I ever saw. You know, you ought to sell that idea to *Popular Mechanics* or one of those magazines. They'd give you some money for an idea like that. I *mean* it, they really would."

I looked at him warily for a moment but finally decided he was quite sincere. "Maybe someday when I get time I will."

Seventeen

When I finished nailing the last rafter into place, I got down off the ladder and walked a short distance into the meadow to look at my work. The rafters ran in close parallel rows of white, looking neat and clean as an architectural drawing, and the studs stood straight and sturdy. As before when building The Shed I was amused momentarily with the notion that the framing and the rafters complete the outline of a house and the sheathing that comes next is really redundant. But the idea fleeted quickly with the approach of practical consideration. The skeleton of my house was complete. Now I must move on to covering the bones.

In line with orthodox building practice, when I had finished the rafters, I turned to sheathing the roof, a procedure which provides shelter for your materials and for subsequent work. My choice of roof sheathing, however, was very unorthodox: I decided to go back to my standby, used flooring. I knew it would take me two or three times longer to lay on than conventional sheathing, but I also knew that its tongue-and-groove construction would make a very tight roof. The real clincher, though, was the incredibly cheap price. Lumber from Rose's sawmill would cost three times as much, and standard roof sheathing would cost five times as much.

Bob Housel greeted my decision enthusiastically. It had just that combination of unorthodoxy and practicality which appealed to him. "Ought to make wonderful sheathing. Take you a little longer to lay it but what difference does that make. You got more time than money anyhow." As a matter of fact, I suspect that in Bob's eyes I came of age as a builder on the strength of that decision. Bud was a great deal more skeptical, not to say scornful, when he saw me nailing three-inch width boards to my rafters. "Man, it will take you till next Christmas to sheath the roof with that stuff!" But he came around pretty quickly when I told him the price: "Twenty-five dollars a thousand! Why, you can't even buy kindling wood for that price!"

More important than the approval of my more better informed friends was the knowledge I was using only a very small portion of precious cash while making an important stride toward a habitable structure, the goal established by my bank manager before more funds would be forthcoming. Somehow I must stretch that $300 to carry me to a framed, roofed, sheathed, and windowed structure in which human beings could live. I was by no means certain I could win this race, in essence a race against money instead of time, but I knew the money I saved by slowly and laboriously laying used flooring as roof sheathing might be the difference between making it and not.

And so I spent all my free time in March and the first part of April, hauling the flooring in my station wagon and then painstakingly nailing it to the rafters. March was not a propitious month for progress. It was a time of great activity at work and of illness at home, both of which slowed me up. But worse still was the weather. It seemed to me it rained nearly all the time, pausing to replenish the supply of cold, dreary rainwater only when it was completely impossible for me to work on the house. I was willing to work in the rain, and frequently did, but it undeniably slowed my pace. Moreover I was apprehensive about usino the electric saw when everything was soaking wet.

This apprehension was shared by Rosemary and was made considerably more acute one Sunday evening in late March. I had spent the weekend working in the rain. In mid-afternoon the rain stopped and the wind began to blow.

For a while it looked as though the wind might clear the skies of rain clouds, but then the sky began to darken until it was almost black and about five o'clock the rain began to fall in great sheets of water. I watched it for a while and then reluctantly decided I was through for the day. I packed my tools away in The Shed and loaded my things into the car. While I was warming the engine briefly, I looked over the meadow, slightly dubious about driving the car out on the track I had been using. I had slithered and wallowed a little more than usual when I drove across in the morning, and after almost a whole day of steady rainfall there were broad ponds and swamps of water standing over the track. I decided to go around on a previously unused portion of the meadow, thus avoiding the the muddy ruts.

All went well at first as I took the station wagon in second gear, along the edge of the meadow on the brown grass, but then the car began to slow despite my efforts to keep its speed steady and finally it sank to a stop. I tried to reverse but the car merely shivered slightly. I got out in ankle-deep water and tried in the growing darkness to see what the situation was. All I could see was standing water, pocked with falling raindrops. More from a sense of duty than hope I got a shovel from The Shed and tried to dig inclines out of the holes the wheels sat in.

I might as well have been shovelling cream of wheat for all the good I did. I gave up for the night and splashed out across the field to the road and headed for Bud's house a half mile away. The wind tore at my coat and lashed my face with cold rain. and I was a forlorn. muddy creature when I knocked on Bud's door. When he recovered from seeing me in my semi-drowned condition, he said, "We'll pull your car out with the tractor in the morning. I'll take you home now."

When Rosemary saw a strange car pulling up to our house in the wild night, her fears mounted sky high, and she was certain I had been electrocuted, amputated, or otherwise maimed. And then, when it became clear I was whole and sound but merely fearfully wet, her fear made a womanly transition to anger and she berated me roundlv. "I was worried to death about you. I didn't know whether to call the police or what. Don't you ever let this happen again!"

Manlike, I took this scolding as no more than my due. As I hurried to take off my sodden clothes and sink into a hot tub, I made firm promises not to let it happen again. "Next time," I said, while stripping off a soaking wet shirt "I'll park the car out near the road."

With the coming of April, the skies cleared at least momentarily and the sun shone with the peculiar brilliance of springtime. The meadow dried rapidly and the yellow brown grass of the hillside subtly transformed itself into the yellow green that is the quintessence of April. All along the creek the trees shot forth tiny green leaves which at first gave an impression of green mist against the dark trunks and then, as the leaves unfurled and grew larger and darker in color, took on a maidenly air, the young green of April flecked with new sunlight. Through the meadow the songs of newly arrived birds began to sound, the cascading song of the song sparrow, the sharp rasping trill of the red-winged blackbird, and the water-cool clear notes of the phoebe. A towhee built a nest on the hillside no more than twenty feet from my building site and protested sharply whenever I ventured near her private construction project. Back in the woods, I heard from time to time the noisy rompings of the grey squirrels chasing each other up and down the tall oak trees and scampering furiously across the dry, brown leaves in their springtime play. Jocko took great exception to this furry levity in our woods and raced madly about from tree to tree in hot pursuit of the miscreants, barking loudly as he bounced along on his black-furred legs.

With the drying of the soggy countryside and the surge of vernal activity I suddenly began to make progress on The Playhouse. During the first weekend of April I got the roof completely sheathed. I had great assistance from all sides. Stephen worked with me all Saturday morning, and we were gay as larks as we sat in the young sunshine, the sound of our pounding hammers echoing in the bright, new-washed air. Somehow we got to singing,

"Oh, the Er-i-e was arising,
The gin was a-gitting low,
And I scarcely think,
We'll get a drink,
Till we get to Buffalo-o-o."

Saturday afternoon Rosemary helped and on Sunday a whole succession of people came by, glad to be released from their suburban houses by the bright weather and curious to see what I really had been doing during the dark winter months. Most of them came merely to look but nearly all succumbed to the lure, almost as universal as the taste for chocolate, of driving nails into flat (well, nearly flat) boards. By late afternoon Sunday we were laying the last board along the front edge of the overhang, looking down from what seemed an alarming height at the pine tree Bud had circled with his tractor. Stephen insisted on having the honor of driving the last nail.

During the ensuing week I consulted Bob Housel about what kind of roofing to lay over the boards. "I would like," I said, "to put down shingles or something permanent but I'm very short of money and I thought I'd put down roll roofing now and replace it in a couple of years. What do you think of that? Is it an economical thing to do or should I manage somehow to get the money together now?"

"Well, it just so happens," he said in his flat, nasal voice, "I'm in a position to do you some good. I've got eight rolls of 90-pound roofing I've had for some time. I'll let you have them at a dollar a roll, just to get rid of them. With those eight rolls as a starter, I'm certain it's an economical thing to do."

Next Saturday morning I shouldered one of the rolls and climbed the ladder to the roof. Steve followed me with the coffee can containing roofing nails and the smaller cans of roofing cement. In a few minutes we were once again hammering away in the spring sunshine and the strains of "The Er-i-e Canal" mingled with the purer songs of the birds in the woods and the meadow.

Applying roll roofing is not very difficult; the only problem is to get it down flat and straight. But it does take a certain amount of time to drive the nails at two-inch intervals, and by Saturday evening we had finished only about a third of the roof. Sunday brought a return of the rain. Unlike the steady, slanting rain of March, this was packaged in sudden, squally showers. By dodging in and out through the showers Stephen and I succeeded in getting half the total job done. But then it settled down to a steady, persistent drizzle, and I decided to take Stephen home out of the wet. I returned myself, bringing with me on a sudden inspiration a small radio from our bedroom. I set it on a box under the roofed portion of the house and tuned in to an exhibition baseball game the Washington Nats were playing in Pittsburgh. I spent the rest of the afternoon cutting and nailing girts (small 2 by 4 pieces that run horizontally between the studs for stiffening) and listening to the exploits of Yost and Vernon. The rain fell steadily in soft patters on the roof over my head and ran in silver streams and big ploshy drops off the new roof. Beneath it I was dry and happily progressing with The Playhouse. Meanwhile, the Nats lost.

It took another weekend to finish the roofing. The last session, on a Sunday afternoon, was attended by Rosemary, our neighbor Barbara Donnelly and myself. Both girls were enthusiastic pounders of nails, but indifferent measurers of two-inch intervals. I solved the problem by putting the nails down at four-inch intervals and asking them to nail in the spaces remaining.

I was ready then for fenestration—in a word, windows. I had thought a fair amount about windows by that time, and I had searched through all the building magazines for the kind of window I wanted. It seemed to me that, next to the proportions of the house and the lines of the roof, the size and shape of the windows would be the most significant feature in determining the appearance of the house. If the outlines of the house were the set of its shoulders and the roofline its hairline. then the windows were its facial features: its eyes, eyebrows, and nose. The main window across the front of the living room was simple: it would consist of oblong sheets of glass set directly in against the studs. The bottom row would probably be a set of louvers, a plan for which I had found in *Popular Mechanics* magazine. The windows on the other side of the living room, in the kitchen ell, and in the bunkrooms, were another matter. In keeping with the long low lines of the house the shallow roof pitch and the overhang, I wanted them to be rectangular in shape and approximately twice as wide as they were high. I also wanted them, for simplicity of construction, to be the awning type which swung in or out of the building.

Unfortunatelv. as I discovered, the average lumber yard did not supply windows of this style. I looked around at several places without success and finally decided the thing to do was to see what I could find at the annual Home Show, an exhibition of housing materials and builders tools. This was an entirely successful expedition. I found precisely the windows I wanted: simple wooden construction of exactly the right shape. They were listed as obtainable at one of the large lumber dealers in Washington.

Later that week I went to the dealer. I had done a certain amount of bookkeeping work beforehand and had come up with the following set of figures:

551.80	Materials & labor for foundation and subfloor
42.70	610 feet, 2 by 4 framing
31.92	456 feet, 2 by 6 rafters
35.95	385, extra rafters, lumber for girts, etc.
2.80	40 feet, 1 by 4 bracing
2.10	30 feet, 1 by 6 ridge pole
1.20	15 pounds, 16-penny galvanized nails
2.00	10 pounds, 8-penny galvanized nails
36.70	labor and parts for entrance switch, fuse box
25.00	1000 feet used flooring for roof sheathing
6.00	6 rolls 90-pound roofing @ $1 each roll
11.85	3 rolls 90-pound roofing
2.00	10 pounds roofing nails
.75	1 pound, roofing cement
$752.77	Foundation, subfloor, framing, roof sheathing, and roofing

These figures disclosed that I had already spent $200 of

the $300 lump sum I had with which to reach the "habitable" stage, and I knew by rough calculation that the siding I intended to buy from Rose's sawmill would cost approximately a hundred dollars. I decided that my best move was to approach the lumber dealer for credit. After all, a big lumber yard was in a better position to offer me credit than old man Rose was.

During my next lunch hour, I went to the lumberyard and selected the pre-built windows: $139.48. I ordered two exterior door frames for $35, total $174.48. Then I asked for the credit manager and waited for action. "Just why do you want credit?" he asked. "Is it for convenience because you may not be there when the material is delivered?"

"No," I said. "Frankly, it's because I don't have the money now to pay for them. In sixty days or so I expect to."

"Well," said the credit manager, a pleasant, handsome man, "we're in the lumber business, not the banking business. And we find that if we leave banking to the bankers we're all better off."

" That's all ver-y -well-," I replied, "but here is my situation. I am building a house with my own hands because I don't have any capital. I have a fairly good income, and I am a good credit risk. A banker has promised me that when I have a tight house he will advance me enough cash to finish it off. If you can advance me credit for these windows for about sixty days, possibly ninety days, I am sure I can pay you then."

The credit manager looked at me very directly for several moments. Then he said, "You know, I like to gamble on people, and I'm going to gamble on you. Go ahead and take the windows. We will bill you every thirty days, but you pay for them whenever you get the money."

"If you would prefer," I said, "I will wait until you have checked my credit references."

"No. Take them now. I'm not going to lose any sleep

over them, either."

Taking him at his word, I loaded the windows, packed in large cartons, into the station wagon and drove out to my woods. There I loaded them into The Shed and carefully padlocked the door. On the following weekend, I put the first window in place. It was the bathroom window on the south wall, and I agonized over it nearly the whole morning. I read and re-read the directions, set the window in temporarily, measured and remeasured the opening and the size of the window. I simply could not believe the operation was as simple as it seemed. In the end, of course, it turned out to be just that simple, and I made rapid progress once I had accepted that fact.

When I had finished putting all the *store-boughten* windows in place, I was ready to put on the siding. I had held several long conversations with old Mr. Rose on the subject. He had no doubt that poplar was the lumber for siding—his own barn had stood there without a coat of paint for thirty-five year—but there was some give and take on the dimensions on the boards. Boards that were 1 by 12 were fine but they sometimes split up the center. On the other hand, 1 by 10's were also fine but possibly too narrow to give a proper appearance. In the end, I chose 1 by 10's. But after all this parlaying and indecision, Rose delivered 1 by 12's because he did not have enough 1 by 10's to fill my order. When I arrived at the woods on a dewy Saturday morning of the last weekend in April, a monstrous pile of lumber consisting of a thousand square feet of poplar planking was lying on the hillside slightly above The Playhouse. To give it protection and to have it handy for sawing, I stacked it inside the house on 2 by 4 strips laid on the subfloor. It was a nuisance, carrying it piece by piece down the hillside and in through the framed doorway, but I felt it was worth the effort to have clean, dry material when I was ready to work it.

Then I began to nail the siding onto the north end of the house, a place I had picked for beginning the new operation because the north wall was unbroken and therefore free from any special fitting problems caused by windows. It was a simple, satisfying job. First, I tacked on the building paper, fitting it carefully top and bottom and making certain it overlapped the adjoining piece by a full eight inches. Then I measured the length required for the piece of board, squared a plank off at the bottom and cut it to fit the rising angle of the roof at the top. I fitted it as tightly as possible to the board beside it, driving the nails in at an angle always in the direction of the previous plank. The only hard part of the job was to support the ladder securely on the hillside. Rosemary was working with me, and she got very adept at finding just the right combination of cinder blocks and discarded pieces of wood which would give the downhill foot of the ladder a solid base. By Sunday evening, we finished off the north end of the building. The sun was casting a cool yellow light through the young leaves in the woods and a robin was caroling serenely from a treetop. We stood well back to inspect the new siding, which was a surprising mixture of tawny brown and yellow green with a handsomely textured grain. The wood looked so attractive in its unfinished state that we were tempted with the thought of varnishing it instead of painting it. "It looks perfectly scrumptious," said Rosemary. "I had no idea it would be so handsome."

The rest of the siding was not so simple because it had to be fitted around the windows and door openings. It went on considerably more slowly but I received unexpected aid to my progress with the arrival on a weekend visit of Dick Mote, my original mentor and examplar. Dick and his family had moved away to Pittsburgh, and his return to the neighborhood was the occasion of great festivity and rejoicing. For me, however, added to the pleasure of Dick's exuberant humanity and vitality was the trepidation you might feel if your scoutmaster turned up after a long absence and asked how you were getting on with tying knots. Dick and Marian arrived with a typical dramatic flourish one Saturday afternoon in mid-May. It was a warm, pleasant afternoon, the air soft and fragrant with dogwood blossoms and Maytime, and I had worked diligently and profitably all day long on the west wall. I heard a car coming in my lane and by the time I had laid my hammer down and walked across the floor to look out, the car was roaring past the front and there were shouts of hello and the wave of a large Stetson hat. Dick leaped out of the car carrying a bottle of whisky and a bottle of soda, and Marian and Rosemary followed behind with an ice bucket and glasses.

"Well, I want to tell you," said Dick with his warm voice and his expansive manner, as broad as the whole Pacific Northwest, "I wanted to come over here first thing and have a look at how you're coming. We brought along a little festive cheer to celebrate the occasion." He shook hands and looked around my plain little building with the air of a man who is inspecting the main lobby of a fabulously expensive dude-ranch.

"Say, this place is looking mighty fine, and you're doing a wonderful job here! What do you say we have a drink on it?"

With Dick's help, I laid some poplar planks across the joists which projected from the front of the house for the deck. Shortly, we were sitting on boxes and stools, drink in hand, christening our deck, welcoming Dick and Marian back to Virginia, toasting The Playhouse, and generally enjoying the ripe spring afternoon. Across the meadow, the little hillside on Mort's side of the creek basked in the warm tones of the late afternoon sunshine and the tall poplar tree at the top of the ridge stood straight and precisely articulated in the flooding yellow light.

"Say, now," said Dick, "I want to tell you this is mighty fine. You've got a wonderful spot here."

It was a point with which I entirely agreed.

Late the next morning, after we had recovered from the gay party we gave in Dick's honor, he and I worked together on The Playhouse and, in a word, we made it jump. The services of a carpenter as skilled as Dick needed to be exploited, so I chose the portion of the siding job which would be the hardest for me to do singlehandedly, the part across the front. Here, where the building was two stories high, the pieces of poplar planking were sixteen feet long, and they were heavy to handle and hard to fit tight. Dick and I soon worked out an efficient routine. We set the sawhorses up under the pine tree and ran the extension cord for the electric saw out through the framed doorway. Dick passed me down a half dozen or more pieces of siding and then we set quickly to work. I did the measuring and the sawing (Dick regarding the powerful saw with as much wholesome respect as I did) and Dick did the nailing while I held the board in place. We put the siding across the entire front of the house in little more than an afternoon, or approximately a quarter of the time it would have taken me working alone.

As Dick shook hands before departing for Pittsburgh, he said in his sincere way, "I'm sure awful sorry I can't stay and help you some more on that house. We could get the whole thing finished in a couple of weeks." He turned and got in his car and said, "But you're coming all right, and you're doing a wonderful job. You're going to have a mighty snug and pretty little place there when you get it all done."

With that and another flourish of his big Stetson hat, he was off. "What a wonderful guy!" I said to Rosemary as we walked back to the house together. "I feel as though he just awarded me my Boy Scout merit badge for carpentry."

It took me another weekend and somewhat more to finish putting the siding on the west and south walls. Then I paused momentarily to take stock before making my next move. With the siding on the walls and the *store boughten* windows in place, what needed to be done before I could go back to the bank manager and tell him I had a tight house? The answer was easy, I needed to put on the doors and I needed to install the glass for the fixed windows in the window-wall of the living room and the lower half of the front. Rosemary interjected at this point that it would be nice to finish off the deck and put a rail around it so that we could eat weekend luncheons there without fear of our children's breaking their necks. I agreed to its desirability but pointed out, with iron discipline, that top priority had to be placed on making the house tight so we could get more funds for building.

I turned to the windows first. One of my neighbors was an artist who had just finished building a studio on his place. "It's not hard," he said as we inspected his window-wall. "You just nail the molding to the stud, then lay a thin coat of mortar on it, press the glass against it, and tack the molding down on the other side of the glass. It's not hard, but it's very tedious work and it takes forever."

This proved to be a highly accurate characterization. It certainly took me forever, or just this side of forever, and I nearly quit once or twice out of sheer exasperation, particularly after cracking two panes in succession by driving a nail too close to the edge of the glass. But at last, after much gnashing of teeth and explosions of bitter expletives,

I got the last pane in place and tacked the quarter round down. There is one thing certain about most building tasks, once done they are done for good. In this case, done at least until a flying baseball or a rock undid it.

Next the doors. I had done research on doors in such scholarly journals as the Montgomery Ward catalogue and I had searched through the inventory of a number of lumberyards for suitable doors. Practically none of them would do. Most of them had cute designs on them like crescent moons or meaningless slashes of glass to break their blankness. What I wanted was a plain solid door. "Why not a dutch-door?" asked Rosemary. "The kind you can open the top half and still keep children and other small game out by closing the bottom half."

"All right, dutch-doors." But these proved no easier to find than plain, solid doors.

"We'll make them up for you," said the lumber dealers and mentioned prices ranging from thirty-five to fifty dollars each. But by this time my bank balance was sagging pitifully. I had just paid Rose's sawmill $125.44 for the poplar siding and some other lumber and had thereby more than expended the remaining $100 of the original lump sum of $300. I did not want to stretch my credit further until it was absolutely necessary.

"Tell you what I'll do," I told Rosemary, "I'll make them myself. I still have some poplar siding left, and I'll use that."

"Will that do for doors?"

"It will certainly do for temporary doors. And if they aren't all right, we can replace them later."

And so I set about making doors. A neighbor of ours had dutch-doors Rosemary particularly admired, so I visited them and took some measurements. Then I went back to The Playhouse and laid some pieces of planking out on the sawhorses under the pine tree. After cutting them to size, I carefully fitted a row of them side by side. Then I laid a strip of building paper over them and laid another row on top. I nailed the pieces together and ran a single 2 by 4 brace along the outside. In a fairly short time I had two sets of dutch doors of two-inch thickness, looking remarkably sturdy and even handsome in their rough-hewn simplicity. I hung them with 4 by 4 hinges I bought from my local hardware dealer.

When I had provided doors for my house, I had reached a temporary resting place. I had made it to the goal established in January by my bank manager, a habitable dwelling. It did not matter that it lacked plumbing and heating; it was tight and weatherproof. To reach this point I had made the following expenditures:

752.77	Foundation, subfloor, framing, roof sheathing, roofing
125.44	1000 feet 1 by 12 poplar siding, other lumber
8.44	2 rolls building paper
11.95	keg of 8-penny nails for siding
3.40	24 lbs, 6-penny nails
1.40	10 lbs, 10-penny nails
21.50	glass for window-wall, basement fixed windows
17.20	430 feet quarter-round molding
.60	putty
.72	4 lbs finishing nails
139.48	12 awning-type windows and screens) items purchased
35.00	2 exterior-door frames but not paid for
11.50	2 door lock sets
5.40	4 pairs, 4 by 4 hinges for dutch doors
1.50	2 brass bolts for dutch doors
3.50	hardware for basement door
$ 1139. 80	Completed shell of The Playhouse

I had arrived at this stage of building The Playhouse with a much smaller outlay of money than I had thought possible, but however small it was it had stretched my current resources almost to the breaking point. My bill at the neighborhood hardware store was alarming, my grocery and milk bills were both a month behind, and we were hard pressed to maintain our insurance premiums. It was painfully clear I needed some long-term credit to dig me out of my present hole and to provide funds for further building. My best hope was the bank manager at the nearby suburban bank. A great deal depended on whether he would honor in May the promise he made in January.

Eighteen

"You say you've got a habitable dwelling, a tight shell?"

I nodded my head, my mouth dry with anxiety. Around me were the sounds of the busy bank, the click of adding machines, the shuffle of feet on the marble floor, the murmur of voices, and the thin clink of silver money.

"How big is it?"

"Eighteen by thirty-six, outside dimensions."

"One floor or two ?"

"Two."

His pencil did some quick calculating on the pad before him. "Let's see. Twelve hundred ninety-six square feet." He looked up at me questioningly a moment. "How much money are you going to need?"

"Well, what is the maximum you can let me have?"

He paused before answering, clicking his pencil lightly against his teeth. "Well, on this type of loan, the maximum is $2500. We don't always go that high, but that's the ceiling. He looked at me meditatively. "What would you use the money for?"

"Well," I said, as dozens of ways money could be spent

on The Playhouse came flooding into my mind, "I need to dig a well, put in plumbing, a septic tank and a septic field, wire the house, put in a heating system and a fireplace, build a driveway—"

"Okay, that's enough." He grinned at me. "You seem to have plenty of use for it. Let's write some of those down on this application." He made several notations, his face gradually losing its grin and becoming serious as he wrote. When he finished, he studied the form before him. Finally, he spoke, his face somber, "Well, I don't know. We're pretty short of funds right at this time, and—"

Just then his telephone rang with a sharp, insistent note. He picked it up and began a monosyllabic conversation consisting of "yes", "no" , "how much" , "when". I sat in a torment of impatience and uncertainty and began frantically summoning all the arguments I could marshal in support of his granting me the loan. My mouth had got dryer still and my heart was pounding in my throat. The conversation on the telephone came to an abrupt close. "No," the bank manager said emphatically,"We can't do it!" He put the telephone back on its cradle firmly and turned to me. "Now let's see," he said. He paused for a long moment. "Twelve hundred ninety-six square feet. I think we can let you have $2500 on that if you want it."

Caught by surprise, I almost stammered. "You wha— ? I gulped hard and got control of myself. "That's fine," I said, striving to sound matter-of-fact and businesslike, "That's fine."

Just how fine it was I had no intention of letting the bank manager know. I walked out of the bank wearing the silly smile of a small boy who had just fallen in the mud and found it was chocolate ice cream. I was over the big, big hurdle. Or rather, to return to the familiar metaphor, I had swung through the air across the wide gap and had caught the swinging trapeze bar with my outstretched hands. I had made it; we were safe. The Playhouse was an assured thing. All that remained now was to translate my newly acquired $2500 into lumber, pipe, plumbing fixtures, and the other accouterments of a finished house. And that I was confident I could surely do. I got in my car in a daze of euphoria and drove slowly home, savoring the good news. On the way I stopped at the liquor store and bought a bottle of Virginia Gentleman, the excellent bourbon whisky made by a small family-owned distillery only two or three miles from my land. Because it was relatively expensive, Rosemary and I bought it only for holiday parties and other festive occasions.

"And so he turned to me with a scowl on his face," I was telling Rosemary, while pouring us each a drink, "and he said without changing his expressing, 'Sure, you can have $2500."

"Oh honey, isn't that wonderful! We've made it! Here's to the dandy Bank Manager!" she said, raising her glass of Virginia Gentleman.

"Here's to him!" I said fervently. And I took a sip of rich, dark whisky.

While I was still rolling the whisky over my tongue, Rosemary asked, "How soon do you think you'll be able to finish The Playhouse?"

"How soon? I don't know. Haven't thought much about it. It will be a long time yet."

"Well, I know you can't know exactly, but I was wondering if we could not get a rough idea. We ought to be doing some planning. For one thing, the lease on this house runs out on September 1st. They probably won't let us have it unless we take it for another year."

"Another year! Oh no, we'll be in The Playhouse long before then."

"Well, then, we'll have to tell them, and we'll probably have to move out of here on the first of September. Where will we go then?"

Quite right, where indeed? Rosemary had uncovered a genuine dilemma. And there seemed to be only one sensible solution available. "Well, I guess the thing to do is to get The Playhouse sufficiently finished so we can move in on September 1st."

"But can you do that? That's not very long from now."

"I don't know but I think it's possible. I'm going to take a month's leave from the office for the month of June. I can tell better after I see what progress I make during that month. But I think we ought to plan on it. Sure, let's do. Let's make September 1st our target date!"

"Okay, here's to September 1st!"

"September 1st!"

My first move in the campaign to get us ensconced in The Playhouse on September 1st was to go to the county seat and get straightened out on the building permit. I had left them with the impression my building project was destined to become a storage shed, and now I must inform them that it seemed to be transforming itself into a Play— well, a sort of cottage. That's it, a weekend cottage. I wanted to set in motion the various activities I intended to sub-contract: the well-digging, the plumbing, the electric wiring, the septic tank and field. If I could get those operations going during the month of June, I could be present to supervise them while I was working on The Playhouse. Before they could begin, however, I needed special permits and to get these I needed to clarify the actual status of my building.

I created a fair amount of confusion in the building inspector's office in this clarification process. "You say you now intend to make this building a cottage, and you want to put in plumbing. Is it properly built for a dwelling?"

"Yes, I think so. I've followed the building code all the way." I thought with quiet pride of the oak beams and joists, the underpinning my friends told me was strong enough to support a freight train. "Yes, I'm sure it's strong and well built."

"Well, it's probably all right," said the inspector, a kindly white-haired man, "but we'll have to inspect it before we can grant you a permit to build a dwelling."

"All right, anytime."

It was a broad, sunny June day when the inspector drove in across my field, the grass lush and waving slightly in a gentle breeze. As before I felt some trepidation but nothing like the degree I felt when the electrical inspector came. As far as the construction of the building was concerned, I felt I could speak with some authority. I had sawed every individual piece and had driven very nearly all the nails. The inspector smiled engagingly as he walked up, saying, "Pretty place you got here." He looked the building over carefully and in detail, noting the full-sized lumber and exclaiming over the clean, sound oak. After his inspection, he said, "The only thing I see you need to do is to run a few more cross beams to tie the sides of the building together. These oak pieces here are probably strong enough but the code says you ought to run cross beams every six feet."

"Okay."

"You put those in and we'll approve it for a dwelling."

"Fine."

After that, another important hurdle I had passed, it was straight-forward. I next went to the health and sanitation office to apply for my septic field permit. A plump young lady handed me the necessary forms, saying as she did so," And here are the instructions for making your percolation test." Percolation test! A number of my friends who had built houses in Virginia had spoken at various times of their percolation tests. It had become synonymous in my mind with the really serious phase of house-building. "Everything depends on it," my friends had told me. What it consisted of, in essence, was a test to determine how rapidly your soil could absorb moisture, a necessary fact in deciding upon the suitability of your ground for a drainage field. "When you are ready for your percolation test," the plumpish young lady said, "call us and we'll give you an appointment."

On the way home I stopped by the office of a contractor for septic fields. "Had your percolation test yet?" he asked. "Can't decide nothing until you have." When I told him I had not achieved that eminence, he replied, "Well, better hurry up and get it done. We've got an awful lot of work coming up. A school and two housing developments. When you've had your percolation test give us a ring and we'll tell you when we can get at it."

With so much of the world hanging upon the results of my percolation test, I lost little time in preparing for it. I had already decided to lay the drainage field out on the hillside to the south of the building, and I proceeded, in accordance with the instructions I had received, to dig three holes of 30 inches depth at the points of a triangle 45 feet across and one hole 5 feet deep. Only the five-foot hole gave me any difficulty. It was so deep the handles of the posthole digger were below the surface of the ground when I finished. Then I put two inches of gravel in the bottom of the holes (borrowed from the driveway of Charley Donnelly), and I was ready for the test.

My father had come to visit us at this time, and his excitement matched mine as I poured the water into the holes on the morning of the *Great Test* an hour before the arrival of the inspector. The water drained away so rapidly it had entirely disappeared when the inspector came. A handsome young man with a soft southern Virginia accent, he told me he was working on his master's degree in order to become a teacher. "This looks like a good drainage site, with that creek down there at the bottom of the hill," he said as he poured in fresh buckets of water and timed the rate at which it descended in the holes. "Oh, yes," he said, "no trouble at all here. Good loose soil. I guess we can certify you for a minimum-sized drainage field: 300 feet."

"Wonderful," I said, beaming proudly over this latest achievement of my land. Apparently the meadow that had once been the best field on the farm had lost none of its prowess. Here it was, after years of idleness and neglect, turning up as a champion drainage field. And all the while, so beautiful!

I telephoned the contractor that afternoon and told him to come ahead. "Well, it'll be another week or so," he said. "But we'll get to you just as soon as we can."

The next problem was to locate a well-digger. Bob Housel, who almost always had strong preferences and stated them vehemently, described with unaccustomed impartiality the relative merits of the two chief candidates. "Well, there's Blane Brothers, they're the big outfit. They've got fifteen rigs and they'll come right in and do you a job in no time. Only trouble with them is they don't fool around trying to save you money by not going any deeper than they have to. They go right on down until they get the maximum flow. But you'll get a good well." He looked at me intently with his small, intensely blue eyes. "Then there's old Hoppe. Been digging wells around here for forty years, and he's got an old, beat-up rig that looks as though it is the one he started with. He's hard to get hold of, having just the one rig, and he's a slow worker. But he's honest as the day is long and he won't go one foot deeper than necessary to give you the flow you need."

"Sounds like the man for me."

"Well, I guess I'd take old Hoppe if I could get him.

But you won't go wrong with Blane Brothers. Just cost you a little more money."

After several fruitless telephone calls at noon and at six o'clock, the only times, I was assured, Mr. Hoppe was reachable, I finally caught him late one afternoon. The voice that answered on the other end of the telephone line was brusk, deep, and weary. I told him I wanted a well dug sometime during the month of June and described in general the location of my property. There was a considerable pause.

"You mean, down there on the edge of the Oliver property?"

"That's it."

"All right, I'll be around there tomorrow about noon to look at your place."

Next day, shortly after twelve o'clock, Dad and I looked up from our separate small carpentry jobs as a car drove in across my field. I got up and walked down to meet Mr. Hoppe. He got out of the car, a tall, proud man who looked as though he were beginning to fail physically.

"I'm Hoppe," he said. "Understand you want a well dug."

"That's right."

He looked around at the hillside and the unfinished building. "Where were you thinking of having it dug?"

"Well, where do you think would be a good place. Where would I be sure to get water?"

Hoppe heaved a deep sigh. "It's all the same to me, mister. You tell me where you want your well dug, and I'll dig it."

"But can you be sure of getting water just any place?"

"One place is as good as another. Of course, you can get one of them water diviners if you want. I never put much stock in them myself. But however you decide it, just tell me where you want the well and that's where I'll start to dig."

"Well, in that case, let's put it up there on the hillside where it can service this little house and the bigger one I intend to build eventually."

"Hmmm. Okay. Up there where that little grove of pines starts? I guess I can get my rig up in there all right."

"Well, fine. When do you think you could get started on it?"

Mr. Hoppe shook his head, conveying a vast uncertainty. "Right now we're deepening a well for a man. He was getting five gallons a minute and the health people tell him he'll need ten gallons a minute before he can double the size of his present milk herd. We're down to a little over 400 feet now and we're still getting only five gallons a minute. So I don't know. Soon's we're through with him we'll come to you. Your place is the nearest one to our present job. But it will probably be another week or so."

"That's okay. Just come when you can."

"All right, sir. But I'd like to get it understood before we start. My prices are $4 a foot where I'm using casing, $3 a foot into rock. I like to get these things straight at the beginning so's there's no hard words later. That satisfactory with you?"

"Perfectly. That's fine."

"How you fixed for a pump?"

"What?"

"A pump. To get the water out of the well. I can get you a mighty good price on one."

"Well, I guess we'll let that wait till later."

"Okay. Just keep me in mind when the time comes." He stalked back to his car, a big, proud man who could easily have been a leader of great armies but somehow got transfixed as a well-digger. "We'll be around here at your place in another week or so."

My next problem was to hire a plumber. No one seemed to have any specific suggestions, so I telephoned a plumber in the neighborhood who had once come to do a small job in a house I was renting. I had been taken by his direct, cheerful manner. Also, I was well aware of the advantage of having a plumber who lived nearby and thus could probably be relied upon for emergency calls at odd hours. We made an appointment over the telephone and Mr. Bragg came bouncing in across the meadow in an old Chevy truck late one afternoon.

Dad and I rose from our separate tasks, and I described the dimension of the plumbing job I wanted done. I pointed out that the plumbing job for The Playhouse was possibly only preliminary to the plumbing for the main house. I said I wanted good work, but I also wanted it to be as inexpensive as possible. Mr. Bragg, a compact man with a crinkly smile, nodded his head and began taking measurements and jotting down notes. Now and then he took a metal rule out of his jacket, whistling through his teeth in a tuneless way as he laid the rule on the floor and slid it along from point to point. After about fifteen minutes of this activity, he turned to me and said, "Well, I figure I can do this job for you at about $300.

"Fixtures included?"

"Oh, no. This just includes the pipe, the labor, and all the fittings. I can *get* the fixtures for you at builders' prices but that will be extry."

"Well, Mr. Bragg, I'll let you know after I check around."

My checking consisted of a conversation with Housel. I told him that Bragg had made an estimate.

"How did he make it?" asked Bob, pouncing on my remark like a terrier on a rat.

"Why, he just took some measurements and made some notes and did some figuring."

"How long did he take?"

"Oh, I'd say about 15 minutes."

Bob threw his head back and roared. "Some estimate!"

he said. "Sounds just like the ones I used to make. I'd pretend I was measuring all these things and making notes. All the time I was looking at the kind of car the fellow had and whether he had a grand piano. If he did, I'd put the estimate as high as the traffic would bear and then I'd go back and tell the wife—who was my secretary—Give him the 'A' Treatment."

I was confused. In fact, I was mortified. "You mean he didn't make an estimate at all?"

"Oh, he has some rough idea of what it'll cost him to do the job. And he just set a figure that'll give him a margin of profit."

"Well, what do you think? Is that a fair price or not?"

"Well," said Bob, "I haven't taken any measurements on your place but just guessing, not estimating"—this with a sly grin—"I'd say you got about the "B" treatment." He paused a moment, speculatively. "That sounds pretty good to me. You might as well take it."

I passed this decision along to Mr. Bragg. "Well, fine, he replied. "Soon's you get your partitions up and know where you want them fixtures put, I'll come along and rough it in for you."

With all my sub-contracting done, I was ready to go back to serious carpentry. During my negotiating period, I had done some secondary jobs like laying the oak planking on the deck and putting on the railing. Dad, meanwhile, was doing such time-consuming and worthwhile jobs as putting knobs on the doors and catches on the window screens. But now we were ready for a more fundamental undertaking: putting in the partitions.

As a matter of fact, the job was even more basic than that because I had only very general ideas regarding the size of the several rooms. The real task, then, was to design the interior. Rosemary and I did it, with Dad's counsel, in the most practical way possible—by laying 2-by- 4's on the floor and then walking around in the *rooms* we had thereby created, trying them on for size. The main idea was to make the living room as large as possible because it would serve as drawing room, family room, dining room, bedroom (for Rosemary and me), and, at one end, as kitchen. We needed two bunkrooms of the smallest possible size and a bathroom of medium size which could double as a dressing room for the two adults. After considerable adjusting, soul-searching, and a small amount of marital bickering, we decided the smallest feasible size for the bunkrooms was five feet-by-eight feet. The bathroom we made eight-by-eight. We placed the bunkrooms on the southeast corner of the building and the bathroom on the southwest corner. This left a two-foot hallway dividing them, at the end of which we placed a closet six feet long, to be entered both from the hallway and the end bunkroom. This left a living room eighteen by twenty-four, extended along the west side by another four feet to provide a kitchen area approximately eight by ten.

The planning done, the work of putting in the partitions was very straightforward. It was just like the framing for the outside wall, the only difference being that the partitions extended to the slanting line of the roof because I intended to make the ceilings sloping, running them along the underside of the rafters. It took me only two days to build the partitions. When I finished, they looked clean and straight, and the new lumber gave off a pleasant pungency. The wood fragrance suddenly reminded me, as I stood looking at my finished work, of boyhood days spent climbing around in new houses—a wonderful sport.

The next step was insulation. At first, I had been dubious about the economy of putting in insulation in a Playhouse. but Housel had been very firm about it. "Don't be silly. Insulation costs practically nothing, and you will get your money back in fuel savings in the first year or, at the most, the first two years And after that it's all paid for, and you'll still save money on fuel. Be a lot more comfortable in the summer too. Buy the best insulation money can buy and I'll bet it won't cost you much over a hundred dollars."

Research in my favorite bibliography of building materials the Montgomery Ward catalogue, proved Bob to be right. I read the description of the best insulation Ward's offered. It possessed admirable attributes: "combines flame-resistance cotton and a highly reflective surface, provides very low rate of heat transmission. Three-way insulation: (1) Surface reflects radiant heat. (2) Millions of air cells retard loss of heat by conduction. (3) Unbroken blanket cuts down draft and air leakage Does not settle, pack, or deteriorate. Resists vermin and insect attack." Here were qualities of character and fortitude I have never dreamed insulation possessed. Who would have thought that in addition to resisting cold and heat it could find time and energy to resist vermin as well? And when I came to estimate the cost, it came to $108.40.

I had made the decision about insulation in late May and had sent in my order. At the same time I ordered some white fibre board with which I planned to cover the bedroom partitions and the ceiling of the whole house. I also ordered some marine plywood for the walls and ceiling of the bathroom.

Word came at the end of the second week in June that my order had arrived at the railroad freight office of a nearby small town. That Friday morning I saddled up my trusty old station wagon and drove over to the little town. The freight office was an authentic old-time railroad office, complete with pot-belly stove and clicking telegraph instruments. It was so real it looked like a stage setting or a Norman Rockwell illustration. The stationmaster, a small bent man, greeted me kindly. "You got a big shipment there," he said, "and some of it looks mighty heavy. You're going to need some help loading it, and I don't know whether I can give it to you. My back has been giving me a lot of trouble the last week or so."

"Oh, I'll manage it all right, thanks. I'll wrestle it on somehow."

"What are you going to haul it in?"

I pointed to my car standing in the shade of the old railroad station. "The wagon."

"Think you can get it all inside?"

"Sure. May take two trips."

But subsequent experience showed me to be only partially right. It did take two trips, just to haul the insulation. Though extremely light and neatly packed in cartons, it was remarkably bulky, as I might have realized if I had thought about it. The fibre board and plywood would not, however, fit in the form they were packaged, and unless I was willing to unpack the packages of ten sheets each and place them individually in the car, I could not haul them in the station wagon.

"Tell you what," said the stationmaster who had been watching my efforts with solicitude and who had been shoving and lifting with me despite my injunctions not to, "There's a fella's a friend of mine who drives the truck for the furniture store. He'll stop by on his way home and haul this stuff for you in the truck."

"That sounds fine. How do I get hold of him?"

"Oh, I'll call him for you. Tell you what. I'll tell him to be here at 5:30, if that's okay with you. I'm supposed to close up here at 5 but he's not through till later. I don't mind staying a little but don't be any later than that because my wife and I are going to the movies tonight and she wants to have supper at 6 o'clock."

I promised to be on time and promptly at 5:30 I arrived back at the station. A *Brown's Furniture* truck stood in front of the station and a round-faced, dark-skinned man leaned against the truck. He walked over as I got out of my car. "Mister Long tell me you want some stuff moved."

"Yes. Do you think we can get it all on the truck?"

The round dark face chuckled. "I ain't seen what you got to move yet," he said gently, "so I can't hardly tell."

"Well, come inside here and look."

We walked inside the freight room of the station to assess the situation. He ran his eye rapidly over the sheets of plywood and the fibre board. "Oh, sure. We can get all that on easy. Only trouble is," he said, stepping to the doorway and casting an uneasy eye up at the sky, "it look like rain and they ain't no tarpaulin to go onto that open truck. We going to have to hurry or your stuff's going to get wet."

"Okay, let's go!"

We loaded the heavy and awkward sheets of material onto the bed of the open truck as quickly as we could, sliding the long packages over the smooth floor. When we finished I jumped down off the loading dock and got in my car. "Follow me," I said.

I started my engine and headed off across the countryside toward the woods. I drove as fast as I could on the narrow, high-crowned roads, while the skies grew darker and more lowering, but the truck hung on my rear as though I was towing it. We made the trip faster than I had ever made it before, and we roared across the meadow just as the first fat raindrops began to spatter against my windshield. I wheeled my wagon off to the right of The Playhouse and jumped out. "Back your truck up the hill behind the house!" As the fat drops began to fall more thickly we took the heavy packages of fibre board off the truck, ducked under the pine branches of the small trees, and crossed the planks bridging the unfilled ditch behind the foundation wall. There we dumped the awkward loads, and before the rain really began to fall we had all the fibre board under cover. That was what counted because it was porous and could become rain-soaked. The plywood could not be damaged by a little rain, but we hurried in unloading that too, mostly out of an irrational desire not to get rained on though we were both dripping with sweat and panting.

When we finished, we stood for a moment in the open doorway, watching the rain pelting the truck and running in silvery streams off the eaves. "How much do I owe you?" I asked the heavy-set dark man beside me, his chest still heaving from our exertions.

"I guess about three dollars."

"Okay, fine." I handed him three dollar bills which he folded and put in his shirt pocket.

"Thank you kindly," he said. He stood for a moment looking uncertainly at the rain. "Well, I guess I better be hurrying along. Got a big turkey dinner down at the church tonight." He lumbered out into the rain and drove off down the hill and out across my meadow. I stayed for a few minutes checking the newly-arrived building materials to see that they were not improperly stacked or leaned at an angle which would bend them.

Nineteen

Two days later, about 4:30 in the afternoon when the cool deep shadow of the woods behind The Playhouse was just beginning to slide over the peak of the roof, old Mr. Hoppe drove in across the field in his Dodge. He got out of his car quickly and came striding up the hill toward me, his stiff dignity somehow out of keeping with his heavy work clothes.

"Going to bring the rig in tomorrow," he said abruptly, almost as though he were threatening me. "Finally got that other job done. Had to go down to 1200 feet and still didn't get him the ten gallons a minute he wanted. Got eight, though. I guess he'll have to make that do."

I whistled. "Twelve hundred feet! I hope you don't have anything like that in mind for me."

"No, no. You won't have anything like that. Most the wells around here go around a hundred fifteen, hundred twenty-five. You only want five gallons a minute anyway. You won't have any trouble." He looked up the hill towards the woods. "Now, let's see. You want that well up there behind the house?"

"Yes, right there on the edge of the clearing."

"All right. I guess we can get the rig up in there. Anyway, we'll be starting on it tomorrow."

I made it a point to be on hand early in the morning. I had just got the tools laid out and was starting to work on the bridging between the floor joists when I heard a heavy truck engine laboring in across the meadow. I went outside and beheld the most outlandish contraption I have ever seen. Mounted on an old truck chassis (from the cut of the radiator I judged it to be approximately World War I vintage) was a heavy crane-like affair made of enormous oak beams. The crane was lying partly collapsed so that it could be moved down the country roads, and it lay in a welter of cables and pulleys. The rig was driven by a young man whom I took to be the nephew Mr. Hoppe had spoken of. Behind the rig came Mr. Hoppe in a small panelled truck.

We held a parley once again about the location of the well. I continued throughout this discussion, as I had been in the others, to be amazed at the casual way one chooses the site for a well. I had always thought that whether it was done through the application of occult or geological principles, the method was to some extent scientific and required a certain amount of study. These gentlemen, who between them had been digging wells for over a third of a century, seemed to think it involved nothing more than pointing the index finger. "There," I said. "Okay," they replied, "we may have a little trouble getting the rig up the side of that hill but we'll make it."

And they did, somewhat to my astonishment after having seen the ungainly and heavy machine. There was a lot of engine roaring and some skidding of the wheels but finally, oak beams, pulleys, and all, it came to rest on the chosen spot. They spent the rest of the morning clearing shrub around the work place, digging holes for the wheels so the crane would stand vertically on the sloping hillside, and erecting the heavy oak beams into an enormous tripod arrangement. By early afternoon, they were ready to start. The nephew, who had been introduced to me as Robert, came down to The Playhouse and asked me, "Where Is the best place to get water out of your streams?"

"Water? Do you need water to dig a well?"

"Sure. You use it to soften up the ground so she'll dig easier. I fill up these drums in the back of the truck and then ladle it in every now and then."

"Well, that's something I never knew. You have to have water to find water. Why, the best place is right down there at the edge of the field where the stream loops out a little. That's the handiest place and the water is deeper there than almost anywhere else."

He drove the little truck down and filled up his drums. In another half hour, the engine of the rig was running and the bit of the well-driver was rising and falling with a steady rhythm and a clanking noise that became extraordinarily familiar over the next several days.

The next day about mid-morning, Mr. Bragg the plumber showed up. He was grinning and a matchstick came out of the middle of the grin. I had called him as soon as the partitions were up, and he had replied he would be over as soon as he finished a job he was working on. "Thought I'd do a little work," he said as he stood in the doorway. "I see you got old Hoppe to dig your well. He'll give you a good one."

"Hope so. I'm glad you came by. I'm getting a little concerned about the way time is passing. I want to get started on the insulation and the finish flooring, and I can't do it until you get the plumbing roughed in."

"Got your wiring done?"

"No, but he's coming this Saturday. If the two of you get done over the weekend, I can start insulating next Monday. How long will it take you to rough in the plumbing?"

"Couple of days if I don't run into trouble."

"Well, I hope you don't. Time is going by, and I've got to have most of this house done by the end of this month."

Mr. Bragg grinned at me engagingly, the corners of his blue eyes crinkling. "Well, I don't plan to hold you up any. Just show me where these fixtures go, and I'll have your plumbing roughed in no time."

I pointed out the chalk marks Rosemary had made on the floor for the locations of the kitchen sink, the toilet, washbowl, and bathtub. "Okay," he said, and got out his rule and began taking measurements. While I went back to my odds and ends of carpentry, he disappeared into the basement. In a few minutes he was back. "I think I can get it all in for you by cutting only one joist. You'll have to put in a header there." He led me down below and showed me where it would be necessary to cut the joist in order to let the drain pipe pass through.

"That looks okay. You want me to cut the joist?"

"No, I'll cut it for you. I just wanted to get your approval."

"You got it. Cut away!"

On Saturday morning, Mr. Fones showed up with a crew of four, one of them being Irving Honesty who had helped Bud dig the excavation, and another being Alvin Brown, my mason. I had marked on the studs with red crayon the locations of the various switches, outlets, and fixtures. Mr. Fones' grasp of the meaning I intended by these markings did not seem very precise, however, so I decided my time could best be spent in close supervision of his work. All this while, the well-digger's rig was droning and clanking outside and down below Mr. Bragg was cutting pipe and bending copper tubing. I had the momentary feeling I was the ring-master of a three-ring circus. Actually, I was performer as well because when I reminded Mr. Fones I wished to do some of the work and thereby reduce the cost he handed me a large electric drill and said, "You can drill holes for the wire to go through."

That Saturday morning in June saw more activity and a larger display of manpower than any previous time in the brief history of The Playhouse. At noon, Mr. Bragg came up to me with a disarming grin. "I got it all roughed in up here, and there are only a couple of hours more work down below. I'll finish it off Monday morning."

"Okay." Mr. Fones, Robert the Well-Digger, and I, not being bound by the more genteel traditions of the plumbing trade, worked on through the afternoon. By six, the pace of the electrical crew was noticeably slacking. Mr. Fones took note of this situation and gave the word to his cohorts they could knock off for the day. "Ace and Irving and me will be back tomorrow morning to finish it up," he stammered with great difficulty. "Alvin, he don't work on Sunday."

"Fine." I gathered my own tools together and then walked up the hillside to have a chat with Robert who was spreading tarpaulin over the engine of his rig. Overhead, a robin was caroling in long cool notes, and there were twittering sounds coming out of the deep shadows of the woods as the afternoon drew on to a close.

"How is it coming?" I asked Robert.

"Oh, fine." He looked up quickly and turned back to fastening the tarp. He had the same quick, abrupt manner as his uncle, but in a somewhat modified, softened version. "I'm down to 45 feet. Hit rock at 42. We're getting some water now but I can't tell yet whether this is the real thing or whether there is another vein farther down."

"That sounds wonderful. Sounds to me as though things are going fine."

"All except one thing. I can't get any sleep at night."

"No sleep. How does that happen?"

"Chiggers."

"What?"

"You've got the worst infestation of chiggers I've ever seen. I stay awake half the night clawing my legs. My uncle, he won't come up here unless it's absolutely necessary."

"Well, why in the world didn't you tell me sooner? I've got some spray down there in The Shed to use against chiggers. I'll spray this whole area here for you. Matter of fact, I'll do it right now."

"Might help."

The next day being Sunday, the well-digging rig was silent, and I worked throughout the day on the myriad of small carpentry jobs that seemed to present themselves: braces, bridging, and joints. Mr. Fones and his somewhat motley crew came in about 10 o'clock and finished roughing in the wiring. By nightfall Sunday, I had all the odd jobs tidied up, and I was ready for the next big jobs — insulation and finish flooring.

I spent part of Monday morning buying flooring. I returned to the used lumberyard where I had had such spectacular success buying used flooring and explained that this time I wanted something I could use as finish floor.

"Well, as a matter of fact," said the yard manager," "we're tearing down a building right now that's got some mighty fine flooring in it. It's pine but it's not badly worn, and it's that good wide stuff. We've got a few hundred feet of it here. Would you like to see some of it?"

"Sure."

He led me over to a stack of flooring, saying, "This stuff ought to sell for ten cents a foot, but if you're interested in taking some of it right away, we'll load it on the truck right on the job and take it out to your place. That way, we can give you a better price."

"How much?"

"Well, what would you say to six cents a foot?"

I picked up a piece and examined it. It was four inches broad and looked as dry and clean as new wood. "I would say, Sold!"

By mid afternoon, Rosemary and I were making a tentative and uncertain beginning with the insulation. It came in long, blanket-like rolls, approximately twenty-four inches wide. You measured the wall space between the studs and cut off a piece a little longer than the distance from floor to top plate. Then you set to work with a stapler—a device almost exactly like the thing you see on office desks—fastening it down to the framing. At first, it went exasperatingly slowly. Mostly it was the old story. The operation was easier than we could imagine it to be, and we spent a fair amount of time trying to make it harder than it was. When we finally understood the remarkable simplicity of the operation, everything went very fast and easily. The only remaining difficulty revolved around the vagaries of the stapler which would suddenly and inexplicably stop spitting out staples. At that point we pounded it, took it apart and looked at it, and sometimes blew on it. Suddenly, without any more logical explanation than had first obliged it to clam up, the stapler would begin to emit staples from its small, metallic mouth, and we were back in business.

After the first afternoon, it became clear that stapling down insulation was a task Rosemary could handle nicely. So I left it to her and the helping hand of sundry friends and acquaintances while I began to lay finish flooring.

The next afternoon, I was working away on hands and knees when Robert appeared in the doorway wearing a peculiar grin. Somehow I was reminded of the way nurses had looked when they had emerged from the maternity ward with news of my newest offspring. "I think we've got it," said Robert.

I jumped to my feet in excitement. "How far down are

you?" I asked.

"Just fifty-eight feet."

"And how much water have you got?"

"Well, bailing at the rate of ten gallons a minute we can't bail it out. So you must have something over ten gallons a minute."

I whistled in astonishment. "At fifty-eight feet! And you thought it would go well over a hundred. That's really amazing."

We walked up the hill to the rig. Old Mr. Hoppe was standing beside the black steel pipe running down into the ground. His expression was sour.

"I hear you've got over ten gallons a minute for me at less than sixty feet. That's really wonderful."

"Yep," snapped Mr. Hoppe, "pretty lucky. Too bad that fellow who needed it so bad for his dairy herd couldn't have had some of it instead of you. I looked for your well to go at least a hundred fifteen."

"Well, that is really grand. How is the water? Have you tasted it?"

"I haven't tasted it, but it's good water. You've got a good well. And that casing is seated good and solid against that rock down there. You won't have any trouble with pollution or surface water draining in."

"Fine."

"But it sure fooled me, coming in like that in at fifty eight feet. That's hardly worthwhile setting the rig up for."

"I don't mind. I can sure stand to save the money."

Mr. Hoppe made a quick gesture as though he had remembered something. "Oh, say, now that I think of it. How are you -fixed for a pump? I've got the catalogue here." He reached into the car and brought out a brightly-colored folder. He flipped the pages and pointed a broad thumb at an illustration. "Here's the model you need. You see they're all rated according to the depth of the well. You can use the smallest model."

I had not faced up to the question of buying a pump as yet, although I had held exploratory and informational discussions with my knowledgeable friend, Housel, and with Mr. Bragg the plumber. Their views were diametrically opposed. Bob, ever the heretic, favored the old-style piston-type pump. He argued they were easier to maintain and more reliable in operation. Mr. Bragg had grinned in disbelief when I had said I was thinking of getting a piston-type pump.

"Why, I don't know anyone who puts in those old-fashioned pumps any more. I haven't put one on a well in years. Everyone uses jet-pumps nowadays. They're faster, no trouble to maintain, and cheaper to operate." Mr. Bragg had also let it be known he hoped to sell me a pump.

Against this background, I was uncertain what to say to old Mr. Hoppe. I decided to fall back on the old reliable method of price comparison. "How do they run in cost?" I asked.

"I sell them for cost plus ten percent. I'll show you the bill of lading they send me with the pump, and you just add ten percent."

"Awful hard to beat that. What is this model run?"

"Well, let's see. That's model 10 B. Uh, that one runs $92.00. You add ten percent to that and you get about $111.00 altogether."

I nodded my head while trying not to show my surprise. The price he quoted was thirty or forty dollars less than I had expected to pay. "Give me a little while to think about it."

I walked back down the hill to The Playhouse and went down below to find Mr. Bragg who was finishing off the job of roughing in the plumbing. I reported my conversation with Mr. Hoppe to him and named the price he had quoted for the pump. He shook his head. "I can't beat that. That's an awfully good price. " Then he grinned and added characteristically, "If it's a good pump."

"Well, how about it? Is it a good pump?"

"Tell you the truth, I don't know anything about it. I handle another kind." Then his face grew unaccustomedly solemn. "But I'll tell you this. Mr. Hoppe is an honest man. If he says it's a good pump, it's all right."

"Guess I'll take it," I said and walked back up the hill. Besides the favorable price Mr. Hoppe offered, I was swayed by a desire to make up in some way or another for the unexpectedly low cost of the well itself.

Mr. Hoppe greeted my reply with abrupt equanimity, displaying neither surprise nor pleasure. "I'll bring it over in the truck tomorrow," he said. I was a little taken aback by this matter-of-factness, even from Mr. Hoppe, and I had got back to my task of nailing down flooring before my mind returned to the remarkably good news about the well. I sat up suddenly and smiled to myself, sitting alone in the partially complete little house, hot in the late June afternoon, redolent of new wood and sawdust and new electric wiring. A well is a highly symbolic thing at any time. A new well, particularly in the country, seems to connote new beginnings, the flowing vitality of a country home, independence from urban machinery and municipal accounting, and the purity and abundance of clear, unchlorinated water. Add to all this, the extraordinary fact that a *deep* well, a driven well, had been established on a hillside at a depth of less than sixty feet, and here was real cause for rejoicing. I decided to knock off work a little early.

"Wonderful!" said Rosemary. "Did you taste it?"

"Is it flowing out of the ground like an oil well?" asked Stephen.

"No, it's just sitting there at the bottom of the pipe.

You can see it all right. No, I didn't taste it. I didn't have any way to get it out."

"Well, I'll give you a cup and a long piece of string, and you can dip some out. You ought to taste it."

"Guess you're right. We'll do it tomorrow."

Next day, we did. Rosemary gave me an old coffee mug, and I tied it to a long piece of light rope and gently lowered it down the black steel pipe. Then I carefully drew it up—Stephen giving vent to a cheer with his right arm raised high in the air as it came to the top—and we all tasted it. It was crystalline clear water and sparklingly cold and it tasted exactly like black steel pipe.

While Rosemary turned back to the insulation job with the help of Tom and Mary Wood, two friends who were visiting us from Florida, I redoubled my efforts on the flooring. It was a long, slow, and exacting task. The material itself was fine—clean and dry and sound. But I was very mindful that I was putting down finish flooring, and I was extremely careful to match the pieces, to fit them so tightly no cracks showed, and to avoid denting or bashing the wood with careless hammer blows. I laid a strip of building paper down over the subfloor, intending it to serve both as insulation against drafts and as sound deadener. Then I nailed the flooring down with blunt-tipped nails, driving them at an angle on the shoulder of the tongue. The remarkable thing was how slowly it moved. I started at the west, or uphill side, of the house, and ran the strips of flooring from the north end of the living room across and through the kitchen ell, a distance of approximately 28 feet. At the end of three or four hours of steady work, I would have gained only about a foot or eighteen inches of the way across the width of the living room. I kept thinking to myself that there must be a faster way of laying finish flooring, but if one exists I never found it.

The end of my month's leave from the office came and

found me still making a snail's progress across the living room floor. On the evening before my return to the nine-to-five routine, I took stock of my situation and what remained to do. July was upon me. Less than two months of weekends and evenings were available before September, the day on which I intended to move my family into The Playhouse. I made out a list of the absolutely essential jobs to be finished by that date:

1. Get septic tank and drainage field done.
2. Dig pit for well pump and build cinder block housing for it.
3. Dig trench from well to house for water line.
4. Finish insulation and flooring.
5. Order cabinets for kitchen and bathroom.
6. Lay linoleum in bunkrooms and bathroom.
7. Have electricity and plumbing finished off.
8. Put wallboard on walls and ceiling.

This looked to be a formidable but perhaps not quite insurmountable array of tasks. It was clear that I would have to make every available moment count. The first thing to do was to jog the septic field people. This I did on Monday morning.

"Awful glad you called. We're planning on coming into your place on Wednesday or Thursday of this week. Will you be there?"

"No, but my wife will. She can show you where everything goes. By the way, while you're here, can you have your crew do a little digging for me? Dig a well pit and a trench for the water pipe to run from the well to the house?"

"Well, you'll have to ask my brother, the foreman on the job about that. You tell him what you want done and he'll see whether they can do it."

"Okay."

As it turned out, it was Friday before the crew came to

my place but with their modern equipment they got the septic tank installed, the drainage field laid, and the earth back in place, all in one day. "It was wonderful to watch them work," Rosemary told me over supper that night. "They had two big machines, a ditch-digger and a bull-dozer, and they just dug those trenches in nothing flat. Then a bunch of men placed the tiles in the trenches, and the bulldozer pushed the dirt back and they were through."

"I'm certaintly sorry I missed it. It's the only operation on The Playhouse I've missed yet. Did they dig the pit and the trench down from the well?"

"They couldn't dig the pit with their machine. They did dig the trench but only about half-way. They couldn't get the machine any farther because of the overhead wires."

On the following Saturday I was back at the old stand. I wanted to get on with the flooring which was in danger of becoming an obsession with me, but common sense told me that the wise thing was to get the pit dug for the well pump so that Mr. Bragg could go ahead and connect up the plumbing. My aversion to the pick and shovel had grown to monumental proportions during the last stages of finishing off the excavation, but my efforts to persuade any of the neighborhood hired hands to take on the job had been unsuccessful. They were too polite to say they considered ditch-digging to be beneath their talents, but they found various excuses for not accepting my offer of employment. Alvin said he had been having "a right smart amount of trouble" with his back. Ace said he was so busy helping Mr. Fones he simply did not have the time. Irving pointed out that he also was building a house and his problem was not unlike mine: he just had to get his family moved in before first frost.

And so, more reluctantly than I can say, I went to The Shed and got out my ditch-digging tools. I carried them up through the heavy green growth of grass and weeds while the July sun, already hot in the still and clear sky, struck down on the hillside. Then with a groan I set to work digging a pit approximately four feet square and three feet deep. These were absolutely minimal dimensions for the situation, and Mr. Bragg demurred slightly over them. In my mood at that moment, however, I would not have enlarged them an inch for anyone. I found the going very difficult at first. A long dry June had baked the topsoil into a stiff crust down for the first foot or so. After that the digging suddenly and surprisingly became easy—as easy, that is, as shovelling dirt ever gets—and the red, loose soil came out on my shovel like soft loam. In less than two hours of furious digging, I had it dug out and squared off. The ditch leading to the house remained to be done, but I decided to leave that till later. I turned back to flooring and succeeded in making another 18 inches across the living room before quitting time. On my way home, I stopped by Alvin's house and asked him whether he would be willing to build a cinder block enclosure for the pump house. He accepted the job and to my surprise got it completed three days later.

The trench to the house was the object of an evening's work during the ensuing week. It very nearly proved to be the proverbial straw. Rosemary and I went up to The Playhouse one night after supper. We hooked up the fifty-foot extension cord and looped it over one of the branches of a nearby pine tree so that it would hold the floodlight in position. Then I set to digging. It was a hot, close night in July, and the night-flying insects were out in force. The ground was baked to a cement-like hardness, and it turned back my mattock and shovel so firmly that I felt as though I were digging with my finger nails. Such was the heat, the irritation of the crawling masses of bugs, as well as my anxiety about the mound of problems remaining to be solved before September, and my bone-deep fatigue which was mounting daily, that I felt once or twice it was going to prove too much for me. I came within inches several times of throwing the tools down on the ground. That night I came closer than any other time to quitting.

Somehow, though, I did not. Rosemary's solicitude and the awareness somewhere in the back of my mind that I had got through more difficult moments previously were the sources of strength that kept me going. Right until the very end, though, it was a struggle. At a point no more than twenty-four inches from the house the ground suddenly became harder than granite. I clawed and hacked at it until the sweat blinded my eyes, but the trench seemed to remain at almost exactly the same depth. Finally, I stopped. It did not seem possible to go on any longer.

"That will have to be good enough," I panted.

Rosemary looked down at the shallow trench. It was certainly no deeper than fourteen inches, if that. She looked up at me, troubled. "But, honey, is that deep enough? Won't the water freeze in the pipe if it isn't any deeper than that?"

I looked down hopelessly at the ditch. Yes, goddammit to hell and obscenity and carry two, it certainly would freeze. Without any question whatever, that miserable, card-carrying ditch *had* to be—at least four inches deeper. Without saying anything, I picked up the mattock again and began to swing with all my remaining strength. After five more minutes I had made another inch, after another twenty I had made the necessary four. I was limp and exhausted and somehow deeply resentful of the necessity I had been under of doing the digging myself. But I was finished and that was all that mattered. "Let's quit," I said. "Let's get the hell out of here."

Twenty

When the next Saturday morning rolled around, It seemed that everything conspired to make me forget the unpleasantness of the preceding week. The weather had been heavy and humid until early Friday evening when a thunderstorm of great violence had broken the heaviness sharply. In the wake of the jagged, flashing lightning, the deep, vibrating shocks of thunder, and the heavy, splashing rain had come a northwest wind carrying cool air straight from the pine forests and the cold lakes of Canada. As I drove in across the meadow before 8 o'clock the next morning, the grass of the field and the woods above it stood in sharp relief as the white gold sun rose in the eastern sky. The needles of the pine trees around The Playhouse were all tipped with little drops of rain that sparkled and prismed in the morning light. It was enough to make me feel ashamed of my outburst of several nights before, and I found that down beneath the ingrained fatigue and the sense of desperation a healthy surge of enthusiasm and energy still remained.

To my surprise, I found Mr. Bragg already at work. He was mounting the pump on the well casing. He looked up with that engaging self-deprecatory grin. "Thought I'd try to get this job done before it gets too hot," he said. He was standing inside the little cement block enclosure Alvin had built, and even I could see that the dimensions were just about as small as they could be. Mr. Bragg, not a large man, filled the available space and had to curl himself around to work at the base of the well casing. "Cozy in here," he said. "One thing about it, though, you won't be able to change plumbers unless you can find one smaller than me."

"That's right."

He worked on silently for a moment while I watched. "Say, one thing. I'll have this pump on here by noon. How are you planning to cover this pump house?"

"I'll build a cover for it," I said, wincing inwardly as I set myself still another job to be done. "I've got some siding I didn't use and some two-by-fours, and I'll make a wooden cover you can lift off. I'll put a couple of layers of roll roofing on to make it watertight."

"Well, you'll need it before nightfall."

"Okay."

I walked down the hill and stood in the doorway surveying the amount of flooring left to be done. I was a little more than half way across. Judging by the pace it had gone so far, not even the new surge of energy that had ridden in on the fresh northwest wind would be enough to finish the job over the weekend. Still, my friend, Hat Ford, was coming out to work all day with me, and we would see what we could accomplish together.

I still was pounding away on the first row I had begun when Hal arrived. Within a few minutes of his arrival, it was clear that his presence was as tonic as the rain-washed atmosphere. He was no great carpenter, but he was filled with the joy of living and overflowing with quips and jokes. He brought a new approach to the problem too and in short order had us organized into a two-man team.

"Look," he said, "I can pound nails like crazy, but I don't get this matching up the sizes stuff and I'm scared to death of that damned buzz saw you've got in your hand. Why don't you select the pieces and cut them into the proper lengths, and I'll nail them down. Won't that be quicker?"

It turned out to be unbelievably quicker. It proved once again that in small house building two men work not merely twice as fast as one but four times as fast. Our progress was phenomenal, and by noon we had made just less than four feet. It was a pace I could not expect us to maintain though. Hal, lacking both the urgent motivation I had and the muscles hardened by a year or more of this activity, naturally had less stamina. By noon, when we settled down with some sandwiches and cold beer, he was ready to take it easy for a while. He had brought along a book, so I suggested after we had finished eating that he read his book while I built the cover for the pump house. He quickly agreed.

I walked up the hill and found Mr. Bragg just putting the finishing touches on the pump, the small pressure tank, and the copper pipe running down to the house. "How's it coming? Think that pump will work?"

Mr. Bragg grinned up at me. "I reckon it will. Work for a month or two anyway. Won't work at all, though, until you get the electrician to lay that lead cable and hook the pump up to the electricity. When you going to get that done?"

"Well, as a matter of fact, I told Mr. Fones to buy that lead cable this morning, and he's coming by this afternoon or tomorrow morning to hook it up."

"I got this job just about finished up. I can't do no more now until you get the bathroom ready for the fixtures and the kitches cabinets in."

I nodded, trying to keep back a big wave of weariness.

"Yes, I know. I guess it will be another week or two before I get to that stage. I can't get on to anything else until I get that damned floor laid."

While Mr. Bragg finished tightening down the last joint, I went down to the basement and rounded up some lumber with which to build the cover. I carried the pieces up behind the house and set up the saw horses. I cut the two-by-fours and nailed them together to form a square frame. Then, having cut the one by twelves, I nailed them onto the frame with eight-penny nails. I had a cover built in less than half an hour. I went back to The Shed and got out a partially used roll of roofing. I cut off three pieces slightly more than four feet long and tacked them on the top of the cover. Hal came out to watch as I was finishing.

"I find this reading routine pretty dull compared with laying floor," he said. "When are we going to be able to get back to the ole assembly line?"

"Soon as I get this cover set in place. Help me load it up on the wheelbarrow and we'll put it on the pump house."

The cover turned out to be remarkably heavy, but with some groaning we got it on the wheelbarrow. Then, with Hal holding it in place, I pushed the wheelbarrow up beside the well, and with considerably more groaning we got it over onto the cinder block walls and fitted into place. It dropped on as snugly as though I had been building well house covers all my life.

"C'mon," said Hal, "let's get back to that flooring. I want to see whether we can knock it off this afternoon."

We went back to the flooring and worked at it until 6 o'clock. By that time, we had less than two feet to go, but Hal was dragging and I felt I had enough. Hal looked ruefully at that two-foot gap. "I thought sure we could make it," he said. "I feel I've let you down. We were going to finish this job off." He looked at me thoughtfully a moment. "Are you going to be working here again tomorrow?"

"Silly boy."

"Yeah. Well, in that case, why don't I come back tomorrow morning? I've got something to do tomorrow afternoon, but I could work all morning."

"Better still, why don't you stay with us tonight? Your family is away, and you can eat supper with us and spend the night. I'll lend you some pajamas. That way, you can save driving into town and back out again tomorrow morning."

"Just one thing. What are we having for supper?"

"Well, old-fashioneds and por—"

"Say no more. You've got a house guest."

With no more discussion we packed up the tools and loaded the empty beer bottles in the car and headed for home. Rosemary was as delighted as I knew she would be to have Hal for a guest. We both showered and changed clothes—Hal putting on one of my old shirts and a pair of slacks—and a half hour later we were all three sitting with old-fashioneds in our hands.

"Something bothers me," said Hal.

"What Is that?"

"Just this—what in the world are you going to do with all your spare time after you get this house built'?"

I snorted. "I would call that the least of my troubles. Boy, oh boy, when I get that Playhouse built I'm going to buy a case of beer a week and I'm going to sit out on that deck and drink it. I'm not going to lift a finger."

Rosemary looked at me over the top of her glass, her eyes sparkling with that peculiar gaiety of a wife who has just heard her husband say something transparently absurd. "Pooh," she said. "You say that now because you're tired. That would last just about a week. Then you would start looking around for another project to throw yourself into."

"No, sir," I said staunchly, "not this time. All I want is to sit on that deck with a glass of cold beer in my hand and watch the birds fly back and forth from the woods to the meadow."

"We'll see," she said. "Why, I'll bet that within one month you'll be talking about starting on the main house up the hill."

I paused, caught by a succession of thoughts that flowed from this remark. "Well, as a matter of fact," I said, trying to be objective about the matter, "I was thinking just the other day it wouldn't hurt to get started clearing, so we won't lose time later—"

"You see!" Rosemary said triumphantly to Hal. "You see?"

"I see," said Hal. "Sad case."

In the morning, Hal and I returned to the flooring. The combination of the experience we had gained the day before and the zest of the morning made the work move very fast, and we had the job completed before noon.

"Now what do you do to it?" asked Hal, looking across the completed floor. "Looks a little uneven here and there."

"Sand it till it is even and smooth. Then stain it lightly with a penetrating wood finish. But that's some way off yet. I've got a lot of other things to get done first." I looked up as I finished speaking and saw old Mr. Fones standing in the doorway. He and Ace had been at work laying the lead cable from the house to the well for an hour or so. Mr. Fones was trying with great difficulty to tell me something, and at last it came out.

"All hooked up," he said. "You can try her now."

"Hey! Let's see how it works." We walked up the hill to the well, and I got down inside the little pump house. I had told Mr. Bragg to put a faucet inside the pump house so that I could fasten a hose onto it which would be available for gardening or fires or any emergency. I opened the valve cautiously and instantly the compact jet pump on top of the steel casing began to whir and vibrate and water rushed out of the faucet at my feet.

"It works!" said Hal. "What will they think of next! Say, let's have a drink of it and see how it tastes. It looks all right, but you never can tell. It might be hundred octane gasoline."

"Might be. But the last time I tried, it was liquid steel pipe. We can try again. Let's get a cup." We got one and made a test. Our verdict was unanimous: it still tasted more like steel casing than water. "Mr. Bragg says you have to run the water for sometime before that goes away. I've got a length of hose down in The Shed I can hook up and then leave it running."

I got the hose from The Shed and in a few minutes the water was trickling and sparkling down the hillside through the pine grove. Rosemary arrived about this time with lunch, and we sat ourselves down on the deck and ate a delicious luncheon of iced sherry and cold roast beef sandwiches with mayonnaise and dill pickle. When we finished, Hal departed, and Rosemary and I discussed how to spend the afternoon.

"I thought I would put the insulation on the ceiling if you are game," I said. "It's a two-man job. How about it?"

"Okay, let's do it." We got out the ladder, opened a fresh carton of the aluminum roll insulation, and set to work. Rosemary used the stapler we had rented from Montgomery Ward, and I used one I had rented from the local hardware store for the weekend. We fumbled a little at the beginning, but very soon we had evolved a smooth system. I laid planks across the sawhorses and we stood on those to reach where the rafters came low near the walls. In the center, where the roof peaked, we used the step-ladder, sometimes standing on opposite sides of the ladder at the same time. We somehow managed to make a game of it, and the work went very fast. I found myself thinking that anyone who can staple together a long memorandum can staple insulation. The aluminum rolls were fitted with flexible flanges along the sides which we stapled directly onto the sides of the rafters on a line just above the bottom edge. We tried to place a staple approximately every foot or so, but whenever we noticed a place where the edge of the flange bulged away from the rafter, leaving a space, we drove one or more staples there. I had read or been told, that insulation is just like a bucket. If there is a hole anywhere, heat or cold leaks through like water through a hole in the bucket. We tried to leave no holes. It was a hot and still afternoon, and until 3:30 or so the mid-July sun struck the black roof over our heads with violence. As we fastened down the insulation we could feel it immediately blocking off the heat, and it was noticeably cooler under the part we had done than under the remaining part.

The work went so quickly, in contrast to the laborious progress on the flooring, and we had so much fun scrambling up and down the ladder, that we put on a race with ourselves. To my astonishment, we were within sight of the end by 5:30, the time Rosemary had told the baby-sitter to expect us home. But there was no stopping at that point, so we pushed on for another 25 minutes and finished the job.

"What a thing! Who would have thought we could finish the insulation in one afternoon? I thought it would take two or three."

"Teamwork, that's what does it."

"Now, just before we go," I said, changing the subject entirely, "what are we going to do about kitchen and bathroom cabinets? Everything is all set now for Mr. Bragg to hook the water up to the house and finish the plumbing, but he can't go ahead until we decide about cabinets. Have you decided on any of the things we looked at in the Montgomery Ward catalogue?"

"No, and I've been thinking about this whole question of cabinets. I know we are trying to build The Playhouse as cheaply as possible, but it seems to me that we would be justified in spending a little money on cabinets. The house is going to have a lot of charm because of its setting and its lines, and I think the one thing that would really finish it off would be some really nice cabinets in the kitchen and the bathroom. The rest of the house can look simple and rustic and if the cabinetwork is good it will really set it off. Homemade or cheap cabinets would ruin the whole effect, I think."

"Well," I said cautiously, wondering apprehensively whether all the savings I had achieved by using inexpensive but recalcitrant materials—like used flooring for sheathing—were about to be washed down the drain, "what do you have in mind?"

"I don't have anything particular in mind, but there's a custom cabinet-maker over in the next town who is supposed to be very good. I would like to see what he would recommend for us here and what it would cost."

"Well, I can tell you now, it would cost plenty. Nothing is more expensive than cabinet work, particularly custom cabinet work."

"Still it wouldn't cost anything to try. I would just like to get him to come over here and give us his ideas. If they're not any good or if he is too expensive, we'll just skip it. It won't cost anything to find out."

"Okay by me, just so long as you find out soon. But don't be surprised if you are terribly disappointed by his price." And with that word of profound wisdom, we packed up and went home to our Sunday night supper of baked beans and hot dogs.

During the ensuing week, Rosemary made an appointment for the cabinet-maker in the next town to come over and see The Playhouse. She found him imaginative and understanding of every idea she presented. He made some sketches on the spot and by Friday of that week he had presented them in a package together with an estimate of the cost. We got out the Montgomery Ward catalogue on Friday night and made a point-by-point comparison. To my very considerable surprise and some chagrin, the prices he quoted for custom-made cabinets compared very favorably with the Montgomery Ward prices. "And," Rosemary pointed out, "these would be custom-made and fitted to our particular situation."

"I think we ought to do it," I said. "Let's go ahead."

At this point, it was time to take stock and re-appraise my situation. I had finished off several of the essential tasks I had set for myself at the beginning of the month: the flooring, the insulation, the well house and the trench to the house. We had decided on ordering the cabinets. What remained to do then on that list of essentials was to put the wallboard and plywood on the walls and finish the floors. My strategic concept in determining these priorities was based on the idea that those things which were absolutely essential before we moved in on 1 September must be done first. Thus, it was essential that the walls of the bunkrooms and bathroom be covered, at least on one side of the partition. It was not essential, however, that the living room and kitchen walls be covered, and it was likewise not essential that the doors to the bunkrooms and bathroom be hung, however desirable it might be to have something solid instead of a hanging curtain. It obviously was not essential that the ceilings be covered, although it was essential that the floors be finished.

I encountered some resistance from the troops regarding this strategic plan. Rosemary was particularly disturbed about the deep trench immediately behind the back wall of the foundation. She had persuaded me some time back to backfill at the back door so that we had been able to discard the plank bridge that had served for many months to cross the abyss. But on either side of the doorway there was a gaping chasm, almost six feet deep and two feet wide, between the foundation wall and the original back wall of the excavation. "I'm afraid some child will fall in there and hurt himself very badly," she said.

But I stood rock-firm. "Not essential," I said. "We can move into the house without doing it. And I've got only time enough and strength enough to do the absolutely essential."

During the course of the next week or two I discovered, as has many a man before me, that masculine firmness and logic are anything but impervious to feminine persistence. Rosemary did not argue the point further, but she began by herself to hack away at the ground behind the house and to shovel dirt into the deep trench. She persuaded Stephen to lend a hand, and the two of them worked at the enormous job from time to time. This of course melted my rigid determination, and I agreed to spend a half hour at the end of my day's work shovelling backfill. "If we will all just do ten shovelfuls each time we are here," Rosemary said, "we will have it filled up in no time." My rather considerable experience in moving quantities of dirt native to the area surrounding The Playhouse led me to believe this was a highly optimistic assessment of the problem, but I had learned—at least for the moment—not to value too highly my masculine approach to the whole matter.

For the most part, however, I was able to keep to my established priorities. I put the white wallboard up on the inside of the bunkrooms without serious difficulty, although there were some fitting problems where the slanting ceiling met the wall and I sometimes missed the studs with the nail I was driving blindly through the wallboard. Because of the cramped working conditions and the fitting problems, the job took much longer than I had estimated, as it did to apply the marine plywood in the bathroom. Here also I felt it necessary to put up the ceiling as well in order to protect the studs and the insulation from the spray of the shower. By the time I had finished these unexpectedly slow jobs and had put up wallboard in the kitchen area, we were well into August and the panic was beginning to mount.

With the wallboard and plywood up in bunkrooms and bathroom, I had something to fasten electric fixtures to, so I called old Mr. Fones and told him to come in and finish off the electricity. Rosemary and I went to an electric supply store and selected simple wall lights for the bunkrooms and fluorescent light fixtures for the bathroom and kitchen. All other illumination in the house would be provided by floor lamps and table lamps to be connected up with the generous number of wall plugs I had put in. We also got four floodlights, one for each corner of the house, which were to be controlled by a switch beside the door.

Mr. Fones arrived on a Saturday morning with a larger contingent than usual of dark and helping hands. It developed rather quickly that some of the hands were unskilled, or at least somewhat rough, in handling electrical fixtures, and I decided I would be well advised to supervise closely to keep them from bending and scarring our carefully selected lights. During the course of the morning a fair amount of confusion seemed to develop over wiring method, and one very handsome, dark brown young man whom I had not seen previously, but who was named Montague and obviously was intelligent, appeared very insistent that a major error was being committed. I took care not to get involved in the controversy. As a matter of fact, I did not even understand it. In the end, however, it seemed that Mr. Fones had his way and young Montague was reduced to shaking his head over the decision.

Shortly before noon, everything seemed to be hooked up, and it was agreed to test it. There was a fair amount of hilarity over this event, and Montague told all of us laughingly, "Man, when he throws that switch I'm going to be taking off into that woods. No telling what's going to happen when the current hits those wires."

But as a matter of fact, nothing startling did happen when Mr. Fones threw the switch. We all stood expectant, looking at Montague for some sign of alarm, but there were no flashes or loud reports and outside the house there was only the soft twitterings of the birds in the nearby woods and the calls and cries of children playing over the hill. We went around from fixture to fixture and from wall plug to wall plug and tested them. There appeared to be only three defects: the fluorescent light over the kitchen sink refused to light, two of the outside floodlights gave off only a dim glow, and the fluorescent light over the stove could be turned on only by the same switch which turned on the bathroom light.

We presented this accounting to Mr. Fones who greeted the news with surprised relief. "Is that *all*?" he asked incredulously. "Why that's go-o-o-d!" This struck us all as monstrously funny, and Mr. Fones' helpers slapped themselves and each other on the leg and back, giving vent to deep, visceral, dark-hued laughter. "That's go-o-o-d!" one of them would say and off would go a new round of guffaws and cackles. When sobriety returned, a counsel was held on the causes for the defects, and it developed that the problems of the non-functioning kitchen light and the inter-related bathroom switch and stove light were directly connected. They were in fact precisely the points over which Montague and Mr. Fones had been debating. In the new discussion, bolstered as he was by concrete evidence,

Montague had no difficulty in carrying the day. Mr. Fones retired from the controversy graciously, and Montague led the crew in rectifying the difficulty. In another half hour, we tested the two kitchen lights and found them working perfectly. The two outside floodlights, however, were quite another thing. Even Montague seemed baffled by them and was reduced to hinting that the lights were defective. In the end, we agreed to leave the problem for solution to the county electrical inspector.

About the middle of the next week, the kitchen and bathroom cabinets were delivered. They arrived late in the afternoon, looking sleek and beautifully finished. They were a beautiful tawny-and-saffron-colored pine and the counter top was formica bound with stainless steel, the top in the kitchen being yellow and the one in the bathroom, gray. "They're really handsome, we assured each other. "We really did the right thing in having them made." We had them set in place and that evening I called Mr. Bragg to tell him he could come in and finish off the plumbing.

Sanding and finishing the floor had next priority, and I began work on it the following weekend. I rented a floor sander from the local hardware store and loaded it into the station wagon on Saturday morning and took it out to The Playhouse. It was a heavy, powerful machine. I lugged it into the house and fastened a sheet of the roughest grade sandpaper on it. It jumped and whined, when I pressed the pistol grip switch, and began to move forward. It exerted a strong pull, with the traction it had with the very heavy sandpaper, and I had to brace my feet solidly to reverse its direction and swing it around.

Actually, the task I was undertaking was much more than merely smoothing the floor prior to finishing it. The used flooring I had put down was in excellent condition and not badly worn, but even so it was considerably more uneven than new flooring would have been. Some pieces stood as much as an eighth of an inch higher than their immediate neighbors. To bring these pieces down even and to make the whole floor uniformly smooth was in reality a job of planing, not merely sanding. The floor sander was capable of doing the job with the soft pine, but it was slow and heavy going. I consumed innumerable sheets of sandpaper during the process.

I was deeply engrossed in the job at one point during mid-morning when some movement near the doorway caught the corner of my eye, and I looked up and there stood Bud Bradley. He had been away for two or three months, and I had not seen him for longer than that. I switched off the sander, and it slowly came to a stop with a long descending whine and a final shudder.

"You've really made progress since I was here last!" said Bud.

"Well, I guess so, but it seems awful slow to me. I'm trying to get it far enough done so we can move in."

"When's that going to happen?"

"First September."

Bud whistled and looked around at the uncovered walls and ceilings, the aluminum insulation glistening in the light. "Still, though, that's not so bad. You could almost move in now if you had to."

"Well, as soon as I get the floor sanded and finished we could. The water will be hooked up by tonight probably, so we'll have light and plumbing."

"What are you going to do about heat?"

"Haven't thought that far really. Probably forced hot air, but I'll wait until after we are moved in and then settle that problem sometime during the month of September."

Bud nodded and looked around again. "Boy, you've really done a wonderful job. Seems to me you've done the whole thing just right." Before I could find my tongue and make some reply to this tremendous compliment from Bud, he swung around and noticed the kitchen cabinet. "Where did you get that? That's a beautiful cabinet!" We walked on around the rest of the little house, Bud asking alert, intelligent questions about the choice of materials and construction details. "The thing I like about the house is the lines and proportions. It's really beautiful from the outside and it sits in this hillside as though it really belongs, as though it had always been here. And inside, it has a wonderful feeling. That big window looking out across the meadow. The proportions of the room are good. It gives you a snug feeling without being small or tight."

"Well, Bud, you know I owe an awful lot of that to you."

He snorted. "Heck, I didn't do anything except move some dirt around for you. You probably would have got it dug out somehow."

"No, that's not true. You practically forced me to excavate the basement and make it a two-story building set in against the hillside. I never would have done it if it had not been for you. That's the most important and the most sensible decision I made during the whole process of building The Playhouse. And you did it for practically nothing too. I'll never forget the favor you did me in digging that excavation."

Bud laughed his dry, cackling laugh. "Well, I'll say this. It's not only the cheapest excavation I've ever done. It's the *only* excavation I've ever done. Learned my lesson on that one."

We were silent a moment and then I said, "By the way, I'd like you to do some more earth-moving for me if you would." I walked to the window in front and pointed down at the ground outside. "That embankment there in front of the house is pretty badly eroded. If you would bring in your tractor and blade and grade it off, I thought I would plant some rye grass this fall and get some roots established there to hold it down. Oh yes, and Rosemary would like a garden plot plowed up so we can prepare the ground for planting next spring."

Bud nodded his head. "Sure I can do that for you. I won't get it done this week and maybe not the next, but I'll get it done in time for you to plant some rye there." He turned around then and walked slowly over to the door. "Got to be moving along. I'm on my way over to get some lumber from old Rose for stalls in my horse barn."

I grinned and shook my head. "You won't get much done today. Old Rose will keep you there talking all day."

"I know. Always talks my arm off. Wonderful old man, though. I sure get a kick out of talking to him." He stood in the doorway a moment, a spare, engaging figure, with the quizzical expression on his lean and leathery face. "See you later," he said and was off. I stood for a moment reflecting about the quality of fundamental goodness and humanity that seemed to emanate from Bud, that inner harmony and magnanimity of purpose that flows so strongly and positively from some people and not at all from others. Then I squeezed the pistol grip on the sanding machine and went back to work.

Twenty One

L ater in the day I had another visitor. This one was a total stranger, and he appeared suddenly in the doorway, a young man of about 22 or 23, dressed in a blue shirt open at the neck, with a tee-shirt showing at the base of his throat. "I don't guess you know who I am," he said, standing hesitantly in the doorway. "I'm Wilbur Dodds."

Wilbur Dodds! Yes, indeed, I knew who he was. I had seen his name on the surveyor's plot for my land. "The Acre!" I said. "You're the man who owns that acre up there on the corner."

"Yes, that's right. You see, I was practically brought up on this farm, and when my great uncle sold it he deeded an acre to me. He wanted to keep some family connected with the land, and he knew I really loved it."

"Yeah. It certainly is nice land." There was a silence then. I waited for him to continue.

"You got a nice place here," the young man said politely. "Sure is hard for me to realize someone is building a house right here on this field. Why, I've driven a plow and a harrow up and down this field a hundred times. And that woods back there. The hunting I've done there! Rabbit and squirrel. Partridges, too. Used to be lotsa partridges. Even got a fox back in there once." He shook his head as the old memories flooded into his mind. "I used to think I was going to build a house here someday, just like you're doing, but the trouble is my wife, she don't like the country. She's a nice girl. Likes to go swimming and fishing and all that, but she's always lived in town and she can't see living way out here. 'Nother thing, we're going to have another baby next spring—we already got one, a little girl—and we're going to have to add on a bedroom to our house in Arlington. I guess I'll enclose the back porch and make a nice little bedroom out of it. But that's going to take some money, and I was wondering whether you would be interested in buying that acre from me."

My heart came up into my throat. Buy that acre! There was nothing in the world I wanted more to do. The Acre was really a vital piece of land, torn out of the body of my woods. The little logging road which ran across it provided easy access to the back part of my land and offered the normal entrance for a drive to the main house I hoped someday to build. Besides, that acre was a valuable long-range investment with its long road frontage. It was all the more valuable to me because anyone who built a house on it would be looking right down the back of my neck.

I tried to appear casual. "Well, I wouldn't mind having it, but at the present time my credit is stretched right out almost to the breaking point. As a matter of fact, I had just about made up my mind to get along without that acre. After all, I've got seven acres of my own."

The young man looked uncertain and shifted his weight. "Well," he said, "I've just got to get ahold some money. I hoped you would want to buy that piece of land. It's the only thing I own to raise some money on. I guess maybe I can sell it all right to somebody, but I thought you would like to be the first to know before I sell it to someone else"

"Well, I certainly appreciate that. I'm glad you did." I paused a moment, thinking. I did not have a doubt in the world he could sell the Acre to somebody. One-acre pieces were extremely difficult to find in the area, and this one with its long frontage was a plum. Moreover, I knew that Dodds would not be particular about who bought the land, and this represented another threat to my peace and security. Again, I tried to be as calm as possible. "I tell you what I wish you would do. I might be interested in buying that piece from you but I'll have to look around first to see if I can raise some money. I wish you would give me a few days to do that."

Dodds brightened. "Why, yes, sure, I'll be glad to do that. You see what you can do and let me know. Do you think you'll be able to find out before next weekend?"

"Yes. I'll know definitely one way or the other by then."

"Well, fine. That sounds good. I sure hope you decide to buy it."

"I'll let you know," I said and let him go without mentioning anything about price. I saw no advantage in getting a negotiation started which might end with his adopting a rigid position. I wanted, when the talking actually began, to have the tactical advantage of having the money in my hand to offer him.

I went back to sanding shortly, swinging the powerful machine back and forth with rigidly braced feet until my leg and back muscles ached. And the longer I worked and the more I thought about it, the more depressed I became. If only he had come to me at some other time. If only I could stall him until the following spring. I knew that virtually every resource I owned was tied up at that time. The Acre was worth, in round numbers, a thousand dollars. Good bargaining might bring it down as much as two hundred dollars, but how much chance did I have of rounding together eight hundred to a thousand dollars?

That evening after dinner I got out the journal in which I had been jotting down notes regarding the progress of The Playhouse. I also had kept an account of expenditures in it, and I noted down on a separate piece of paper the following items:

1139.80	Completed shell of The Playhouse
2.39	18 six-inch lag bolts for deck stanchions
220.50	Mr. Hoppe's services in digging well
189.50	Well pump ($111), pressure tank, plastic pipe
18.50	Cinder block & mortar for well house
16.50	5 tons construction sand
15.00	Services Alvin Brown constructing well house
480.00	750 gal septic tank, 300-ft septic field, & services
50.72	12 sheets 4x8 plywood for bath & bunkroom linoleum underlay
107.40	12 cartons aluminum foil-cotton blanket insulation
7.00	Staples for stapling insulation
6.70	Stapler rental
1.15	Bag of rock wool insulation
90.24	21 Sheets insulating wallboard
18.11	88 feet lead BX for underground conduit to well house
39.36	Electric fixtures
100.00	Services of electrician (25 openings @ $4)
60.00	1000 feet used pine flooring
$ 2562.87	Shell, well, sanitation, insulation, electricity

These calculations disclosed that I had spent approximately $1500 of the money I had borrowed from the bank on my last loan. This left another $1000 but with that money I needed to buy the plumbing fixtures, pay the plumber, install a heating system, buy a hot water heater, pay for the cabinet work, and equip the kitchen with a stove and a refrigerator. I did not even bother to add up this list of items. Without any question the bills for these things would mop up my remaining $1000 and put me in debt besides.

What to do? Rosemary and I talked it over at length that night. The only resource I could bring to mind was to go back to the lawyer at the county seat and present the problem to him. I was not hopeful that he would be interested in lending me $1000 with which to buy just one acre, but he would be more likely to do so than anybody else. He knew the background of the situation at least and that might count for something. And what if that failed? We discussed the possibility of trying to raise $1000 among our families, and we tried futilely to think of something we might sell—anything—to get that much money. I thought of one or two wealthy friends I might go to in my desperation. But each of these alternatives was one I would resort to only in the direst necessity, and I was not certain, in the last analysis, that The Acre really belonged in that category. We decided to try the lawyer on Monday. If the approach to him failed, then we might very well have to resign ourselves to get along without that piece of land.

I put in a long and exhausting day sanding the floor on Sunday. My spirits were at low ebb anyway, and the heavy pull of the sanding machine and the noise and the dust and the heat had tired me to the lowest point I had yet reached. Our friends Mary and Jim Victory, my most faithful visitors and most laudatory audience, came by about 4:30. They had got into the habit of dropping in to see my progress on Sunday afternoon. They were very perceiving about how much had been done and were always very complimentary about it. This time, by prior arrangement with Rosemary, they had brought along their charcoal grill and all the fixings for a baked bean and hamburger supper.

Before I knew what was happening, Vic was standing in the doorway with a can of beer in his hand, his mouth moving in some kind of message I could not hear above the shrill whine of the sander. I turned off the switch and the whine descended the long scale down and down until it stopped. Vic said in his warm, friendly voice, "Colonel, why don't you take time out long enough to have a cold can of beer?"

This was the kind of morale-building I was greatly in need of. "Nothing I would like more, Vic. As a matter of fact"—I looked around at the floor and saw that I had nearly finished the sanding job—"after I have a can of beer with you I'll do about fifteen minutes more work, and then I'll quit for the day."

"Good." Vic's voice was as kindly and as reassuring as a benevolent uncle. "You look as though you need a little break from the grind."

"Yeah." We walked across the living room and out onto the deck. The mid-August sun streamed across the yellow-green grass of the field and washed the hillside across the stream with hot light. The air was close and still even out on the deck, and the cold beer gurgled out of the sweating metal can and rushed over the parched tissues of my mouth and throat. "Oh, boy, that tastes good."

"Sure does." We were silent a moment and then Vic said, "You're going to make it all right, aren't you. I mean, you're close enough now so that you'll be able to move in all right on September first."

"Yes, I think so."

"Mary and I have been kind of worried about you. You've been looking a little tired and drawn lately. Of course it's no wonder. Frankly, I don't see how you've done all you have. I certainly couldn't have done it. But you don't want to overdo, you know. No sense in wrecking your health. It isn't worth that."

"I'll be all right, Vic. I'm really over the hump now. There are just a certain number of odds and ends I have to get done before September comes, but boy oh boy when I get us moved in here I'm really going to let down and sit on this deck and drink beer by the case."

"Well, I don't blame you."

I tipped the can up in the air and drained the last swallow of the beer. I rolled it around in my mouth and then let it slide down. I stood up slowly and long waves of fatigue rolled down my back and legs. "I'm going in and finish off that little bit left," I said, "and then I'll knock off for the day."

"You do that, and I'll be getting everything all set for the charcoal fire so we can broil the hamburgers."

I went back inside and pulled the sander around into position. Then I squeezed the pistol grip and I was back at work. It took me about fifteen minutes to finish off the remaining portion of the floor. All that remained was the edging which the big sanding machine could not do. For that, I needed to rent a small edger, and I decided I would do that during one of the evenings of the coming week. So I turned off the sander, coiled the long cord, and carried the machine out to the station wagon. Then I went down to the creek and bathed my face, shoulders, and torso in the cold clear water. After that I was ready to relax.

Rosemary, Mary, and Vic had carried our folding chairs down onto the meadow and had arranged them around the charcoal broiler. They also had brought down the sawhorses and had placed some planking on them to create an impromptu table. By this time, the shadows of the woods had silently crossed the meadow and the creek and were stealthily moving up the hillside on the other side. The magnificent poplar tree at the top of the hill stood golden and precise in the late afternoon light. It was still very warm but out of the woods behind us currents of green-cool air came wafting and sliding.

"Have a chair, colonel," said Vic, "and have a beer."

"Nothing I would like more." We sat in a quiet semi-circle while Vic fussed and ministered the charcoal broiler and our hamburgers. The food was delicious and the company was friendly and warm and delightful. After my second (or was it my third?) beer, the green of the hillside standing in shadow and the warm yellow tones of the poplar tree standing against the rich blue sky took on an hypnotic intensity that almost was too beautiful for the eye to bear. In my fatigue and my euphoria, I became almost maudlin, and I found myself thinking silently that even if I could not raise enough money to buy The Acre I would still have my friends and the extraordinary beauty of that hillside in the light of the setting sun.

Next morning, as I was preparing to leave for work, I picked out some recent photographs of The Playhouse and took them along. At the office I telephoned and made an appointment with the lawyer during the noon hour. I left my office just before 12 and was in his office by 12:30.

"Well, what's new?" he greeted me, his long, horse-face creased with a friendly smile. "Did you ever get a house built on that land you bought?"

"Almost built," I said, "but I had to end up by doing it myself."

"What do you mean, doing it yourself?"

"Just that. With my own hands. Look, I'll show you. Here are the pictures." I got out the photographs, taken after I had finished putting on the siding, and showed them to him.

"Well, I'll be darned. I'm really amazed." He looked at the pictures again and shook his head. "Let me tell you, I really take my hat off to you. That's something."

"Well, it's been a lot of work but also a lot of fun. Right now though I've got a problem, and I'm hoping you can help me with it."

"What is it? I'd sure like to help you if I can."

"Well, do you remember that business about an acre being held out of a corner of Mort's land?"

"I certainly do. Old man Oliver wanted his nephew to have an acre so Mort let him take one of the corner ones."

"That's right. Well, that corner acre takes a hunk out of the corner of my land. It's a valuable piece of property and it's worth more to me, naturally, than to anyone else. Right now the nephew wants to sell it and he's come to give me first chance on it. I want to buy it but I'm over the barrel building this house and I need money with which to do it."

"What does he want for it?"

"We haven't discussed price. But it's worth a thousand dollars at least."

"A thousand dollars! Why, there's land right around here, improved land, that costs less than that. Are you sure that is right?"

"Well, twelve acres up the road from me, an open field without road frontage or one tree, just sold for twelve thousand dollars. Yes, I am sure it's worth that. But I might be able to get it for less."

He looked thoughtful for a moment, rubbing his hand over his reddish brown hair. "What's the nephew's name?" he asked suddenly.

"Dodds."

"That's right. I remember now. Dodds." He was silent again, his hand moving slowly over his hair. "Well, I'll tell you what. I think you ought to have that acre. I don't have the slightest idea where I can find any money for you, but I'll find it somewhere. You go ahead and tell Dodds you'll buy it from him. Get the best price on it you can get, and I'll back you for whatever it is. You really ought to have that piece of land."

"Thanks a lot," I said gratefully. "Thanks one hell of a lot."

As I drove back to the office I found myself thinking that fatigue must be warping my judgment. Here I had stewed and worried and very nearly convinced myself it was useless even to try to raise the money to buy that piece of land, and when the actual moment came it was ridiculously simple. I probably should have foreseen that Jim Keith would have grasped immediately the importance of my having that acre and would do everything possible to help me get it. But perhaps, on further reflection, what Jim's quick and favorable reaction really reflected was a fundamental change in the status of my property. Previously, when I had gone cap in hand to borrow money, my assets were the nearest thing to invisible. But now, in the nearly completed Playhouse I had a real resource. My land was no longer unimproved and therefore worthless from a banker's point of view. It was improved land and on it was a habitable dwelling. That undoubtedly was the real lesson of the episode and one which I had not previously grasped.

Later in the week I called young Dodds and told him I had had some success in obtaining funds and made him an initial offer. We negotiated then over the telephone and finally arrived at a figure as good as I could possibly hope to get. He was eager to get the money in his hand and I was eager to get the property nailed down, so we arranged that the actual sale would take place in the lawyer's office on the following Saturday morning. I called Jim, told him what the deal was, and asked whether he could possibly make that.

A low whistle came out of the telephone. "Boy, you really move fast, don't you." He paused and then said, "Yes, I can make that. You and your wife come here 10:30 Saturday morning, and we'll close the deal."

During that same week, I rented a small edger and spent an evening at The Playhouse finishing off the sanding job.

The next problem was to put a coat of finish on the floor. We had decided to use penetrating wood finish, which is colorless, and to add a stain to it which would give the floor a pleasing and harmonious color. Our eventual plan was to cover the walls with pine panelling. What we needed, then, was a stain which would bring out the high-lights of knotty pine, preferably something with a yellow-brown cast. Time was growing so short that we decided this was a job Rosemary could do by herself, largely during the daytime. The first afternoon she started on the job she called me at the office about 4 o'clock.

"Honey," she wailed over the telephone in The Play-house, which had been installed just the afternoon before and which sat grandly and simply on the bare floor, "I've got this stain all mixed and when I put it on the floor it turns out bright yellow."

"Well," I said, "I don't know what you can do now. The thing to do is to go ahead and cover the whole floor uniformly. If it is too bright, we can tone it down with another coat of stain. I'll be along in another hour and a half, and we'll have a look at it then. Don't worry about it; just go ahead and we'll fix it later."

After work, I drove straight out to The Playhouse. Rosemary by that time was about halfway across the floor. She and Stephen had been painting it on with a brush and then wiping it off with rags after it had stood for several minutes. She looked up at me as I stood in the doorway. "I think it's all right now. When it dries it isn't quite so bright."

I looked across the floor at the portion already finished. In the light of the late afternoon, augmented by the fluo-rescent lights of the kitchen and an old shadeless floor lamp, the newly stained floor looked unexpectedly colorful. But after a moment or two of getting used to it, I decided that although it was a little high on the mustard side it would do very nicely. If it would not, we could tone it down later. "Cmon," I said. "Let's go home and have supper and come back and finish this tonight." We did just that.

The following Saturday was an extremely hectic day. I wanted to get slabs of cement down where the hot water heater and the laundry tubs were to stand and I also wanted a slab on which to base the furnace. The easiest thing to have done would have been to lay the entire basement floor in one operation, but this was obviously outside my financial grasp at the moment. So I decided to pour the slabs which were absolutely essential for the permanent pieces of equipment I was installing and leave the rest of the floor for another time.

I arrived at The Playhouse at eight. I had scheduled the load of concrete to arrive at 9, thus giving myself an hour in which to build the forms for the two large slabs. Ten minutes after I arrived, I heard the heavy roar of the concrete mixer truck coming in across the field. It stopped before The Playhouse and a sleepy-eyed boy of twenty looked out of the cab. "You're early," I said accusingly. "You were supposed to arrive at 9."

"I know," he said. "I thought you might like it earlier."

"Not at all. I'm not ready for it."

"That's okay. I'll just take a nap until you are ready."

I hurried upstairs and called Rosemary on the phone. "I need you over here just as soon as you can come." Then I called Don Chase, who had volunteered at a square dance a week before to come help, and repeated the message. After that I returned to building the forms. By 8:45 both Rosemary and Don had arrived and by 9 o'clock we were came up out of the leather seat, and he began to rub his eyes. This, I decided, was a sign he was awakening.

In a moment he had the engine started, and I showed him where to back the truck. Then I got the heavy duty wheelbarrow I had borrowed and positioned it before the basement door. He backed the truck up as near as he could come and in another moment we were pouring cement. The driver ran a wheelbarrowful out of the spout; I wheeled the enormously heavy load over the threshold and across the dirt floor of the basement to the forms; and Rosemary and Don pushed it around evenly inside the forms. The whole operation took less than 30 minutes. Two-thirds of the way through the driver announced I had not ordered enough concrete; we were going to run out. Momentarily, I was shaken, but then I remembered how accurately I had figured it for the footings, and I said firmly, "We will have enough." As it turned out, we did have. In fact, we had one or two shovelfuls too many.

By this time it was approaching 10 o'clock, and we were due at the lawyer's office at the county seat at 10:30. Don volunteered to stick around and smooth the cement when it began to set up, so after writing a check for the concrete I ran to the creek with a bar of soap, washed my hands hurriedly, and ran to The Shed to change my clothes. We set off then with a roar, wound our way through the heavy traffic of Saturday morning shoppers, and arrived at the lawyer's office at 10:32. In another fifteen minutes we had signed the necessary papers and started back home, owners of one more acre of land in the Virginia countryside.

During that Saturday afternoon, Rosemary and I encountered a very real snag. I had bought enough white fibre board, or wallboard, to cover the bunkroom walls and the entire ceiling of the house. I reasoned that the fibre board would make the rooms lighter and quieter. I had checked over the master strategic plan of priorities and had satisfied myself that it was all right to spend the last weekend we had in performing a task of such secondary importance as putting on the ceiling. Of the absolutely essential jobs, the linoleum needed to be laid in the bunkrooms and the bathroom, and the hot water heater needed to be set in position and hooked up. Both these jobs had been subcontracted and were scheduled to be done during the forthcoming week. Mr. Bragg was supposed to follow right on the heels of Mr. Fones in tying the heater into the water system and then finishing the plumbing. The refrigerator and stove were supposed to arrive slightly later in the week. Everything else seemingly accounted for, we turned our thoughts to the ceiling. "Better to get it done now. it will be easier before the furniture is in. We'll start in the bunkroom."

I went down into the basement, opened a package of wallboard, and carried one of the 4-by-9 sheets around the end and up into the house. It was light but extremely awkward to manage and to carry. The first snag came in trying to get in the doorway of the bunkroom. After a fair amount of trial and error, combined with some judicious bending of the fairly pliable wallboard, we got a piece inside the bunkroom. We quickly found that two adult people and a 4-by-9 sheet of building material created a congested situation inside a 5-by-8 bunkroom. Suddenly, it began to seem extraordinarily funny trying to wrestle with a piece of recalcitrant material that stood at all angles so that it could fit at all inside the tiny room, and we began to giggle. And amidst all the confusion and the hilarity, fumbling with the awkward piece, stumbling over own feet, trying in vain to find a place to stand where the wallboard was not, we suddenly found to our surprise that we had got the thing up over our heads and ready to nail against the sloping rafters. It was astonishing how quickly and unexpectedly it had happened. We tried then to nail the board in place. Rosemary ran and got the ladder for me while I stood like Hercules with my hands held overhead. Then we inched the board up close, and I drove the first nail in. In getting the board up tight to the rafter for the second nail, we tore the board loose from the first one.

Then, when we finally did manage to get several nails in and holding firm, I got down off the ladder and looked up at it. It was a mess. The fibre board sagged between nails like a wet shirt on a line, and it was obvious that in order to hold it flat to the ceiling I would need to nail it every six or eight inches along every rafter. The sad but inexorable truth was that fibre wallboard in sheet form in not suitable material for a ceiling. Somehow those eulogistic descriptions in the Montgomery Ward catalogue had omitted any mention of this shortcoming, and none of my experienced friends had been told of my plans for the wallboard.

"There's only one thing to do," I said. "Take it down." We started then to pull the wallboard off the ceiling, tearing chunks out of it where the nailheads held it firm to the rafters, and cracking and bending other pieces to get it loose. It was then we discovered that the piece which had almost magically elevated itself above our heads could not be brought down again inside the five-by-eight inclosure of the bunkroom.We wrestled and twisted the board—somehow it no longer seemed the slightest amusing—but without any visible success. I was finally forced to break it into two or three pieces in order to get it down again.

"Well, what will you do with all that wallboard if you are not going to use it on the ceiling?" Rosemary asked.

"Send most of it back I guess. Oh, I can use a package or so of it on the ouside of these bunkroom partitions. Matter of fact, I think I will start that right now."

"How about putting it on the walls of the living room?"

"No. I'm going to put pine panelling on that. We can stand to leave those walls uncovered until after we have been moved in a while."

I spent the rest of the weekend putting wallboard on the partitions and tidying up odds and ends of jobs. When I left The Playhouse Sunday evening, I felt I had done everything I could do before *The Big Move* on the following weekend. All that remained were the jobs I had subcontracted.

On the following Tuesday, the linoleum men came in and put down the bunkroom and bathroom floors. Rosemary, who was there to watch them work, said the whole operation took no more than an hour and a half. The hot water heater was delivered that same day, and I got old Mr. Fones to come in and hook it up to the electrical system. On Wednesday, Mr. Bragg came in and connected the water heater with the rest of the plumbing. When I came by at 6 o'clock on my way home from work, I found Rosemary happily working the faucets in the kitchen sink and trying the other plumbing outlets. They all worked. On Thursday, the stove and refrigerator arrived, gleaming white and handsome, and Mr. Fones came back to connect up the stove. That concluded all the subcontracted operations, and everything was connected and operating in anticipation of our moving in.

Meanwhile, the walls of the living room, or two-thirds of The Playhouse, remained uncovered. The studs stood naked and exposed with the flashing silver of the aluminum foil insulation lying between them. By contrast with the walls of the bunkrooms, covered by the immaculate white of the wallboard, the living room walls looked unfinished and crude. "Look," I said on a sudden inspiration, "let's cover those walls with wallboard. We can get half of it done tonight and we will still have tomorrow night, Friday, before we move in on Saturday."

"I'm awfully glad you suggested that," said Rosemary. "I wanted to but I didn't feel I should, considering the expense."

"Oh, the expense is very small. Costs only about 2 cents a square foot. Besides, it will give us just that much more insulation, and in the meantime, we will have covered walls instead of these ugly blanks. Let's do it!"

We started working on Thursday night and by 10:30 had covered what seemed a good half of the wall space. It must have been the easier half, however. The next night we worked at top speed until 1:30 in the morning finishing the job. By that time we were groggy and reeling, but we had covered walls everywhere in The Playhouse.

"Let's go home, dear," I said. "We've got to pack. The movers are coming at 8 o'clock this morning, exactly six and a half hours from now."

We were so obsessed with the importance of finishing the immediate job of covering the walls that we failed utterly to realize the tremendous significance of the moment. We had completed the task of making The Playhouse a habitable dwelling. From that moment on, it had ceased to be a building project and had become a house. All that remained was for us to move in.

Twenty Two

The day of *The Big Move* dawned bright and hot. I got up at 6:30, my head empty and tight from lack of sleep, ate a hasty breakfast, and pulled some things together before the movers arrived. They came shortly before 8, a young ex-Navy man who told me he took moving jobs on weekends to fill out his income and three middle-aged black men who moved with the shambling ease of professional movers. With easy efficiency, they loaded aboard the piano, the washing machine, the sofa, and some other heavy items in about twenty minutes. I led them over to the woods in the station wagon. They backed the big van part way up the hill behind The Playhouse and began to unload. In a remarkably short time, they had everything off the truck and sitting somewhat haphazardly about the living room floor on the reddish kraft paper I had laid on the newly finished surface. I paid them off by 10 o'clock and they were on their way.

After that, my work really began. Looking back on it, my system for moving was probably a dubious economy, but it certainly was a lot of fun, or at least as much fun as moving can ever be. I had hired the van only to move the large and heavy items. For the rest, I had mobilized a flotilla of station wagons from among my generous and accommodating friends. At the time, it seemed like a good idea because we had been so frantically engaged in building the house until the very last moment that we had not had time to pack anything. With many hands and many cars we could carry things loose and put them down again by hand wherever they belonged.

When I got back to the house from the woods, I found Chet Cooper and Jack Shaffer already loading things into their cars. They were coming out of the door laden with lamps, chairs, pictures, card tables, cribs, book ends, waste baskets, and all the accumulated paraphernalia of a household. We all helped each other pack this disjointed and awkward assortment of items into each other's cars, taking great delight in finding some unused chink of space. We had just got the three cars packed to everyone's satisfaction when Barbara Donnelly arrived in her station wagon. We all joined in packing her car with pots and pans and other accouterments of the kitchen. Then at last we set off on our two-mile passage with a squadron of four station wagons.

We quickly discovered, once we had drawn up this imposing array of vehicles, that unloading posed greater problems than loading because each piece had to be set down in some orderly fashion. The problem was made all the more acute by the fact we were moving from a five bedroom house into a house of three rooms in all. As a matter of fact, our possessions simply would not fit into the living space of The Playhouse, and the only way we could get everything we owned under cover was to store some things in the basement and some in The Shed. This required a steady stream of decisions as to where each piece was to go. We met this problem by setting Rosemary on a stool under a tree where she could direct the flow of traffic as it came by. "Upstairs," she would say. "Basement. Shed—uh, no, wait a minute, better make that basement."

And so our moving went throughout the day. I had put a case of beer in each of the refrigerators at the two ends of our journey, and there was no evidence that anyone went thirsty. At noontime, Rosemary and Barbara offered cold meat sandwiches at The Playhouse. After lunch, Chet and Jack went back to their normal lives, and Paul Borel and Jim Victory took their places at various times of the afternoon. Paul specialized in books and records, succeeding in transporting all my bookcases and books in two trips. Vic made a specialty of children's toys and equipment and, when that resource ran dry, turned with considerable versatility to Rosemary's and my clothing.

As the son of a restless father who moved eight times during the first ten years of his marriage, and as a householder who carried on that itinerant tradition by moving eleven times in fourteen years, I had acquired a certain expertise in moving household possessions. When 4:30 in the afternoon came, I knew it was time to set up the beds. Once the beds are up, progress can continue or not, depending on what strength you have left, but whenever complete exhaustion strikes you can fall in without further effort. By six o'clock, the beds were up and made. Our regular baby sitter, Salome Jane, came in to feed the children and put them to bed.

Shortly before seven, Janie and Bob Komer arrived with an impressive array of hampers and receptacles containing our supper. Slightly less than a year before, they had moved into a new house, and Rosemary and I had taken dinner to them their first night. They were returning the favor, doubled in spades. First we were treated to martinis made with vodka. Then, to an extremely complex and magnificently-flavored casserole, Italian-style, flanked with wine and followed by an enormous and equally complex salad. And finally, coffee and cognac.

By midnight, Rosemary and I were blotto, what with the accumulated fatigue of months of hard work, the day's excitement and exhausting activity, and the wonderful food and drink. Bob and Jane loaded everything back into the hampers, including even the dirty dishes, and made a hasty exit. We followed them out to their car and stood watching, numb and spent, as they drove away. Then we walked slowly back up the little path leading to The Playhouse — oblivious to the soft, country night and the stars winking in the black sky overhead—closed and locked the door behind us, and fell wordlessly into bed.

When my eyes opened next morning the first thing they saw was the glistening aluminum insulation over my head. They followed the rafter directly above me down to the side wall and then down to the large window stretching across the front of The Playhouse. Across the meadow stood the hillside in the early morning light, cool and serene and enhanced by the slight mist rising from the low ground and the running streams. Behind the house, the woods sounded murmurously and tranquilly as the birds took up again the innumerable and feathery activities they had abandoned at dusk of the day before. Inside the house it was still and peaceful with only the soft whirring of the new refrigerator to mark the completeness of the quiet. I found myself thinking that this moment of waking in the silent little house with my family sleeping about me in snug peace was the culmination toward which I had been struggling with so much ardor and sweat for so many months. Here, in the tranquillity and secure shelter, with the morning beauty standing round about waiting only for awakened eyes to look upon it, was the realized goal, the long pursued and arduous dream. This was the end of the strenuous journey that had begun in Mort and Barbara's living room and had led me by many an indirect and tortuous route—even including several hazardous flights on a metaphorical trapeze through momentary insecurity and back to firm landing—into new endeavors I had never imagined were within my powers or my strength.

But as I had found before, realization does not come immediately at one's bidding, and I was not able as I lay there in bed to bring into its fullest meaning the realization that I had built my own house and moved in. Throughout that day and the others that followed in swift succession, realization came alive in a number of unexpected moments. It came when I walked down the meadow in the early morning to get the newspaper waiting in the mailbox by the gate. It came when breakfast, with its fragrance of sizzling bacon and bubbling coffee, was cooking on the spanking new stove. It came when we all sat down to Sunday lunch at the dining table in the middle of the living room, with its handsome views out either side of leafy woods or grassy field. It came the first night I arrived home from work and turned in at the gate and parked my car in the little logging road beside The Shed. It came the first time it rained all night and we were warm and dry in our beds while the raindrops splashed on the leaves in the woods and pattered on the roof overhead. It came the first time we entertained in The Playhouse and the gently sloping roof and the surrounding pine trees were blanketed in a sudden six-inch fall of snow and the little house evoked exclamations of admiration from our guests as it stood on the hillside looking like a Swiss chalet. It came when my little boy, Scott, celebrated his third birthday and the living room resounded with shrill giggles and laughter. It came when we celebrated Christmas and the house stood resplendent with pine boughs and holly branches from our woods. It came repeatedly but always when it came it was new and I felt all over again the surprise and the pride: this is *my* house. I *built* it.

Rosemary and I spent the rest of the Labor Day week-end finishing the move and organizing things into place. When Monday night came, we were in tolerably good condition, and I was readying myself to go back to work on the following morning. "Well, we're here," said Rose-mary, "and pretty much in one piece. What do we do next?"

"Well, of course, there are lots of little odds and ends to clean up around the house and I can very comfortably fill up all my weekends till Christmas with small carpen-try jobs, but the only things I know which *must* be done fairly urgently are the grading out in front and installing the furnace."

"I hope you will get at the furnace first. The grading can wait but it gets awfully cold at night in October."

My first move in the direction of a furnace was a fa-miliar one. I went to talk to Bob Housel, my knowledge-able and heretical friend. "Get an oil burner with forced hot air," he said. "They're the only kind for your house. Compact, economical, and these modern ones have filters built into them so you don't get all that dust blowing around. Matter of fact, I'll tell you what I'll do," he said in his staccato way, his pale blue eyes boring intently into mine, "I'll get one for you at wholesale price. I got an old friend in the plumbing and heating business. I'll look into it and let you know."

"How much do they cost?"

"I'll let you know."

Before I saw Bob again, I got Bud Bradley to come in and do the grading and plow up a garden patch. This was straightforward work except that Rosemary seemed to have certain ideas about how to contour one portion which she had great difficulty in communicating to Bud. They would discuss it and Bud would nod as though he understood.

After several minutes of maneuvering tractor and blade around, he would stop and raise his eyebrows questioningly. Rosemary would shake her head and explain again what she wanted done, her voice shrill over the sound of the idling tractor engine. Bud would try again with a similar result. After several repetitions, Bud and Rosemary broke down in convulsions of laughter. "That's gotta be right now," Bud said, "I got this dirt here all wore out just moving it around!" They finally agreed that although the last degree of artistic perfection had not been achieved, it was as near that as Bud's tractor and blade could bring it.

"What are you going to do with it now?" Bud asked.

"I've got ten pounds of rye grass seed to put on it. That will grow very quickly, and I hope to get a roots system established here to hold that bank in place."

"Sure, that's a good idea. Tell you another thing that would help. Put some straw on it to help hold it down. I've got some over at the barn and I've also got some loose hay that's starting to go bad. Take all that you want."

"Thanks a lot." After sowing the grass seed, I drove the station wagon over to Bud's barn and loaded it full of straw and hay. As I stood in the barn and threw the hay over the tailgate into the wagon, I found myself marvelling again at the versatility of the station wagon and the innumerable uses I had put mine to. Without any question, it was the most useful tool I had employed in the whole process of building The Playhouse, even more useful than the power saw.

Some days later, Bob Housel and I had lunch together in town, and we discussed again the question of the furnace. "Got you all fixed up," he said. "This guy's got one the size you need, and the first chance he gets he'll have his truck haul it out to my place. You and I can move it down from there in your wagon."

"Sounds fine. How much does it cost?"

"$200."

I nodded, remembering that in the Montgomery Ward catalogue such furnaces cost approximately $350. "Now, I have another question to ask. Who do I get to set the furnace up for me?"

"Do it yourself."

"Oh, no. Look, you've got me into doing all kinds of things I never thought I could do, but sheet metal work is the end. None of that for me."

"But there's nothing to it. Look, you don't need to use anything fancy in that set-up you've got. You can just take round stove pipe, fit it together like tinker toys, and run it around between the joists to the floor registers."

"Not for me, boy. I'll stick to wood carpentry."

"Okay, if you want to spend your money. There's a fellow out our way, Willard Oliver, who'll hook it up for you okay, but he's not much good at ducts and sheet metal. He'll just connect up the oil lines and the electric power to the burner and blower."

"Fine. I'll get hold of him when the time comes."

Several weeks passed and October and nippy nights were rapidly approaching before I finally got Bob to fix a date for moving the furnace into the Playhouse. We picked it up on a Saturday morning and had it sitting in place very shortly. I had Mr. Oliver standing by to begin work that afternoon.

"What are you going to do for a chimney?" asked Bob.

"Well, if I don't run out of money I'm hoping to get Lyons to build me a fireplace in the north end of the living room. I'll put another flue in that for the furnace. If I do run out of money, I'll guess I'll have to put in a temporary chimney of some sort."

Bob cast an appraising eye at the north end of The Playhouse. "If it was mine and I was short of money, I'd just put up a galvanized pipe chimney. Keep it out away from the house a foot or so with a metal strap, put a china cap on top, and it'll get you through this winter very nicely."

"Well, I hope I can get the fireplace in this fall, but if I can't I may do that."

When I came to look into the economic feasibility of building a fireplace and brick chimney that fall, I found the decision about the chimney had already been made for me. Reviewing the expenditures I came up with this set of figures:

2562.87	Shell, well, sanitation, etc.
4.00	40 lbs. flooring nails
12.70	sanding machine rental, sandpaper
8.30	two rolls building paper
1.95	roll of rosin-coated kraft paper
36.11	23 feet of 36" linoleum
22.00	services linoleum layers
14.00	2 gals. penetrating wood finish
21.70	1 cubic yard concrete for basement slabs
126.88	50 gal. glass-lined hot water heater
245.56	plumbing fixtures
320.40	refrigerator, electric stove
312.30	plumber's services installation system
230.25	kitchen, bathroom cabinets
$ 3920.02	Shell, well, sanitation, plumbing, kitchen equipment

Confronted with the hard fact that I had once again used up all my capital, I had no trouble deciding that the fireplace would have to wait until next spring. It was disappointing because Rosemary and I had looked forward to enjoying winter nights beside our fireplace, but our disappointment was moderated by a fundamental change in our outlook toward the future. For the first time in our married life, we were living in our own house and we had the rest of our lives to make changes and improvements.

Moreover, the outlook for a fairly rapid economic recovery had greatly improved because we were no longer paying out rent every month. The $150 that normally would have gone to the rental agent on 1 September had stayed in our account and had helped to pay off building and moving bills. And this would be true in October, November, December, and all the succeeding months. We could do without a fireplace for one winter.

And so I went to a large wholesale outlet for plumbing and heating supplies and bought enough 8-inch galvanized smokepipe to make a temporary chimney. It took me less than an hour to hook it up to the galvanized flue Mr. Oliver had cemented into the cinder block wall. I wired it to the gable end of the roof with a metal plate set into a block, and I stayed it each way with more wire running to the fascia. I had also bought floor registers at the same time, and I set to work cutting openings in the floor for them. By this time, Mr. Oliver had the furnace hooked up and ready to run, but I still had not found anyone to do the sheet metal and duct work. Moreover, the pressure of work at the office had become very great, and I could not find time for several weeks to do it myself. Meanwhile, the nights were becoming frosty.

When I asked Bob Housel what to do about it, his reply was typical. "Just turn the furnace on," he said. "You've got the registers set in the floor, haven't you? Well, the heat will rise all right through those openings. You'll use a little more oil than you should, but I'll guarantee you this: you won't be cold."

As usual, he turned out to be right. We kept the thermostat set at 70, and when the temperature in the room dropped two degrees the furnace came on and ran for thirty minutes or more at a time. The basement got extraordinarily warm but the upstairs temperature remained remarkably constant. In fact, as Rosemary and I soon began to realize as the autumn changed to winter and the winds rose in velocity while the mercury steadily dropped, The Playhouse for all its simple board and batten construction was a tighter, snugger house, more free from drafts, than any house we had lived in before. The winter was about half gone when I bought a pair of tinsnips and followed Bob's advice about running in my own ducts with round 6-inch pipe. I had a little sheet metal work done by a local shop, the tricky part, which consisted of taking the forced hot air off the top of the furnace and running over the top of the girder and around a 90-degree bend, thus enabling the main line to run down the center of the house. I also had small register pans made. The rest I did myself, and as Bob had told me, it's as simple as putting tinker toys together.

When spring came we held a painting bee one Sunday afternoon. When dusk fell and we assembled in the living room for old-fashioneds and a spaghetti dinner, the entire outside of The Playhouse was glistening with new paint, barn red with white trim, and had been transformed into The Little Red House. All ten of us had had a gay time, standing three-deep on the ladder on occasion, sloshing paint on the house and each other with abandon, and it was several minutes after we had finished rinsing ourselves off with turpentine before we noticed one of our citizens was missing. It was Jim Victory, and we finally located him in the basement, still cleaning paint brushes. He was working on the last one and he had all the others laid out before him. I counted them and reached the horrifying number of sixteen. "There, colonel," he said, giving the last one a final flip, "I don't suppose any other living man has ever cleaned sixteen paint brushes at one sitting but I did it and I'm glad. And now, sir, I would like an old fashioned."

Later in the spring I began shopping around for knotty pine panelling, and at last I found some for twelve cents a board foot. I bought a thousand square feet and began laying it on the walls over the top of the white wallboard. This was easily the most satisfying job of all. The beautiful pine boards in varying widths of 6, 8, 10, and 12 inches slid smoothly into place and instantly transformed the appearance of the wall. The longer I worked with knotty pine, the higher it rose in my esteem. As a decorator's device, it has been so over-used that it has become a cliche, but as a utilitarian wall surface it is almost impossible to beat. It is very cheap, and it needs only a coat of shellac or floor varnish to seal it. Bumps and nicks, which it absorbs without pain, tend to enhance its appearance, and it needs practically no upkeep once it is in place. To go with the pine walls, I put pine plywood panels on the ceiling, thereby covering up the aluminum insulation at last.

During the summer I hired a contractor to pour a concrete floor in the basement and to put up a brick chimney and fireplace. It took him only three days in all, and when he finished we built a fire in the fireplace even though it was a hot summer night. When I paid the contractor off, I had completed all the expenditures on The Playhouse. My final reckoning looked like this:

3920.02	Shell, well, sanitation, plumbing, kitchen equipment
120.00	1000 feet, knotty pine panelling
200.00	forced hot air oil furnace and oil tan
7.50	temporary chimney
40.00	services, furnace installation
546.64	services, materials for fireplace, chimney basement floor
$ 4834.16	Completed Playhouse (renamed the Little Red House)

Several Sunday evenings later, Vic and I were sitting on the deck having a beer. Our kids were playing down below in the huge sandpile—what remained of my final order of four tons of construction sand—and in the kitchen our wives were making an enormous garden salad to go with our charcoal-broiled hamburgers. One of Mary's justifiably famous chocolate pies was sitting in the refrigerator. From the living room came the sound of the record player giving forth the sophisticated and ingratiating music of George Shearing. Jocko, the only living being besides myself who had been present when every nail was driven into The Playhouse, lay beside my chair. Across the meadow, standing beside the brook in the last rays of the late summer sun, the neat rows of our garden—the garden whose produce was at that very moment being leafed and chopped into salad—cast long shadows.

"You know, colonel," said Vic, "it was just about this time a year ago that we were talking here one evening. Seems to me you said something about putting your feet up on that rail and drinking a case of beer a week after you got moved in."

"I'm still going to do it. Just as soon as I get things tidied up."

"Umm hmmm." Vic took another swallow of his beer. "Tell me honestly, now that it's all over and you've got your house built, would you do it again if you had it to do over?"

My first impulse was to say, "Hell, no!" It was what many people expected me to say, but it certainly was not true to my actual feeling. "I guess the only honest answer, Vic, is that I wouldn't have missed it for anything."

"You really mean that, don't you? Well, I suppose it must give you an awful lot of satisfaction to know you've built your own house."

"It does." I paused for a moment, watching three crows in a ragged formation flying over the woods in the last rays of the sun. "But more than that, it has given me a wonderful project for the past two years. I'm going to miss it. You know, I've wondered more than once what people who are not engaged in building their own house do with their spare time. There were times when I almost felt sorry for them."

"Well, what's the next move? Are you going to build a large house up the hill and leave this attractive little place standing empty except for occasional parties?"

"I really don't know. And as a matter of fact, I really don't intend to worry much about it. That's one of the most gratifying aspects of the whole business. I've got a very flexible position now with several alternate choices, all of which I find attractive. I can if I want, merely add on to this house, using this part as a wing. Or, if I wish, I can build the other house up the hill and rent this. With a small amount of remodeling it could be a highly desirable rental and the source of considerable income. And finally, if things work out so that I can afford it, I can build the main house and keep this for a guest house. But no matter which of those I choose, I've got a base here and a place to live."

"That's right." We were silent then while we both took a sip of beer. "Well, what do you think about this. When the time comes to do some more building, are you going to do it yourself?"

I paused for a moment before answering. "I don't really know. I suppose there is some question whether a man has more than one house in his system. I don't know whether you can go through the ordeal twice without regretting it."

"What's this?" asked Rosemary, coming out on the deck with Mary. "Did I hear you talking about building the next house yourself?"

Vic and I grinned at each other. "Well, I guess it's fair to say the subject was under discussion."

"Don't you even think about it! We're going to have

the next one built by a builder, and we're going to sit right here and watch it being built. Once is enough!"

Vic and I grinned again. "Well, my dear, fortunately it is not a decision that needs to be made right now. We've got approximately two years before the time comes. And I really don't have much intention of building the next one single handedly anyway. But I might do my own contracting and I might hire a journey-man carpenter and work along with him on the rough carpentry. I just have a feeling that when we compare a builder's estimate with what it will cost if I do some of the work, we'll find we can get quite a bit more house for our money."

"Well, maybe so. Anyway, as you say, we don't need to decide for another two years. Let's leave it till then."

And that is precisely what we did. Meanwhile between tasks like mowing the field, plowing the garden, chopping the firewood, and building a stone wall around the terrace behind The Playhouse, now renamed The Little Red House, I have been spending a number of hours on that deck watching the birds fly back and forth between the woods and the meadow. I still think there is nothing like it—except possibly building your own house.